D0596248

The Time Cellar

DISCARD

By Marc Emory © 2012

Copyright © 2012 by Marc Emory

All Rights Reserved.

Reproduction or translation of any part of this
work without permission of the copyright owner
is unlawful. Requests for permission or further
information should be addressed to:

Ivy Press, Inc.
3500 Maple Ave, 17ᵗʰ Floor
Dallas, Texas 75219-3941
U.S.A.

All images are courtesy of Heritage Auction
Galleries, except where otherwise noted.

ISBN 978-1–59967-971-6

Manufactured in the United States of America

website: www.the-time-cellar.com

Facebook page: TheTimeCellar

Film rights: The Time Cellar c/o the Ivy Press
3500 Maple Avenue, 17th floor
Dallas, Texas 75219-3941
USA

First Edition

IvyPress, Inc.

Read what people are saying
after their visit to the Time Cellar!

Adrian Cronauer, portrayed by Robin Williams in "Good Morning Vietnam:"
"I'm not sure what I expected, but it was great!
Then, again, what would one expect from a book that begins with, 'For the record, if there ever is
one, the body in my basement with the pitchfork sticking out of his back isn't mine.' What a fine
opening line!..........

"All in all, it is an excellent piece of work......you probably have another career
awaiting you as a sci-fi/fantasy writer."

Gov. Howard Dean, M.D.:
"Marc Emory has written a unique story that will delight fans of Thomas Jefferson, but also
enthusiasts of time travel, collectible wine and rare coins. Told in a unique dry, humorous style,
with researched, believable conversations with characters from centuries past,
Emory draws the reader into Robert Packard's suspenseful attempts to stay one step ahead
(or 150 years behind!) of divorce lawyers and educated hired thugs. I highly recommend this
entertaining book to anyone who loves history, collectibles, or just a good romance!"

Karlyn Thayer, twenty-year instructor for Writer's Digest University:
"Marc Emory's novel, The Time Cellar, is the best story to cross my desk in twenty years.
The strongest factor in Emory's favor is his ability to create suspense—at its best. This truly is one
of those stories that keeps the reader turning the pages, desperate to find out how the story ends.
Pacing is excellent, with no down time. The story zips along at dizzying speed, despite forays into
Thomas Jefferson's sitting room. Readers can't help but root for Robert, the protagonist. In all my
years as a writing mentor, this is the first time I've had reason to recommend a book, and that
reason is just plain terrific story-telling!"

David Harper, editor, **Numismatic News** and **World Coin News**:
"I grew up reading science fiction. Combining it with numismatics and wine makes the plot a
winner in my mind. Maybe someone will want to make a movie out of it."

Stan Lee, creator of **Spider-Man**:
"Hey, Marc—I hate you! Now I can't even look at a glass of wine without thinking of your
furshlugginer story!!!"

"Le secret du bonheur et le comble de l'art, c'est de vivre

comme tout le monde, en n'étant comme personne."

(The secret of happiness, and the pinnacle of art, is to

live like everyone else, while not being like anyone else.)

--Simone de Beauvoir

"Most people....fail to realize that style and form are everything,

and substance a passing myth."

--Rodney Whitaker ("Trevanian," speaking as Nicholai Hel)

For the record, if there ever is one, the body in my basement with the pitchfork sticking out of its back isn't mine. It used to be some thug whose name I never knew, one of Stef's buddies. The pitchfork is at least 150 years old, and it was put there by someone who was born 178 years ago, i.e., 1832, who kindly decided to save my life. If you think *that* sounds far-fetched, wait till you hear the rest. I thought I'd have a little more time to elaborate, but apparently not. I figure I have maybe a few minutes left to do what I gotta do, hit "send," and do a fast fade. Thank goodness I changed clothes already. Stef—you'll read about Stef later—will be on his way here to check on his fellow goon the second the Brinks armored truck is gone from my driveway, so no time for a lengthy introduction now. You'll figure it out soon enough. Regards to the cops and, I hope, the fire department. As for me, Elvis has left the building.

******

Summer, 2010

"Mister President?"

The great man turned. "Well, good afternoon to you, Robert. All went well after our initial encounter, I trust?"

I was almost getting used to his pattern of speech. Almost.

"Good afternoon, sir. Yes, without a hitch."

"A hitch?"

I had to keep reminding myself. My slang would never be his slang. "I mean, yes, all went well, thank you. Actually, I was hoping for another round, so to speak."

"So was I, I'll confess," he replied. "As I said when we first met, my personal finances are not in the best of order."

I still had difficulty swallowing this, although it had never been any kind of national secret. Here was a man who dared so much, from controversial moves that nearly emptied the U.S. Treasury to sending ships to fight pirates off the coast of Africa, and yet he had trouble balancing his personal checkbook, something I rather doubt he had anyway.

"The sale of my books did help a few years back," he went on. "Some in Congress were going on about some of them promoting an 'infidel philosophy,' if you can imagine that," he said.

I could.

"Since our last meeting, I did locate some bottles I think you will appreciate. I still did have some Lafite and Mouton. They needed a little dusting off, but other than that, they are as I bought them, and that was around thirty years ago. I do have more, so I'll not be emptying my cellar by selling them to you. I think they should have mellowed out nicely by now, don't you?"

By now. Oh, yes, they should definitely have mellowed out nicely by now. VERY nicely, in fact. Organize a wine tasting with ten of *those* bottles, and oenologists would come from the four corners of the earth just to see them.

"Same quantity, same price?"

"That would be perfectly acceptable," I nodded.

"I suspect the same method of delivery, as well?" We both had chuckle at that one. "I see no reason to vary the method of delivery," I confirmed.

"No, I suppose not," the great man said. "Even at my age, I think I can manage that maneuver on my own."

I told him I had every confidence, and that I didn't consider his age to be so terribly old. He smiled.

"Very well, then. How long would you need to complete your end of the bargain this time?"

"Maybe two hours," I estimated. Actually, it would probably be half that, but you never knew what traffic was going to be like, and I still had to make sure that I would be able to conform to the former president's unique requirements as to form of payment.

"Agreed. I'll see you back here in two hours."

"I look forward to it," I smiled. I reached for my car keys, and he turned to retreat to the inner reaches of Monticello.

✻ ✻ ✻ ✻ ✻ ✻

1.

I might as well tell you my name. It's not like I'll have much to fear from identity theft. Plus, maybe this will find its way to people I don't mind making scream with rage and frustration. Even the vague possibility warms my heart. *Schadenfreude, mon amour.* My name is Robert H. Packard. Like Hewlett-Packard, but without the money. For most of my life, anyway. The "H" doesn't stand for Hewlett, either—just Harrison, my mom's maiden name. People usually called me "Bob." Soon, a relative term, as you'll see, they'll only call me Robert—"Ro-BAIR," like how Stephen Colbert pronounces his last name. Not that anyone has ever heard of Stephen Colbert where I'm headed, but maybe someone knows his great-great-grandfather. I wouldn't know, and I can't very well walk up to everyone I meet whose name is Colbert and ask if their great-great-grandson will be a famous comedian in America some day, can I?

I was born on June 23, 1974. It's now September, 2010 (I originally started writing this in August, refining as I went along), so I'm now thirty-six years old, and due to a decent set of genes, I look younger than that. I work, or did until recently—as in about three hours ago—for a small law firm in Sherman Oaks, California. I'm not a lawyer, more like an accountant/office manager. Since most people outside of California have never heard of Sherman Oaks, I just say I'm from Los Angeles. Actually, I *was* born within the Los Angeles city limits, but that was because on June 22, 1974, my parents thought they could drive down to San Diego to see my mom's parents for a quick weekend visit and get back before "the baby" (that's me) came. But even back then, there was more traffic on the San Diego Freeway than anyone ever reckoned with. Needless to say, they didn't make it back before I put in my initial appearance.

But my birth went well, unexceptional, and without any great complications—either that or my parents wanted my conscience to be free of guilt and it was actually the most complicated birth that hospital ever had, and my mom and I nearly died. Whatever. They told me it went without a hitch, anyway. I came out and promptly peed all over the obstetrician. Obviously, my disrespect for the rules of etiquette started very early in life. The doctor took it in stride, saying he'd be thrilled if that were the worst thing to happen to him all week. It was on a Sunday afternoon in some hospital whose presence was announced just before some freeway exit within the city of Los Angeles. My dad missed a day of work the following Monday, but that was about as exciting as that part of the story gets. The dark and stormy night part comes later. Be patient.

My dad was the late Andrew Packard of San Francisco, and my mom was the late Patricia Harrison of some small town that got swallowed up by the city of San Diego before my time. They met as sophomores at UCLA, and that was pretty much that. An engineering major, my dad got his first job as an electrician on some construction site north of Los Angeles and decided to settle there. As a *lot* of construction was going on in the area in those days, he left his job and started his own business, weathered a recession or two, but did all right for himself. He was able to afford a decent house of his own, employed some local people and a few Mexicans with legit papers. He was an easygoing guy—not always a given in the construction business, but he was very good at what he did and had a knack for managing projects very efficiently, a talent I apparently inherited to some degree.

Mom liked to go around to book readings, especially if they were in French--I'll get to that--and volunteered for projects at my public high school, whose academic offerings were superior to the national norm (not saying much, I know). I never thought of her as pretty or ugly or any other adjective associated with the superficial judgment of women. She was my mom, my one and only mom, and there was no value assessment attached. She always took time for me when I needed to talk to her, and that was all that mattered to me.

She and my dad were a couple very much at ease with each other, something I came to envy, as in "green with." While they never made a fortune by southern California standards, they, I should say we, were comfortable and didn't lack for much. Dad always saved enough for us to take fancy summer vacations, and when I was a teenager, those vacations were the highlights of my year as well. I know some teenagers hate taking vacations with their parents. Call me a nerd, but I always had a wonderful time with mine. It probably had more to do with where we went than the company, although my parents and I got along famously most of the time. It's not too uncool to say that, is it?

I have heard that southern California has a reputation for its people being laid-back, and that the catch phrase of the sixties and seventies was, "I'm OK, you're OK." That certainly describes my parents, and it rubbed off, I like to think, on me to a certain degree. But I can't imagine that we had a monopoly on it in California. Look at Minnesota. Now, I have never been to Minnesota, but it produced a writer like Garrison Keillor, politicians like Walter Mondale and Al Franken, and musicians like Bob Dylan and Leo Kottke. So I figure there are other places on this planet besides California that produce interesting, laid-back people.

As my life progressed, "unexceptional" was a more fitting description of me than I would have preferred. I was good in school, but this earned me no points with anyone other than my parents and my teachers. As every kid from first to twelfth grade knows, those are the people who matter least of all in the life of an American school kid. To those who mattered, i.e., my classmates, I was not an athletic star, or the child of extremely wealthy parents, or exceptionally hot-looking in the eyes of the girls in school. In other words, I was nobody. The symptoms weren't fatal, but it sucked. I was the Larry Kroger of the National Lampoon High School Yearbook parody, except that I got good grades—"Dacron, Ohio," meet Sherman Oaks, California.

If there was anything at all exceptional in my growing up as the only, and very unremarkable, child of undistinguished parents in southern California, it was our summer trips to France. My mom and dad were both enthusiastic fans of the place. My dad had taken French as his required foreign language at UCLA, and my mom had even majored in it there. She wasn't a fanatic, don't get me wrong. She loved the language and the culture, but did not shove Voltaire or Rousseau down my throat. While on vacation, she was just as happy to be strolling in the Quartier Latin in Paris or down the Cours Mirabeau in Aix-en-Provence as she was to be touring famous cathedrals. This was very important to me, because in the Quartier Latin and on the Cours Mirabeau, nice-looking French girls occasionally smiled at me, whereas the nuns in the cathedrals didn't smile at anyone.

One thing in France *did* catch my fancy just as much as the (unfortunately) novel phenomenon of attractive girls my age smiling at me, and it was far more accessible, even if that was not my order of preference at the time. That was wine. The drinking age in California prohibits teenagers from legal access to wine, but in France, kids start sampling it before they hit puberty. As "enlightened" Francophiles, my parents let me drink wine with meals while on vacation in France. I was taking French in high school, and, like with my other subjects, did well in it. Speaking French on vacation became second nature to me.

But being able to order wine at French restaurants in the *lingua franca* was nothing compared to the taste. Man, was **that** a revelation. Just sipping it, letting it lay out a landscape of sensations on my tongue, it was a pleasure that absolutely blew me away. So many different varieties and vintages, too! Years before I ever learned to pronounce "oenology," I had read up and knew that wine was both a science and a culture in France. Even so, that didn't prepare me for the sheer pleasure of tasting it myself. To many people back in southern California, wine was just something made for $150 bottles at restaurants only some of our parents could afford, or else in gallon glass jugs costing $2.59. The difference between the two was not always discernable. The gallon jugs, of course, were accessible to anyone with a friend who was at least twenty-one years old. I knew that up in the Napa Valley, north of San Francisco, they were already making respectable wine, and even down in the Texas Hill country, I had heard that a few vineyards were starting to get some deserved recognition. But at age seventeen in America, that did me about as much good as seeking the presidency. I just wasn't old enough, and that was that. But wine was to become important enough to me to cause me a lot of headaches as well as a lot of pleasure. I'll need to fill you in on some background so you can understand why I am where I am now, but knowledge and appreciation of wine is what ultimately got me there.

To those who don't have a taste for wine, it's hard to explain, and surely comes across as pompous and pretentious. For that matter, at some wine tastings later on, I used to roll my eyes when some connoisseurs would sip some vintage and start professing to know what brand of coffee or what kind of tropical fruit they detected in the bouquet. But for all that, there *is* a difference between Mouton-Rothschild and Cheval Blanc, between Latour and Margaux, and so on, and they *do* differ from year to year. I know some people can't taste the difference, and nor do they care. I could, and I cared. In the late 1980s and early 1990s, the dollar was worth more in Europe than it is now, and my parents did their share of splurging on good wine while in France. I don't know if my enthusiasm really delighted them or just amused them, but they reacted positively to my interest and indulged it while we were there. One of my greatest thrills was when we visited the Beychevelle area and got to visit, and taste, Château Branaire Ducru, made famous in Roald Dahl's short story, "Taste."

Back at school in California, wine—available though nominally prohibited to my age group, along with all other alcohol (mostly beer, which I loathe still)—was to be had, but only served as a means to an end. It was deemed by my male classmates to be mostly useful for abusing girls' favors on dates and/or self-stupefaction. Although self-stupefaction was low on my list of favorite pastimes, winning girls' favors was right at the top. Unfortunately, winning *my* favors always seemed to be at the bottom of their lists, and I would have been *so* willing to bestow them, too! I was just put off by the idea of trying to achieve my goal by getting some girl rip-roaring drunk. I'm not sure that I was *really* that chivalrous, but I never even got the chance to find out if I was or not, pathetic as that may seem in macho circles.

I went to a local high school, and though American public schools may not have the greatest of reputations as a group, mine was actually not bad; we actually learned about certain subjects. I had some guy friends at school, of course, but my social situation was a perfect storm combination of them all being either totally uninterested in girls, or living too far away to make going out to fun events with them practical, or them having social schedules that never seemed to include me. I didn't go out of my way to be uncool, whatever that meant, but I was too stubborn or proud to go out of my way to be "cool," too. My parents were supportive, which I appreciated to no end, but somehow, I never appealed to girls who appealed to me. I ended up being one of those thirty-three per cent (or whatever the statistic is) of American kids who graduate from high school before having their first sexual experience.

2.

I'm going to fast forward here a little, as my unrequited youthful yearnings for romance are not really important to the story I want to tell. Suffice it to say that I followed in my parents' footsteps to UCLA, except that I majored in physics and minored in both French and a convincing imitation of the lead roles in "Revenge of the Nerds," though, alas, *sans* the revenge. I also had my first sexual experience (sound the trumpets!). Her name was Marnie Wexler.

Marnie Wexler was one year ahead of me. She was not beautiful, not ugly, not skinny, not chubby, but had gorgeous, thick, dark brown hair that hung down below her shoulders. She was pleasant enough, although she would not have been valedictorian at Charm School, and cared not one bit about wine. OK, nobody's perfect. Marnie had one outstanding trait—she talked incessantly. Her mouth did not have an off switch. As I was too polite to shout to get a word in edgewise, talkative though I can be, I apparently made an impression on her as a "good listener," and while I would have rather had my first sexually intimate encounter with a soft-spoken, passionate model type, Marnie was kind and very understanding of my inexperience. She also talked through most of "the act" and started up again pretty soon afterward, too. Was this normal? Where's Dr. Ruth when you need her? I had no experience of my own to draw on, of course, and I wasn't about to ask my mom or my dad about it, but I was pretty sure this was not how it was supposed to be. It wasn't how I wanted it to be for me, anyway. So, much as I missed the intimacy, I gradually stopped calling, and Marnie found herself another "good listener" in short order. "Good listeners" are apparently in ample supply in the male college population. I think it has to do with hormones, and I'm pretty sure that the hormones in question have very little effect on the function of the auditory nerve.

11

Through my college years, I got a few more Marnies under my belt (in more ways than one). I passed some of my free time by going to some wine tastings I could afford, and with watching old movies. Undergrad colleges offer a lot of old movies, and this was, after all, UCLA, with one of the best film schools in the country. The film that captured my fancy the most was "The Fly" with Vincent Price and David Hedison. Besides the story line, the idea of teleporting things from one place to another somehow seemed more conceivable to me than just "beam me up, Scotty." I intuitively thought molecular disassembly and reassembly should somehow be indeed possible, although I really didn't have a good grasp of how or why. Other than my constant interest in wine, especially now that I could drink it legally without traveling to France, my little theory became almost as much of an obsession with me as sex, difficult as that might be to believe of a normal twenty-one-year-old man with an intact hormonal make-up.

By the end of my senior year, while I did not end up beaming up Captain Kirk from the planet Durák, I did end up with a fair knowledge of physics, a broader knowledge of wine, and the companionship of Carolyn Arregui, also a senior. She had been fascinated by the fact that I recognized her name as being Basque the moment I heard it. There are enough Basques in the Bordeaux region of France that I recognized her ethnicity immediately from my many visits there with my parents. But she didn't know that at the time. She was so impressed that she went out with me the first time I asked, and we sort of clicked. She was from Elko, Nevada, which, she explained to me, had a decent-sized population of ethnic Basques. The Basques, for those who don't know, are an ancient people whose ancestral homeland is in the area on both sides of the Spanish/French border at the Atlantic end of the Pyrenees Mountains. The Mediterranean side is the homeland of the Catalans. I don't know if there's any line of demarcation. If there is, it must be patrolled by a brigade of mountain goats.

The Basques have their own version of *"E Pluribus Unum,"* which is *"Zazpiak Bat."* Instead of our *"Out of many, one,"* Zazpiak Bat sort of means *"Out of seven, one."* I did know that you form most plurals in Basque with the ending "-ak," although there was no way I was going to tackle a language that needs to say *"beirrogei ta hamazortzi"* just to say *"fifty-eight."* As it is, *"beirrogei ta hamazortzi"* translates out to *"two twenties and eighteen."* I think the chips in the first pocket calculators must have been patterned after the Basque brain. Fortunately for me, Ms. Arregui did not speak Basque, did not aspire to, and, best of all, did not expect me to.

There are seven Basque provinces (the *"zazpiak," "zazpi"* meaning "seven" in Basque), three of which are in France, which is how I came to know such trivia. To a Basque, by the way, Basque heritage is anything *but* trivial, so be careful who you say that to. The Basques are proud, sensitive and tough. Throughout history, they have been dumped upon by everyone from the ancient Romans through Franco's fascists, who let them be used as bombing practice targets by Hitler's Luftwaffe in 1937 during the Spanish Civil War. Don't try Basque ethnic jokes on a Basque unless you're seven feet tall, have the body mass of a sumo wrestler and the moves of Bruce Lee.

Carolyn was five feet seven and pleasant-looking, had shoulder-length brown hair, lighter than Marnie's, but pretty, nondescript dark eyes, and an aesthetically pleasant figure. This matters a lot to twenty-one-year-old men, even after they turn twenty-two. She was content to be calm and quiet at times (oh, yes!). She also tended to be moody (oh, well), and had an uncanny ability to find fault with anything (including me—I should have heeded the warning). Her mother had always found little faults with everything, including her daughter, who duly picked up the habit from Mamá. But the fact that she could shut up of her own volition, after my several Marnies, nonetheless made her a candidate for canonization in my short-sighted eyes. I totally missed danger signs like her going apoplectic if my shirt hung out just a tiny bit from my waist, or if one of my shoes was untied, or if I didn't have a credit card that made a good impression on her folks. "Offenses" like that just didn't seem worth getting riled up over and, therefore, I didn't realize it constituted a danger sign when Caro lumped them in the general category of crimes against humanity.

She liked to be called Caro, since it meant "dear" in Italian, even if it got her gender wrong. It was also the Italian word for "expensive." I should have heeded *that*, too. Caro's family was a very conservative, fairly well-off group of self-absorbed businesspeople, owning a variety of successful family businesses in and around Elko. Or so they said. The few times I visited the place, the only thing that I saw "around" Elko, Nevada, was desert. Maybe they owned a thriving sand dealership, who knows? The one thing I *did* know is that they didn't seem to think too much of me. Their attitude seemed to mirror that of the girls I liked in high school. I was not a top athlete, not famous or gorgeous, and not wealthy. Three strikes, and you're not good enough for our daughter. They never said it in so many words, of course, but if looks could kill, they would have been lucky to plea-bargain down to manslaughter. If looks could break up an impending marriage, all the better—at worst, they'd be facing fifty hours of community service and reimbursing the justice of the peace for the cost of the marriage license. Like me, Caro was an only child and, therefore, her choice of partner was of great import to her parents. She had plenty of aunts, uncles and cousins, but that didn't lessen the scrutiny with which her parents eyed Caro's boyfriends, including me.

Even so, Caro and I settled into what was if not a deep, passionate love, a comfortable relationship that included satisfying sex, a long-coveted goal of mine. She also liked wine, and this interest of mine even won the grudging approval of her Basque family, even if I didn't drink it out of a goatskin pouch like back in Euzkadi, the old country. I don't even remember what it was that moved me to propose to her, but I did, and she accepted in an equally routine manner. Upon reflection, I think the mutual wine appreciation is what finally persuaded her parents to allow the wedding to take place. Upon reflection, I'm not exactly sure what persuaded *me* to let the wedding take place but—20/20 hindsight and all that—maybe there was a little too much wine in both of us at the time I proposed. I *had* grown to care for her and, I'm pretty sure, she for me. Still, Caro found fault with me all the time, and I never developed thick enough skin to be able to ignore it completely. Like I said, I should have heeded the warning. My parents, as with everything, were cool with it all, but upon looking back, I wonder if they weren't suppressing having a long talk with me along the lines of, "Are you sure you really want to do this?" I thought parents were supposed to jump up and down and cheer when their offspring announced their engagement, but mine never made it off the ground when I told them. I think they were secretly hoping that, some day, I'd hit it off with Chelsea Clinton or something.

3.

The wedding was held in August 1998 in Elko and, I must admit, Caro's family put on quite a show, even though it must have been 110 degrees in the shade—of which Elko, Nevada, has none. I'm not religious and neither is she (her parents still don't know that), but her family made a big deal out of the ceremony, and I went along with it, although all the Catholic rituals were a chore for me to learn. Tom Lehrer's "Vatican Rag" kept running through my head. But hey, family harmony and all that, right? I maintained a straight face, "bowed my head with great respect," and kept the "Vatican Rag" to myself.

My parents got along OK with hers, but didn't make a point of trying to become their best chums or anything. They had their own circle of friends back in California and, politically, they were light years away from the very conservative Basques of Nevada. Caro's folks thought Ronald Reagan was God, or at least a close relative. They had been fervent supporters of another conservative ethnic Basque from Nevada, Paul Laxalt, who had been Nevada's governor and a senator, as well as a close Reagan ally. My folks, on the other hand, thought Bill Clinton was the best thing since sliced bread. As Kipling put it, "Never the twain shall meet." The parents promised to stay in touch, which translated to calls on birthdays (at first) and Christmas cards.

After a parent-funded honeymoon in Hawai'i, the real world started. Too bad. I couldn't find a job I liked as a physicist, and I suppose it didn't help my interviews much when I mentioned my fantasy about "The Fly" and teleportation. After all, by 1996, Star Trek was thirty years old and not only had Scotty not yet beamed anyone up, neither had anyone else, including yours truly. Worse yet, I still didn't have any concrete ideas about how to go about beaming anyone anywhere. My career as a Nobel Prize-winning physicist was going nowhere fast. I needed a day job.

My folks gave us some money (Caro's folks, who were far richer, gave us none), but I could tell they were anxious for me to start supporting myself and Caro on my own. They were right, of course, but it took time for me to admit to myself that I wasn't going to be Scotty, the celebrated beamer-upper, any time soon, and the Enterprise was leaving without me.

I finally got an out-of-the-blue job offer (from a chance encounter at a Starbucks, to be precise) from a former undergrad I had known at UCLA. Jim Hernández had been two years ahead of me, but also a student in my physics class, whom I had helped with lab work. He was about to return the favor. Jim's family had been in California so long, he could trace his ancestry directly back to Spain and firmly corrected anyone who called him "Mexican." He certainly looked the dashing Latin lover, right down to the pencil moustache. I used to call him "Zorro" back in physics lab, which he actually liked, since the fictional Diego de la Vega had been the son of a Spanish nobleman. Jim had gone on to breeze through law school at Stanford, making Law Review in his second year and graduating *magna cum laude*—a bright guy even if he wasn't wired for physics. He had joined a small but growing law firm in Sherman Oaks and told me their office desperately needed someone who was good with numbers and had organizational skills. I didn't know how valuable or useful my meager organizational skills (and apparently useless knowledge of physics) would be to a law firm, but I took the job (steady income!), started studying nights for my CPA, and was able to figure out fairly quickly what Jim's firm needed. They needed someone who grasped math, had a sense of time, and could handle special needs. It seemed to me they needed little more than a CPA who would also serve as a gofer, travel agent, occasional receptionist and interior decorator, but who was I to argue? Never look a gift day job in the mouth, especially if you can't find one anywhere else.

As it turned out, Jim worked with nice people—very nice people, even. I actually fit in quite well and was able to help make his office run smoothly. That, in turn, thrilled the partners. Their appointments no longer overlapped. Their plane reservations coincided with the dates of their hotel bookings, and the bills got paid once instead of twice or not at all. This was not exactly my chosen field and didn't seem to present much of a challenge to my self-assessed intellect, but, hey, they paid me decently ("we need to keep you here!")—way more than I thought they needed to, really. They seemed to think my skills were the catalyst that made the firm run like a softly purring 600 series Mercedes, something enough of them owned to lend serious credibility to the comparison. Besides, they *were* making money like a printing press on steroids. America's addiction to litigation, yay! Due to Jim, no doubt, they made sure I shared in their good fortune, and generously. Personally, I thought any self-respecting secretary would have done the same job for less than half what they were paying me, but I wasn't complaining.

Jim's firm was called Blake and Brock, or "B & B" at the office. Lawyers' reputations being what they are, a cynic might have said "Flake and Crock," but they were genuinely good people and actually seemed to have a conscience, thereby negating all the lawyer jokes I had ever heard since I found out what a lawyer was. I didn't fancy working for the bad guys in a John Grisham novel, anyway, so this was just fine with me.

It was not fine with Caro, though—at least, not fine enough. Oh, she liked the money at first, some always being far better than none. Still, it gradually ate away at her that she was not the wife of a hotshot lawyer, but the wife of a guy who helped hotshot lawyers have an easier time being hotshot lawyers. That was not the same.

18

She knew it, and she let me *know* she knew it. Worse yet, she made quite sure her family knew it, too. They saw me as little more than a male secretary/receptionist with an undeservedly inflated salary (not entirely wrong, I guess). In the beginning, though, it wasn't such a divisive factor as to threaten to split us up. We were able to afford a down payment on a decent-sized house within two years, and Caro did indulge me my two hobbies with no objection. There was a modest lawn out front, which Caro mowed herself, and she tended to a rather respectable garden that was one of her prides. Caro was not a spoiled rich brat, don't get me wrong. She was willing to get her hands dirty. It's just that she craved the social status her family enjoyed in Elko, and my current position wasn't going to provide that.

4.

In our basement, I was able to set up both a small wine cellar plus a modest-sized lab with space for gadgets that I was sure would one day enable me to do the beaming up that Scotty never did in real life. Hey, it was only a matter of time--no, really! Does anybody know off the top of his head if the Nobel Prize for Physics is awarded in Stockholm or Oslo? Maybe it wasn't too soon to look into good deals on advance plane reservations with Scandinavian Airlines? But back in the real world, I was OK with the way things were.

Caro, on the other hand, was *not* OK with my being just "OK." She still wanted to be the wife of the top dog, not the lapdog. She was anxious for me to start coming up in the world. No, let me be more accurate. She was anxious to be the wife of someone who was starting to come up in the world. Maybe it was some inner desire to prove to her parents that she had made the right choice after all, and in her family's eyes, this was measured by the yardstick of our house's square footage and how much our cars cost. I was starting to hear this a little too often for my taste. Unconsciously, I found myself going to wine tastings a little more frequently than I used to, and got even more into the intimacies and intricacies of the various vintages than I ever thought possible. *Escapism, mon amour.* I was to take *that* concept to a much higher level, as it turned out, but I wasn't anywhere near there yet. That part came after the dark and stormy night.

Twice I took Caro to France on vacation. She spoke no French at all and found the country quaint, but preferred Hawaii or Lake Tahoe. Post-honeymoon trips to Hawaii were perks financed by an appreciative Blake and Brock, attorneys at law. They paid me well, but not enough to afford two weeks in a suite at the Mauna Lani. I was in heaven, of course, when we were in France, but I got the impression that Caro was really bothered by the fact that she was somewhat at my mercy in a country where I spoke the language and she didn't. To make matters worse, Caro, with her Basque ancestry, looked far more French than I did, so when people heard us speaking English together, they assumed that if anyone spoke French, it was she and, hence, they would address her first. When I spoke up instead, she thought she passed for an idiot, and finding fault with herself was not something she did voluntarily. Therefore, she found fault with France. Caro had majored in drama at UCLA, and provided more of it than I would have liked.

To Caro, France was too dirty, too small, Paris was too crowded (L.A. wasn't?), and the people were rude. I think she read that in some list of mandatory clichés about France. She liked the food, some of the scenery, and thought the wine tasted "pretty good." I thought the place was pure paradise, and that the wine tasted divine, but my opinion was neither requested nor desired—something that grew in geometric proportions as time wore on. I tried not to do things that made her angry, but some things were just beyond my power to fix. No matter what I did, people in the Loire Valley would always address us in French first. Funny how they do that in France. The nerve!

As my place in the firm starting growing roots, we got invited to gatherings at the houses of some of the people at the firm. Jim, in particular, invited us over a lot. His wife, Janice, was an attractive blonde surfer type who was originally from Kansas City and had no idea how to surf. They were planning to have children some day but "hadn't gotten around to it." Janice taught girls' gymnastics at the same high school where I had gone. I wished Caro had been able to occupy herself with a job, too, but her upbringing had taught her how to be the wife of a rich man, and her schooling had taught her how to make a scene about the fact that she wasn't. Instead of enjoying the company and Jim's great house, Caro grumbled that they had a bigger, fancier house than we did, and where we drove a Camry, they drove a Lexus (at least the brakes and accelerator pedals on our car still worked!). I said it was normal, as Jim was a successful lawyer and was making way more money than I was. I heard the penalty buzzer sound in my head as soon as the words left my mouth.

"And you're happy with that?" Caro demanded angrily. I shut up, because the truth was, I *was* happy with that.

Caro came from a wealthy family that held me in disdain for my relative poverty. Having friends who had way more money than we did was *not* normal for her. It was a major wrong that was in dire need of rectification, and I had no idea how to do it. Worse yet, I had no *desire* to do it. I got raises with embarrassing frequency, generous (in my eyes) bonuses, and was pretty happy with my situation. I felt no pressing need to pull in three million dollars a year, and even if I had my own Lear jet, I wouldn't know how to fly the thing. I didn't see myself commandeering some poor on-call pilot around, either. "Jeeves, I think we'll be lunching in New Orleans today. No, stop. The oil spill might affect the taste of the bluefish filet. I've changed my mind. Make it Seattle, instead. Request a change in the flight plan, there's a good lad." Sorry, that's just not me.

5.

My domestic life was deteriorating, but it was happening so gradually that I was able to not notice it from one day to the next. Besides, it wasn't a straight downhill spiral. Caro and I *did* have some good times together, especially when there were no reminders around as to why my ability to show off material accomplishments was somehow lacking. While hiking around Lake Tahoe, it didn't matter to either of us how many more square feet than ours the Hernández house had. The scenery was the same no matter how much money you had, and the air was just as invigorating for paupers as it was for billionaires. Fortunately, the subject of children never even came up. I had no time to be a stay-at-home dad, and she had no desire to take care of children, anyway. I would have liked a family at some point, but was not exactly devastated by Caro's wish not to. Subconsciously, I think, I was scared of the prospect of needing to protect and comfort our imaginary offspring from her moodiness. At home, I was able to mentally write off particularly unpleasant arguments with rationalizations that Caro was having a bad day or didn't feel well. The main thing was to find some reason that it wasn't really her fault, and it would be OK. Caro, on the other hand, was sure that the causes of all disputes were *my* fault. Even if they were, I didn't really want to expend the emotional energy to constantly be on the defensive, and so I hid by tinkering in the basement lab or going to wine tastings instead of spending evenings in the living room, getting an updated review of the inadequacies of our social status.

I was able to talk to my parents for moral support, and they were willing to provide it, as always. They said they understood where Caro was coming from, having met her parents and relatives, but agreed that I was certainly financially better off than anyone else with my kind of job had a right to expect to be, and they thought she was being unreasonable to blame me for not being wealthier. Her folks eventually did make me a half-hearted offer to join their small family business empire, but I didn't really detect a lot of sincerity in their offer. It was made with an undertone of "feel free to say no," which I did. Besides, I didn't see myself living out my days as a sand mogul in Elko, Nevada, any more than Frank Zappa had really intended to move to Montana soon and be a dental floss tycoon.

By 2005, with the Internet now being as standard as potable tap water or grammatical errors by George W. Bush, I was able to really get into my two hobbies in depth. I had all sorts of exotic gadgetry set up in my lab downstairs, and though I was getting nowhere with my teleportation fantasies, I was learning all sorts of advanced information about molecular physics. I even e-mailed with people who told me they thought my fantasy might just be reality some day and why. I had an idea or two that I thought might work if I could only find some source of ten gazillion volts of electricity (not inconceivable, *"Back to the Future"* notwithstanding) and some circuitry that hadn't been invented yet (less conceivable). Hah! Such minor details. I had also e-mailed with a Nobel Prize-winning physicist who invited us to a yearly New Year's gathering in Charleston, South Carolina. All sorts of VIPs and gifted non-VIPs got together there, and he said I might meet some kindred spirits. It sounded fabulous, but Caro wouldn't hear of it, said we'd just be rejected if we applied, and even if we were accepted to attend, we wouldn't have anything to contribute and would just embarrass ourselves. A real upbeat outlook on life, don't you think? Neither of us had ever been to South Carolina and I thought it sounded like great fun, but Caro managed to think up so many different reasons why it *wouldn't* be, that I eventually abandoned the idea. I now wish I had overruled her, but then, there are a lot of things I wish I had done differently. Besides, if I *had* overruled her and dragged her along, she would just have found a hundred reasons why both of us were not having a good time and made it a self-fulfilling prophecy. It was an argument I couldn't win, so I decided not to have it.

My parents had recently retired and were traveling back to Europe as often as they could, and I envied them mightily. My envy faded when they boarded a Helios Airways flight from Lanarca, Cyprus, to Athens on August 14, 2005, and the plane never arrived. I knew from their last phone call from Lanarca on the thirteenth that they were trying to get on the flight at the last minute. They weren't even on the original official passenger list, and it took some long phone calls to Cyprus to determine that they had indeed been on the plane. I was told that the crew had misread some instruments and made some mistakes. The plane crashed at full speed into the side of a mountain just north of Athens—no survivors. The only thing close to comforting was that I was told that, due to verifiable oxygen deprivation, all the passengers were unconscious at the time the plane went down, so my folks never experienced abject horror in their last moments.

Jim and the guys at the firm were great and said any time I wanted to talk, etc., etc., but I was inconsolable. It didn't help that Caro's shoulder, the one I needed most and should have been able to cry on, was colder than I thought I deserved. Caro seemed more interested in what I would inherit, which was their house and a little stock, but not much else. Looking back upon it, I wonder if I hadn't right then and there seen the omen foretelling the collapse of my marriage and I had just chosen, out of convenience, to overlook it. I had just lost both my parents with whom I had always enjoyed a close relationship—something far from commonplace, from what I had observed. My grief didn't really seem to concern Caro a whole hell of a lot. I wondered, for all the concern her parents had shown for the well-being of their own daughter, if their concern had more to do with her acquiring a high rung on the social ladder than whether or not she was happy. Of course, if they had convinced her that happiness *was* a high rung on the social ladder, then she had a concept of happiness that would be forever irreconcilable with my own. Not that I take myself to be the standard by which spiritual contentment is to be measured; it's not like I had a marriage that was the envy of lovers worldwide. But it seemed to me that I deserved a shot at attaining the comfort and ease that my own parents had (at least, as far as I could tell) with each other, and I didn't have it. Caro's mercenary attitude when I lost Mom and Dad disturbed me at the time. In retrospect, it should have enraged me, and maybe that was the moment where a spark ensued that was to smolder underneath my lethargic surface for a long time. Even now, I can't really feel sputtering rage towards her, just a dull disappointment watered down by an understanding of the values her parents instilled in her, plus very recent events that permanently changed my whole outlook on the matter. I'll get to that.

Mom and Dad had enjoyed life, and when they saw that I was "established," they had spent what they could on themselves. Good for them. I was happy for them, and approved of their attitude wholeheartedly—even more so after they were gone, as they at least got to enjoy a lot of what life had to offer and had what I thought was a really sensible outlook on it all. After all, *que será será*, right? I only wished they had left me an instruction manual.

As their only child, I was appointed executor of their will, which turned out to be fairly uncomplicated. The details were pretty straightforward and don't really have a bearing on my story here, anyway. Suffice it to say that I sold their house through a real estate agent recommended by B&B, and one of Jim's lawyers handled the legal stuff. When they saw that I had a solid job with a law firm, my parents had placed their will there a few years before. I was able to handle the tax part on my own, and by the end of the year, their estate was settled, even if the gaping hole they left in my life was not. In recent years, we hadn't talked every day, or even every week, but the fact that I *could* talk to them whenever I wanted (or felt I needed to) turned out to have been more important to me than I ever realized while they were alive. They were just shy of sixty and both in great health when they died, and it never occurred to me that they wouldn't live to be 100, so I took their eternal presence for granted. That old song was right: you never know what you've got 'til it's gone.

6.

In my unconscious quest for time away from Caro, when not
tinkering in my lab in the basement, I was still seeking refuge at
wine tastings whenever I could fit them in. It did occur to me, as well
as to her, that I was getting just a little obsessed with my affinity
for the wine tastings. But, as Caro was not interested in returning to
France for more vacations and our relationship had not yet gotten so
bad that I was considering taking vacations by myself without her,
this was about as close to France as I was going to get, and I think
she rationalized that it was preferable to having me drag her off to
France again.

At the wine tastings there were stuck-up people, normal people,
completely weird people, nice people, not nice people, and some who
were somewhere in between. It wasn't always obvious who fit into
which category, as I found out. Aha! The plot thickens, and the dark
and stormy night approaches.

For a payment up front, those present at the tastings got to sample
vintages from all over, and sometimes there were some old bottles
from the cellars of serious collectors. There were plenty of stories
about prestige vintage bottles that had been doctored, either with
fake labels or manipulated content, but I had a great time anyway.
I didn't much care for arguments over whether some vintage being
sampled had raspberries or boysenberries in its bouquet (gimme
a break), or whether some other vintage had instant coffee or freshly
ground espresso in its aftertaste (gimme another break). That always
sounded hopelessly pompous to me. I did, however, love to taste
the different types and vintages and let them weave their tapestries
of taste over my tongue at these events. The fascination that hit
me as a teenager vacationing with my parents had only grown
more intense with the passage of time. There were the classics,

of course—Château Lafite, Château Margaux, Mouton-Rothschild, Château Latour, Château Yquem, Pétrus and so on (one specialist from New York called them "the usual suspects"), but also the occasional new California vintages, and once in awhile some exotic ones from Australia, South Africa and Chile, even places like Texas and Cape Cod, Massachusetts. The non-French vintages were not as "mature," of course, but some of them showed promise. Give some of those Napa Valley reds some time to mature and there might be some real classics among them. Of course, anything dated after 1870 was, by definition, "new wave," so to speak, as a plague had practically wiped out the local Bordeaux vineyards that year. That's a long story, but the short version is that any Bordeaux before that time that had been properly stored and well sealed at the time of bottling (most of the few surviving bottles had not) usually outclassed anything that came later, although there was the occasional star among the later vintages (Mouton Rothschild 1945—now a $10,000 bottle in its own right, Cheval Blanc 1947, the fabled 1929 Latour, the legendary 1899 Lafite, etc.).

I gotta watch it here, as it's not my intention to sound as pompous as some of these people, but I swear, if there could ever be a kaleidoscope effect applied to taste, then this was it. Lafite, Margaux, Mouton, Pétrus, Cheval Blanc, Latour, bring 'em on, baby. If I can't get to France whenever I want, then the mountain must come to Mohammed. Sometimes I'd run into French people at these events, and was always proud to hear from them that my French was still near-fluent, and that my accent was good. *"Votre français est vraiment excellent, monsieur!"* *Oh,* yeah. Excellent! You hear that, Elko, Nevada? *Excellent!* And that's pronounced "ex-say-LON." Not as good as great sex in a harmonious relationship (as if I would know, right?), but music to my ears, nonetheless.

If you've never been to a serious wine tasting in southern California, they attract truly *all* kinds of characters, let me tell you. There were guys with Coke-bottle-bottom glasses and *fleur-de-lis* bow ties, or snotty self-declared experts who would ponder some vintage wine's bouquet and then take the word "bouquet" literally, telling you that they detected the unmistakable scent of Aunt Murgatroid's favorite azalea bush, located somewhere between the raspberries and the Lavazzo coffee. Sometimes, you would even meet some really serious collectors, with cellars housing thousands of bottles. I don't know when they ever planned to drink them all, not to mention their basements must have been big enough to house NORAD.

As I was not a famous entertainer or an internationally acknowledged wine expert, I was not accorded much attention at the wine tastings I attended. Not that I craved adulation, but I did my homework and thought I knew what was good and why. I figured it wouldn't kill anyone to acknowledge that. But it wasn't enough that I knew that a Cheval Blanc 1982 was far preferable to a Cheval Blanc 1981. I guess it was just my bad luck that *my* Aunt Murgatroid wasn't a direct descendant of Marie Antoinette (or married, however briefly, to Kirk Douglas).

There were several L.A. area wine dealers who came regularly, and some of them dealt in really prestigious stuff, costing sometimes tens of thousands of dollars per bottle. Some had even handled some of the so-called "Jefferson Bottles," which were purported to have come from the wine collection of Thomas Jefferson, although the origin and provenance of these bottles had been brought into doubt in recent years, and one irate collector was suing the pants off of a group of dealers in exotic wine who, he was sure, had sold him a phony bill of goods for a *lot* of money. Rare wine was no longer a question of $150 bottles of Château *Jamaisentendu* at your local pretentious restaurant. Famous bottles went for six figures nowadays, and a phony $100,000 item was a major fraud in any field of collectibles.

One dealer in particular, Aldous D. George of Rodeo Drive in Beverly Hills, seemed to have an especially extensive knowledge of rare wine, as well as a very well-heeled clientele for super-expensive wine bottles. He attended auctions at Christie's in London and similar events. If you were to hear him go on about the vintages he had sold, you'd think the world of rare wine revolved around him. Hell, give him enough time, and he'd have you thinking Galileo was full of it and the sun itself revolved around him (*"eppur si muove"*). He would toss out names like Michael Broadbent and Hardy Rodenstock as if the three of them got together for poker and adult movies every Friday night. In reality, I have no solid knowledge that he ever hung out with either of them. He knew my name – kinda, sorta – but always gave me the brush-off at tastings, as I was not interested in, or capable of, buying bottles of wine at $40,000 each, nor did I possess any in that kind of price category. Once it became clear I was connected neither to Hewlett-Packard nor to the manufacturer of prized vintage cars, I was at best a presence to be tolerated, and in small doses at that.

I got sort of a secret revenge for his disdain for me in that I found out — but never let on that I knew — that his real name was not Aldous D. George, but Aldo DiGiorgio, and his pompous English name was as phony as his supposed aristocratic British ancestry. For that matter, his looks *were* a lot closer to Danny DeVito than Roger Moore. But so what? Why anyone would be ashamed of a cool ethnic name like Aldo DiGiorgio was beyond me. After all, in 2010 the president of France had a Hungarian name, and the President of the United States had a Kenyan name. Ethnic was in.

But maybe Aldous D. George was the product of another generation, one to whom the Godfather movies were still a little too fresh in their minds. Another wine dealer who knew him from way back told me that George/DiGiorgio was really Sicilian, and had family connections to organized crime. The dealer also said that it wasn't healthy to bring that up in public, no matter what you knew, and I didn't have to be told twice. If I had no intention of getting on the wrong side of Aldous D. George, I certainly was not going to deliberately offend Luca Brasi. Besides, the guy *did* know his stuff, and he *did* sell wine bottles for $40,000 (and more) a pop. That's not small potatoes, even if your dad was Don Corleone. He did look the part, that was for sure. Aldous D. George was not the tall, slender, graying blond, aristocratic English gentleman the name evoked. He was a round-shaped, balding, mustachioed, swarthy man who looked more like what he was. Why that isn't good enough for some people, I'll never know, but I guess southern California has a reputation to live up to. At least he didn't appear to have had any major breast enhancement surgery. But his deliberate ignoring of me was not to be a permanent phenomenon. The estimable Mr. George was to play an important role or two in my life soon enough, anyway – weren't you, Aldo, you greedy son of a bitch?

7.

The firm of Blake and Brock just never seemed to be able to do any wrong, and while I didn't really put in what I considered a lot of overtime, I was on overdrive from eight to six most days at the office. The more legal business there was, the more logistics I had to coordinate, which now included high-level meetings around the world, security in some cases, intercontinental travel, software issues, and, on occasion, personnel issues. I called the rare, inevitably teary firings "tissue issues," poet that I am. By the way, I hereby grant full rights to any aspiring medical student who might wish to steal "tissue issues," unless it turns out that I unwittingly just stole it from someone else.

The year my parents died, I even got to hire an assistant. After six or so interviews, I settled on a short, very plain-looking, slightly plump forty-something woman named Juanita Chang (Guatemalan with a green card, who had married and divorced a failed short-order specialist in General Tsao's chicken). On her written application, she had written, "efficiency and reliability must necessarily be viewed as inseparable assets." This had really impressed me. When I met her at the oral follow-up, I remarked on what she had written. She said, "Jus' like I written down, I gotta be dere to do what djoo need when djoo need it!" Amazing. Juanita had the IQ of Einstein and the energy of Mount St. Helen's at the time of eruption. Her English, when she put it to paper, was fluent and grammatically as good as that of Winston Churchill, but when she opened her mouth, she sounded like a parody of Speedy Gonzales— sort of like having salsa on your fish and chips. Juanita did not have a great education. She was mostly self-taught in English (I think she must have started with Chaucer), or else she would have won her first Nobel Prize ten years earlier.

In the oral interview, as a joke, I asked her if she had learned to speak Mandarin Chinese while she was married. She thought I was being serious, gave me a stern look, and said, "Djoo kiddin' wit' me, Señor Roberto." OK, maybe my little joke crossed the line, although by this time, I had decided on her anyway. But before I could apologize, she continued, perfectly seriously, "My ex-hosban ees from Hong Kong. I only learn to speak Cantonese, no Mandarin." Umm, right. *After deep insertion, remove foot from mouth as gracefully as possible.* But like I said, I had decided on her already.

Once Juanita started, my workload eased back from "hectic" to a comfortable level, and the firm swore they noticed no decline in the efficiency of what was now my nameless "department." They eventually decided to name it "Security and Logistics," and my title as director thereof would be next to my name when the next round of business cards was ordered.

Caro had no problem with Juanita, even saw a step up in her quest for some nebulous prestige that I now had someone working for me, thereby raising my position from low man on the totem pole to second lowest. After all, now I had my own department! The few times that she met Juanita, Caro treated her as if she were a retarded maid, but I made the high esteem in which I held Juanita very clear to her, and she told me she just figured Caro was acting out some kind of required role as colonial master—*"dueña de la hacienda,"* she called it. She might not have reacted as indifferently if she knew that Caro's disdain was all too real, but Juanita was so used to Caro's attitude from countless other Anglos that she paid it little heed, luckily for me.

Still, even with my "enhanced" position--with an underling, no less!—Caro's drift away from her original affection for me seemed to be on a steady ride down a one-way street. I guess the fact that I had once recognized Arregui to be a Basque name got stale

34

with age. We still slept in the same bed, and even got together for sex on occasion, but it increasingly seemed to me to be more for the mutual satisfaction of hormonal needs rather than for affection, which I missed. When not at the firm, I continued to seek asylum in my wine tastings and tinkered more in my lab with greater intensity than ever before, although I got no closer to Nobel Prize-winning success than I had up to then—and I missed France. Occupational therapy was more like it. Even so, it didn't escape me that I was less than heartbroken over the situation, and I didn't feel the pain that I thought such a rift was supposed to cause. I guess I wasn't ready to admit to myself that the patient was dying a slow, natural death, but looking back, that's the most accurate diagnosis I could have given the marriage of Robert and Carolyn Packard.

I won't get into the intricacies of physics, but suffice it to say that I had been building up what I hoped would become a pair of computer-driven force fields that would deconstruct objects fed into one end and reassemble them coming out of the other end, just like the scientist in "The Fly." I got nowhere, of course. I did get what I imagined to be the equivalent of being tasered a couple of times while trying to shove something made of metal through one of the portals with my hand, but that was about it—not even singed eyebrows or hair standing on end. I got myself a big ceramic pizza spatula, all the same. You know, one of those things that Albanians pretending to be Italians use in pizza parlors when they can rent enough space to have a real brick pizza oven in their eatery. Only mine was made of ceramic, not metal, as I was not looking to get tasered on too regular a basis. I tried everything I knew, picked the brains of great minds over the Internet, and *still* got nowhere. Nobel Prize winners offered me a few bits of advice, words of encouragement, and brushed me off with a polite version of "Good luck, kid." I was a little disappointed, to tell the truth. Sixty years ago, these guys split the atom, and after all this time they still couldn't help Scotty (i.e., me) beam up Captain Kirk? My force fields hummed and crackled, but otherwise were not behaving, and I was not in this for the sound effects. Besides, Rice Krispies had already been patented.

Fact: Every object, animate and inanimate, is made up of a collection of molecules, arranged in a certain pattern. I figured everything had to be like a molecular Rubik's cube; no matter how completely you took the original pattern apart, there had to be a way to reverse the deconstruction and reassemble it. Well, it *sounded* logical, anyway, as long as you were an idiot like me. There just *had* to be a way to program and wire the system to disassemble an object to its molecules, send them in a beam somewhere, and have a device on the other end that recognizes the original form, encoded in the transmission, and reassembles that object exactly as it was before. Well, apparently not. Amazing Fantasy Comics number 4896, welcome to my basement lab. Someone go call Stan Lee; I need some help with the details of the plot. Back in late March, the Hadron Collider near Geneva, Switzerland, had succeeded in smashing some protons at just under the speed of light, but somehow they forgot to invite me for the occasion or subsequently inquire if their findings might prove useful in my experiments. A mere oversight on their part, I'm sure.

I didn't really tell Caro what my science project was. It was bad enough that she thought the people I met at the wine tastings were somewhere between pretentious and weird. She came to one once, and that only reinforced her opinion. It would have been far worse far sooner if she knew that I was spending time and money — especially the money — attempting to recreate something I had seen in a 1950s science fiction film. Caro was not miserly with money, but it was important to her to have plenty of it all the same. I guess her family had instilled these values in her as a child. Since her family was one of the wealthiest in their neighborhood and flaunted it, I suspect she missed people *envying* her more than she felt any actual poverty. As I could never comprehend why anyone would crave envy, I had a hard time understanding her point of view, and she faulted me for that, too. I think it's fair to say that we were inescapably headed to what is termed "irreconcilable differences," but fate took care of that before the symptoms became terminal. We never did end up getting a divorce.

8.

IT WAS A DARK AND STORMY NIGHT

Ah, *finally*! Hey, look, I told you it was coming, so chill out. Besides, this is just the start of where things began to get weird. Now comes the part where you start to get happy you didn't click away five minutes ago to Google tomorrow night's local movie listings or the services provided by the five Thai massage parlors in La Paz, Bolivia, or whatever.

It wasn't dark for any abnormal length of time, but stormy? Oh, yeah, stormy we got. I don't know if it was global warming, climate change, or some freak weather pattern that would have happened no matter what. What I *do* know is that every local TV station, radio station, cop car with a bullhorn, and supermarket poster warned everyone that a major, *major* lightning storm was going to hit our area. This was going to be the mother of all lightning storms. I mean, they told us to turn off everything in the house that used electricity, down to your Energizer bunny, if you had one. Unplug your TVs, refrigerators, appliances, answering machines, vibrators, *everything!* If you didn't live in a house equipped with a grounded lightning diverter, then go to one that was. Ours had one, so we stayed put, but we heeded the edict and unplugged everything that had a plug, and made sure to remove the batteries from all battery-powered gadgets. We heard our neighbors scrambling to do the same. Jim Hernández, Juanita and even Richard Brock himself called to remind me, in case I had forgotten. Richard Brock, as in one of the firm's two managing partners!! I would have been less blown over if it had been Barack Obama on the line, saying he had an important message for me, then handing the phone to Hillary Clinton, so she could remind me to shut off my dehumidifier.

Caro and I sat in the living room on the ground level, basically being bored, but not for long. We heard the crashes of thunder a few miles away, but they came closer with a steady, and very scary, pace. The house started to actually shake, as if taking body blows, from the thunder claps, and this was with the actual storm still a few miles away. As it bore down on us, we could feel not only the house trembling, but the ground beneath us as well, intensifying as it closed in. I remembered those old ads for margarine—it is *definitely* not nice to fool Mother Nature, not that I ever consciously tried.

The storm reached us soon enough, and the crashes were deafening. Lightning exploded all around us, and I was sure the house took a few direct hits, saved only by the lightning rods installed during its construction, well before we bought it. Caro, mood or no mood, grabbed onto my arm in genuine fright, and had our gender roles been reversed, I would have done the same to her. We imagined we heard neighborhood children screaming in their houses after every new ground-tossing crash of lightning, and sympathized with every one of them. I had never had such a terrifying experience in my life, before or since. When a tree was hit, a sickening crack could be heard, and the only reason we never heard the thudding of large pieces of wood hitting the ground or our roof was because new bolts were striking before the effects of the previous one could be detected. We heard bits and pieces of shouting from enraged spouses in nearby houses, telling the other off for forgetting to unplug this or that electrical device, which had now been totally fried, along with a goodly portion of their house wiring.

Caro and I held on for dear life, although inside the house we didn't seem to have been in any real danger. The shaking and crashing carried on for a while, and for a moment I wondered if the storm would set off an earthquake, but it finally started to subside and move on. Lightning still boomed and crackled in the distance, but with decreasing frequency, and, finally, ceased altogether.

We eventually dared to peek out of our door to see what damage the neighborhood had suffered. One car had been hit and exploded (Caro noted with some satisfaction that it was a Lexus), and there didn't appear to be one tree that had come away unscathed. Branches were blown off, or blown down altogether, or the whole tree had been blasted into toothpicks—sometimes a combination of all three. Several houses nearby seemed to have suffered minor fires, but nothing bad enough to cause a total loss of the structure.

Turning around from outside our front door, I looked inside our darkened house and prided myself on the efficiency that had earned me so many kudos, as well as an assistant named Juanita Chang, at the office. I had turned off every device on the ground floor and upper floor of our modest-but-roomy house. No electrical device on either floor had escaped my attention, even in our panic, and all there was in the basement, after all, was my lab.

 Oh, crap. My lab. All my instances of getting tasered, all those force fields that I really didn't completely understand (or make function), all those thousands of dollars used to buy electronics, circuitry and all that fancy stuff I never explained to Caro for fear she would ask what they had all cost. I had not turned off the power in my lab.

I had all kinds of circuit breakers to protect from surges, of course, but there are surges and then there are surges. The electrical surges I had sought to protect against were like gently lapping waves on Lake Tahoe. What had just hit our house was a winter sixty-footer at Waimea Bay on Oahu's North Shore. I felt ill, and I hadn't even surveyed the damage yet. I was pretty confident I knew what I would find down there, so I was in no hurry to inspect the damage. As far as Caro was concerned, there couldn't have been any damage, as the loss of anything that only I was interested in did not constitute damage in her mind. We went back into the house, and at around 6:00 a.m. Caro announced that she was drained from the ordeal and was going right to sleep, which she did without so much as asking me if I planned to escort her or not. *Plus ça change*, as they say in France.

I figured things were not going to repair themselves on their own, so I had better get it over with and inspect the damage, or the debris, which was more of what I expected to find. I opened the door to the basement. The first thing I noticed, before even descending the stairs, was that there was no stench of molten anything. I had expected to see my years of electrical experimenting transformed into a bubbling, stinking, toxic grey mozzarella on the concrete floor, so the lack of an overpowering stench was encouraging. I had expected to be hit with the acrid stench of burnt rubber and charred silicon, yet smelled neither. Rather, there was a faint odor of ozone, a musty reminder of an ionized atmosphere. While descending the stairs, I was pleasantly surprised *not* to see broken pieces of electronic devices strewn about the floor. No electrical wiring alla Parmigiana. Better yet, it seemed that nothing at all had been destroyed. Had I really been spared? Nahh, couldn't be, no way. The circuitry was undoubtedly fried beyond repair, and only the shell remained. But if that were so, how come there was no telltale stink? I hadn't turned the house lights back on yet, but I saw that the indicator lights on my wannabe gadget were all green. I wondered if anything other than the indicator lights had survived. After all, the house had to have taken a few gazillion volts of electricity, and that's normally enough to churn the insides of any electrical device, no matter how insulated. I had put in some powerful backup batteries in case of a major power outage, but nothing like a hospital has to keep its operating rooms going in case of a complete power outage. I did not perform hobby appendectomies in my spare time, after all.

9.

I got to the foot of the stairs and noticed immediately that one of my portals, the "taserer," was showing what looked like a big 3-D movie scene plastered onto it. Not only that, but the film was still running. Weirder yet, the characters in the film were all gathering in front of the portal staring back at me. They appeared to be standing at the edge of some field near a copse of trees. OK, maybe I had gotten hit by some lightning and didn't realize it? But Caro had been next to me the whole time, and she had gone right back to being her usual irritable self. If she hadn't been zapped, then neither had I. OK, so what's with the big screen, high-definition DVD player? I certainly didn't install any such thing down there. For lack of any other idea, I addressed the film characters staring at me, saying, "Hi guys, what's the good word?" They looked at me from the other side of the portal as if I had just dropped in from Mars. There were about eight people there, dressed in some kind of antique costumes with what looked like gardening tools, shovels, pitchforks, that kind of thing. Rural gothic, if you will—a few older guys, a middle-aged woman, and a Juliette Binoche-type brunette beauty in her late twenties (I supposed), in a simple frock dress and with a smile that took my breath away. Whatever film this was, I was going to get the DVD and watch the scenes with her in them about twenty times before watching anything else.

She reminded me of a mature version of some of those nameless pretty French girls that smiled at me when my parents took me on vacation while I was a teenager, only somehow purer, more uncorrupted. It's hard to explain, as I had never seen anyone like this up close. This was a film, right? So how come the other people took about two and a half seconds to notice my sudden infatuation (I think my tongue hanging down to my knees gave it away) and got a chuckle out of my staring? If anyone reading this was forced to read Joseph Conrad's

"Victory" in high school (as I was), then even if you hated trudging through it, you might remember the moment where the protagonist, Axel Heyst, sees his woman-to-be and thinks to himself, "A *girl*, by Jove!" I hadn't exactly been celibate up to this point, but that pretty much describes my reaction. I don't blame them for having stared at my staring. Except, how did *they* notice that I was staring?

I was shaken out of my sudden romantic stupor when one of the older men staring at me addressed me with "*Qui êtes vous?*" That's French for "Who are you?" and in any language, it's not what you expect to be asked by a character in a DVD you are watching. A new kind of interactive French language DVD? And if so, who installed it during the lightning storm?

I felt like I was Bill Cosby's Noah trying to figure out if, and why, he was *really* suddenly supposed to build an "ark," whatever that was.

Even so, my French didn't fail me, so I said, "*Je m'appelle Robert. Qui êtes vous, et où êtes vous?*"

The man answered back, "*Je suis Philippe Boudreau, et nous sommes en France, évidemment!*" I had told him my name, and asked him who he was, and where he was. His answer translated out to, "I am Philippe Boudreau, and we're in France, obviously," as if to say, "You idiot, where else could we possibly be?"

I asked him where in France, and he thought I was mocking him, so a little impatiently he said they were in the Bordeaux region ("*dans la région de Bordeaux*") and, while we were on the subject, just where was I? I said I was in Los Angeles. They all looked at each other, drawing a collective blank. He came back with "*C'est où, ça?*"— "Where in the world is that?"

I thought this was getting a little silly and told him to be serious, as everyone in the year 2010 knew where Los Angeles was. They found this hilarious, even my Juliette Binoche smiling beauty. The man said (I'll translate here), "I'm sure they do. Get back to us in 150 years and we'll all know where it is, too."

At this point, I started to consider the vague possibility that my oddball circuitry coupled with the one-off effects wrought by the lightning storm might have just turned my basement into the first and foremost scientific wonder ever, but I still couldn't intellectually grasp what was obviously being played out before my eyes (that's a formal way of saying, "Naaaah, no *way*!"). Things like this happen to characters made up by Stan Lee, not to me. I said I didn't know if it was safe to cross the portal, so they should keep to the other side, but I did my best to explain that Los Angeles was in California on the west coast of the United States of America. Philippe said that from what he heard, it was the best part to be in, what with all the trouble that was supposed to be brewing between the North and the South on the east coast. I had no idea what he meant until I remembered that in 1860, the Civil War was not history, but an impending event. With the southern states trying to buy arms from France, the word had to be out over there, even if Fort Sumter wasn't going to be shelled until the following year. California had become a state in 1850. I was one of the few who actually had paid attention in American history class in high school and knew that kind of thing.

There was so much I wanted to talk with them about, but I remembered the admonishing I had heard in all the science fiction stories about time travel and how fiddling with the past could drastically alter the future, so I bit my tongue for the moment and asked about my other main interest. *"Si vous êtes à Bordeaux, auriez vous une bouteille de vin par hasard?"* (If you're in Bordeaux, might you have a bottle of wine by any chance?)

They had themselves a big laugh over this, too, and said, *"C'est tout ce qu'on a, mon vieux!"* (That's all we *do* have, old boy!)

My Juliette Binoche-type melted me with her laugh. It was melodious, ringing and genuine. It would have been worth memorizing a book of French humor just to hear her laugh like that. I asked their names, not that I cared about anyone but her. She was not Juliette, but Anne. Anne Boudreau, Philippe's daughter. Although the portals were big enough—about fifty-six inches high and thirty-six inches wide--I was terrified of another tasering or worse (worse being losing the portal or getting fried), so I didn't try popping over to 1860 to say howdy, and by the way, might I have your hand in bigamy? I did, however, dare to ask if they would sell me a bottle of local wine. They shrugged and pursed their lips in that particularly Gallic fashion that hasn't changed a bit in 150 years. They said sure, why not? *"Pourquoi pas?"* They asked if one from the château where they worked was OK. I asked what château that was, and they said it was called Lafite.

Holy jackpot, Batman, I was looking at purchasing a mint condition bottle of 150-year-old Château Lafite!!! I asked how much it would cost. This made them pause, and they all huddled in serious discussion as if they had been in the Super Bowl and they were down by a field goal two minutes before halftime. Quarterback Philippe said they would get me a bottle for ten francs. In gold, please.

Uh, right. I explained to Philippe that in the year 2010 (and it really was 2010 where I was, *sans blague* – no joking!!), the typical American household didn't have ten French francs in gold lying around. If this was really the year 1860, it was also a little early to try to explain the Euro to him. I told him I would return in a couple of hours. They gave me their Gallic shrug once more, and turned to get back to whatever it is vineyard workers did in Bordeaux in 1860. Anne turned before joining the rest to give me one more taste of that dazzling smile of hers, and I wilted again. I then went upstairs. By now, it was nine a.m. and Caro was up again.

Passing me in the hall, said she was going off to visit some friend of hers named Wendy to see what damage had befallen her in the storm. Wendy worked in some bank or other. I hadn't paid attention to which one when Caro told me about her. She had apparently been given the day off from work to inspect her home for storm damage and do any emergency repairs that might be needed to keep her house functional. The lightning bolts had provided enough stored energy to keep the portals working, although I still hadn't figured out why the batteries hadn't been blown to bits. There was a little bit of charring around the metal edges of the portals, but that was about it. Maybe all that circuitry I was fiddling with had been good for something. Anyway, with the restoration of electricity to our neighborhood, I had reason to hope that the portals would remain stable. Now that electricity was again working in the rest of the house, I booted up a laptop and went on the Internet to see if there were any shops nearby that sold old coins.

I found one not too far away, maybe a fifteen-minute drive if rush-hour traffic had thinned. It was called California Coin, which sounded like just about what the *docteur* ordered. I called ahead and asked if they had any nineteenth century French 10 franc gold coins, and the guy at the shop on the other end, luckily used to dealing with novices, said he had a few and would I like a bare head, laureate head or Ceres head. Um, yes, good question. He said that he had no Ceres head coins in stock at the moment. OK, scratch the Ceres head. I said it was a present for a friend and that I didn't know much about old French coins. He said that as of 1861, the portrait of Napoleon III on French coinage was crowned with a laureate wreath. The ones from 1854 to 1860 had no wreath and were referred to as "bare heads." If this was going to work, I had to look out for little details like this. I said I wanted a bare head from the 1850s. In the year 1860, coins dated 1860 would be shiny and new, whereas the coins likely to be in a shop in California 150 years later were likely to be used and worn. However, in 1860, coins a few years older would not raise suspicion if they were worn.

The shop owner said that due to the near-record high gold price, the coin would run me $120. I said that was fine and drove down there. The guy on the phone turned out to be named Josh Crane. He was in his mid-forties and a pleasant, patient guy who just liked his hobby, and he was patient with guys like me, who had no clue what they wanted. He let me choose from about ten coins he had that fit the bill ("I'm not Fort Knox," he apologized). He said I could choose between an A mint and a BB mint. I had no idea what he meant. Did he offer new customers hard candy or chewing gum to relax them? I asked if that was like the difference between spearmint and peppermint? He laughed and said the French 10 franc gold coins of that time were minted both in Paris and Strasbourg. The difference was designated by the Paris coins having a little "A" on them, and the Strasbourg coins having a little "BB" on them. I picked one at random, an 1856-A (Paris mint—I catch on fast), thanked him for the explanation and his patience, paid for the coin, and told him we might do some more business later on. He said sure, any time. I exited his shop and sped, literally, back home. The portal was still operating fine. I hadn't even intensively checked the one at the other end yet. I was so blown away by what I was seeing in this one, I just hadn't gotten around to trying to figure out the time and place of the other portal—all I could see there was forest. I would, of course, check it out later—duh.

10.

Back in my basement in front of the portal, I looked for Philippe
or any of the others. While I waited, a lone fly crossed through
from the grounds of Château Lafite into my basement. Just a fly.
But a 150-year-old fly! All this time, I had been fantasizing about
that movie and here, as if nothing were amiss, a fly from the year
1860 just sails right on through as if it were a kitchen window
where someone had forgotten to put down the screen. A fly had
very little volume and was not a mammal, but it was alive and flew
right on through without any visible negative effects, so that gave
me a lot of hope. Even so, with apologies to Vincent Price, the first
thing I would do later that day would be to buy some fly screen
and some wood at a hardware store and build screen doors so that
bugs potentially carrying all sorts of diseases did not start crossing
in droves. I could always shove the screen doors aside when trying to
send something over or receive something back, assuming that would
work with objects bigger than a fly.

 I waited for maybe fifteen minutes and, sure enough, Philippe
wandered back—sadly without Anne. I didn't dare ask where
she was—not yet, anyway. Fantasyland was still pretty new to me
at this point. I said I had his money, and he said he had my bottle.
I guessed that they were charging me several multiples of the
going rate, just in case I was for real, but I didn't care, of course.
Also, I had been in France enough times to know that if you are
buying anything, you show the money first and figured, correctly,
that this was already the case in 1860. *Je connais les français*, after all. I
looked for my pizza spatula.

I put the small gold coin plus a wine bottle-sized wooden box I
had grabbed from my adjacent wine cellar on the pizza spatula
and got my first fright. What if the force field would disappear at

being disturbed by solid matter bigger than a fly? What if some huge surge of electricity would kill me instantly? After all, though gold was inert, the 10% copper in the coin's alloy was not (Josh had showed me the composition in some catalog that looked like the L.A. phone book). But I overcame my fears quickly, before I could think rationally, and shoved the pizza spatula through the portal. Nothing. I might as well have been reaching across the dining room table. Amazing. More than amazing. Like "this-can't-be-happening" amazing. Philippe, now along with his brothers, Jean and Arnaud, who had been there when we first "met," took the coin, examined it, muttered in approval *"Elle est toute à fait bonne"* (It's perfectly genuine), and placed a brand new bottle of wine in the wooden box on the spatula, which I carefully pulled back into my basement. I examined it with a sense of wonder that a sixteen-year-old kid must sense when being told he is getting a new BMW for his birthday.

A perfect, mint condition, 1859 vintage bottle of Château Lafite (the bottles from the current year of production weren't quite ready yet)!! Bold-colored liquid almost right up to the cork, which was an indication that it was fresh—a near impossibility for a bottle that "old," as wine was hardly ever stored completely undisturbed for 150 years without interruption, and even then *some* evaporation was expected to have taken place. I thanked Philippe profusely, asked if he could deliver me more such bottles, and maybe a few from neighboring castles or previous years. He said sure, it would be his pleasure (and financial gain, I assumed). I told him the only thing was, he should tell no one about our little contact, as it could cause a *lot* of trouble if the wrong people found out. My time had terrible weapons, frightening technology that let us fly from one continent to another in hours instead of weeks, etc. He didn't seem to believe me, but he obviously wasn't interested in competition, either, so it was mutually advantageous to keep this our little secret.

He explained that everyone who had seen me was family and would keep a lid on it. I asked him to send my regards to Anne. He smiled what I took (OK, hoped) to be a knowing and approving smile and went off. It was all I could do to keep from jumping through (OK squeezing through—I hadn't originally anticipated being an active participant in the experiment) and hugging him. H.G. Wells, eat your heart out.

I called Juanita, and told her the storm had really rattled me and I was taking a day or two off. She said I was crazy not to take a week or two off, and I realized that it had been a year and a half since I had taken a real vacation. I said I might. She said, *"No te preocupes, chico,"* (Don't you worry, kid,) "I got this." I knew she did, too.

I debated whether to enhance my wallet or my prestige with the bottle. I went for the money. I didn't know exactly what my new bottle was worth, but I was pretty sure it was plenty. Not knowing who else to call about a bottle of this caliber, I called up Aldous George. He was as standoffish as usual until I told him that I had been offered access to a unique, 150-year-old wine cellar, the oldest and most extensive in all the American West. No one else knew about it; my folks had met the family's relatives while in France decades ago, blah, blah. He probably suspected I was making this up as I went and sniffed his doubt right through the telephone. I didn't blame him. But I said I would drive down there and show him a bottle that would blow him away if he thought he could move it. He said it was my gas and parking fee, so I was free to do so if I so desired. I drove down and parked in one of those overpriced parking garages near Rodeo and walked to George's Wine Emporium. No customers were in there at the time, so he said, "So, whatcha got for me?" I opened my little package, and said, "Just this." He stiffened just a bit before regaining his cool, and said, "Wow, this is a pretty remarkable fake. They got all the details except the ullage right. This is way too full to be genuine."

This gets a little technical, but it's an important detail. "Ullage" is the term wine people (oenologists, if you can pronounce it) use to describe the loss of liquid over time due to conditions of storage, evaporation, cork deterioration, and other environmental factors. The term, oh trivia fans, derives from an old French version of the word for "eye," and refers to how far up to the hole in the bottle the wine reached before being sealed. Indeed, the word for "eye" in Catalan, which is still spoken in the French border area with Spain on the Mediterranean side, is "ull," although you shouldn't try to pronounce it correctly in Catalan unless you absolutely have to or have lived half your life in Barcelona. About the only way an old bottle of wine will suffer little to no ullage (i.e., no loss of liquid over the years) was for it to be undisturbed from the day it was bottled, and even then only if stored under ideal conditions, the right temperature, perfectly corked, etc., etc. For a bottle of Bordeaux 150 years old found in North America to be in such phenomenal shape and, therefore, promise to be eminently drinkable, would be next to impossible. Note the "next to" part. Bottles that old had, of course, been opened before, and found to have phenomenal taste, but they had often been opened at some point in the past and then re-corked. If the re-corking had been done at the castle of origin, it was considered to still be original, but if the "shoulder" (i.e., the level of the wine in relation to the cork) was especially high, the bottle was suspected to have had something new added to it. My bottle, being essentially a year old, had a very high shoulder, but no evidence whatsoever of ever having been opened and re-corked.

I told him to look closer before I walked and he just might see that it was in impossibly good condition, but was definitely not a fake. He sighed the sigh of the knowledgeable dealing with the fool, and examined it more closely. He obviously knew what to look for, and what he was looking at, because he didn't stop examining for a good five minutes. Finally he turned to me with a rather unfriendly stare, and said, "OK, where did you *really* get this? Is Khoury starting to sell his collection? And if so, how come through you?"

Tawfiq Khoury, a well-known wine collector down in San Diego, was reputed to have a cellar of tens of thousands of bottles, and he had turned eighty this year. I said that no, it wasn't Khoury's collection, that it was really and truly through a chance family acquaintance that came about because of my good French (not exactly lying, was I?), and now that my parents were gone, I had exclusive access to the cellar for as long as the owner was willing to sell. I said he wanted to raise some serious money, but remain in the background, so he asked me to be his broker. I would get a small fee for doing it, and that was contingent on my keeping his name out of it, or else he would cease dealing with me. Aldous/Aldo looked again, and, with a newly minted respect bordering on friendship about as genuine as a three dollar bill, casually asked the price of the bottle.

Uh-oh. Like I said, I hadn't the faintest idea how much the price of the bottle was. I couldn't very well say so, either, or my flimsy cover would be blown before it had even gotten established. I did some quick thinking, wracking my brain for figures I had seen of elite bottles reported as sold in big auctions. Picking a figure out of thin air, I said, "This one would be $20,000." He looked up and said that my friend with the cellar was pricing his bottles rather aggressively, seeing as how the likelihood of a bottle that old retaining its taste was minimal at best. The one word conspicuously lacking in his response was "No." No ullage, remember? I said I had no idea of the market. I just appreciated the merchandise, and I was expected to represent the interests of my client as best I could. I got my price guidelines from the owner. I was also authorized to consign the bottle to auction if "my contacts" thought the asking price was unrealistically high. In other words, I was bluffing my ass off and hoping he wouldn't catch on. He didn't.

Aldous George was suddenly all smiles, and said, "But not at all, my boy! It's just that I was hoping for a break, this being our first transaction and all. But you say your friend has other bottles?" I said it was a family and their holdings were substantial, and, except for having been transported to the west coast of America about 100 years ago, they were practically untouched since they had been bottled and stored under such perfect conditions as to be as good as in the year they were made. I told him they had shown me a portion of their cellar several years ago, and only a very tiny portion at that. I said I knew it was hard to believe, but here was the living proof in his hands. George admitted that he had examined the bottle every way from here to Sunday and had found no fault with it whatsoever. He took out his checkbook, and wrote me a check for $20,000, reminding me to come see him first any time my "client" wished to part with another of his remarkably preserved bottles. Somewhat rashly, as it later turned out, I said no problem, as they had many thousands of bottles in their cellar. I shook hands with my new best buddy, Aldous D. George, and drove home, with a quick stop at my bank to deposit the check.

11.

When I got out of the car, I looked again at my deposit slip.
I just got $20,000 for a bottle of wine! Yo ho ho and a bottle
thereof, with apologies to Robert Louis Stevenson. In some
collecting circles, this is small potatoes, I know. But this wasn't
a $25 million Rembrandt that would grace the National Gallery
in Washington, or even a 1913 nickel for $3.7 million (I saw on the
Internet that an auction house in Dallas had sold one recently). This
was "just" a bottle of wine, but with one very important detail not to
be overlooked: This was *me!*

The next stop on the way home was a hardware store, where
another $160 investment got me enough wood, a strong hammer,
two boxes of nails, and enough fine wire mesh to build two screen
doors that I could use to cover my two portals. I didn't make the
frames too heavy, as I had to bring them into position all by myself,
but I managed, and it only took me a couple of hours' work to
get them into place. They weren't exact fits, but close enough to
discourage most self-respecting bugs, I hoped. No one was there
as I fitted the screen door over my portal to Château Lafite. I went
around to the second portal and saw nothing but green forest in
the fading daylight. I fitted the second screen door over it and,
resisting temptation, decided to call it a night.

The next evening, I was still contemplating at what speed to
exploit my little bonanza. At a wine tasting where George was
not in attendance, I found out that he had immediately called up
a prominent local collector, and told him what he had. He had
embellished by saying that he might have access to the greatest stash
of old wine in the western United States. Therefore, if the collector
wanted first shot at a mint condition bottle of 1859 Château Lafite
for $35,000, he had better get down to the shop pronto, before some

other connoisseur chanced in. The collector had paid the $35,000 and stashed the Lafite in his own cellar, where he intended to admire it for an hour every day. Some people, I swear. But I didn't swear too loudly. This was going to make me rich—Arregui family rich. Richer, maybe! And I would be a little greedier with my next offering from the mythical wine cellar.

I considered tinkering with my new toy in the basement, thinking maybe I should go visit Vincent van Gogh in Arles in the 1890s and maybe commission a painting or two. But I didn't dare fiddle too much for fear of losing my portal altogether—and, I admit unashamedly, losing my crazy, impossible contact with Anne Boudreau, the French vineyard worker's daughter born a mere 142 years before I was. You may start in with the "older woman" comments any time. I once again remembered the admonishments in every science-fiction book and movie not to mess too much with the past for fear of changing the future (i.e., the present). Fiction or not, it made all the sense in the world to me. I did not want to bring some fabulous wine bottle back, only to suddenly find, an instant later, that I was Sarah Palin. I made a mental note to myself to remind Philippe to keep our little arrangement quiet, not that telling a Frenchman to shut up about the source of undeclared supplemental income has ever been really necessary, even fifty years before they instituted an income tax in France.

I did have control dials on the two portals, but I had designed them for minute spatial calibrations, not a fourth-dimensional Google Earth. Nevertheless, there was one person in the past that I absolutely and desperately wanted to meet if I could. This was the man I always listed on those Internet questionnaires when they asked, "If you could meet one historical personality from the past, who would it be?" Plus, he was reputed to have had a great wine cellar and was always short on money. I decided I would try to find him with the portal on the other side of the room, if I could. I also dearly hoped, in the process of searching, not to find myself in the middle of an above-ground H-bomb test or feeding myself to velociraptors on "Jurassic Park, The Reality Show."

There was no way in the world I was going to tinker with the settings of the first portal that gave me my connection to Château Lafite in 1860. Despite all our difficulties, I had never cheated on Caro, but I had never seen Anne Boudreau's smile before, either. The last thing I wanted to do was attempt to adjust the time and then find I could never get back to Anne, so I didn't even try. If there was a control to vary the time in which I was visiting, I didn't know where it was or how to work it. I had only thought of spatial adjustments, and this was what I had to work with. Having Van Gogh paint me would have to wait for another incarnation.

I went around the room for another look at the other portal. I saw a scene of the same green forest I had seen when I fitted the screen door over it, but I still couldn't tell if it was from the present or if Julius Caesar was fighting the Gauls right around the corner in suburban Lugdunum, or sometime in between. Omnia Gallia in my basement *divisa est*, with apologies to Miss Hobson's ninth grade Latin class, as well as Astérix and Obélix. But it was definitely another portal to *some*where (and some *when*). I had to be careful with this, and wondered if it wouldn't be more prudent to just shut off this one altogether and concentrate solely on Bordeaux in 1860. But I decided to be rash. I wasn't looking to avert Lincoln's assassination or anything. I was looking for Thomas Jefferson. Jefferson was one of the greatest thinkers ever to grace the American continent. The author of the Declaration of Independence, advocate of the separation of church and state, freedom of the press, "he who knows best knows how little he knows." I had read that the Texas School Board had decided that history was better off without

Thomas Jefferson. I thought history was better off without the Texas School Board. In history class, to me, Jefferson was the *man!* He just got everything right, as far as I could tell. Oh, yeah, one other reason I so desperately wanted to find him—he was reputed to have had a fabulous wine cellar, knowing all about wine from his time in France and having imported lots of it to his residence, Monticello. Better yet, he was also known to have been in financial difficulty after his time as president. I have another quote for you, Mr. President: "Knowledge is power"—Francis Bacon, 1597. The "settings," such as they were, had been only slightly different for the second portal, and since the first one had landed me in 1860, I figured the second one had a one in three shot of being sometime during Jefferson's lifetime. The other two possibilities were, given the close to identical settings, either the same time as the other one (i.e., around 1860) or a few decades later, say around the beginning of the twentieth century. Of course, this was pure speculation on my part. For all I knew, I might just as easily find myself trying to talk Oliver Cromwell out of beheading King Charles I of England in 1649.

12.

The control dials that I had installed to line the second portal up with the original portal (and which had never functioned as such) actually did move the "scene" almost as violently as Google Earth, and another knob that was meant for focus now suddenly acted as a zoom function. I had no idea what I was doing, and it was not like I had a manual I could consult. I probably could have consulted the Defense Department, but that might have just as easily gotten the whole thing confiscated in the interest of "national security" or some similar excuse. Besides, they wouldn't have any more of a clue than I would. I couldn't go up to satellite height for fear of getting sucked up into the portal by the thin atmosphere. But one of the spatial dials seemed to influence height, so I could get high enough to see a coastal outline, if I could find a coast and hope to recognize something. Or else a city—if there were already cities! I didn't even have a clue what millennium this was, but I hoped that whatever special rewiring that had taken place with the other portal to give me a window to 1860 hadn't produced too different an effect from the first one. The settings had been slightly different, of course, as one was set to transmit from one side of the room and the other had been set to receive at the other side of the room.

I decided to move higher and west. The dial was extremely sensitive, far more so than pre-storm, and I didn't know if or how any of the others worked. Hell, I didn't know how *any* of this worked! This was no longer the gadget I had been tinkering with all these years.

I moved a little to the north and found a coastline. It was fairly rocky, though not homogeneously so, and appeared to run east to west. I went westward and saw what appeared to be a well-traveled path, though with no pavement anywhere. I followed the path, figuring

I had to be maybe half a mile up. A hundred miles sped by in seconds and suddenly a twin-spired cathedral with a smaller spire in between the two main ones showed up in the distance. I kept following the path, which must have been a major road, westward, until I got to the city where the road ended, which appeared to be close the coast. More people seemed to be on the road toward the city the closer to it I got. This had to be somewhere in Europe, and I was looking for Virginia. I was too high up to get a good look at the people's clothes or hear what they were speaking. But when I saw the contour of the land where the city was, I realized where I had to be. This was Santiago de Compostela at the northwestern tip of Spain. The path was the path of Saint James ("Santiago"). A few miles farther, and the Iberian Peninsula would end at the Atlantic Ocean.

I crossed the Atlantic in pretty much a straight line, veering slightly to the south, as if this were a video game, and came to what had to be the coast of Massachusetts. Sure enough, there was the outline of Cape Cod, though it was somewhat bigger and thicker than I remembered it being on our present-day atlases—more heavily wooded, too. Too bad I couldn't warn them about erosion control, but for all I knew the Pilgrims hadn't yet landed, and my Wampanoag was just a little rusty from lack of practice. I went in closer and slightly to the northwest, to where Boston should have been, and a decent-sized city was there!! The Pilgrims had definitely landed, and not the day before yesterday either. So, I went in closer to look at the architecture. I hoped I was keeping the portal high enough not to spook anyone. The houses looked to be pretty much colonial era or a little later—architecture was not my field of expertise. I didn't know if the USA had been established yet, or if Bunker Hill was a battle waiting to happen. I moved down the coast. New York City was there, but no big bridges yet. So far, so good. Down the coast of New Jersey, Maryland, very rural, no industry at all, this was all good. When I got to the Potomac River, I moved inland and this was where it got hairy, as the distances I was trying to cover were no longer in the hundreds of miles, but relatively small for my clumsy dial. How the hell was I to know what I'd need? I found a modest Washington, D.C., and the White House, but no Washington Monument, so I was after 1812 but before 1848. Jefferson died in 1826, so I might be in luck, although finding him on his deathbed would be gruesome.

Now my search got difficult. There was no I-66 West or Route 29 south that I could follow. I had printed out a map of Virginia, but this was needle in a haystack time. I couldn't exactly swoop down and ask for directions without risking it getting into the history books. Luckily, the map showed me the general direction of Charlottesville, and the domed contour of Monticello was easy to spot. I passed right by it the first time around, but didn't lose it the second time. Moment of truth here. I knew where I was, but I didn't know *when* I was. H.G. Wells is never around when you need him, and Monticello exists as a national monument to this very day.

It appeared to be mid-afternoon in the late spring or early summer, so, practically moving the dials by little more than blowing on them, I looked in on Monticello surrounded by splendid greenery. It was quick, so I won't draw this out into some suspenseful drama. I found him in what looked to be his sitting room, very much alive, although he looked rather worse for the wear. He was engrossed in some book, and, luckily, alone. Everyone knows that for all his enlightenment, he kept slaves, and even had one of them for a mistress. Walls and solid objects didn't appear to present any kind of barrier to the portal when moving it, which had to be defying several laws of physics. I made a mental note never to leave the portal in the middle of a tree or a wall, in case any of the dials decided not to work for some reason. The portal came to rest at the far end of his sitting room, which he called his "cabinet," near the open passage to his bedroom. Some daylight poured in, but he still had a candle burning for extra light. Telescopes and other scientific devices of his day adorned various parts of the room.

13.

Um, right, so here I am, probably about to give Thomas Jefferson a fatal heart attack just by saying howdy. But my history book says he died peacefully in bed on July 4, 1826, fifty years to the day after his Declaration of Independence was signed in Philadelphia. I *really* hoped this wasn't July 3, 1826, but he didn't look like he was in his early eighties yet. He wore what I assumed to be simple garb for his time, appeared to be taller and a little more gaunt than I expected, but otherwise looked very much like a slightly older version of his portrait on the two dollar bill.

I called over to him, "Mr. President?" He started, saw me through the portal, and dropped his book. He got up from what looked like a revolving chair, slowly crossed over to me. Thomas Jefferson!!!!!

I said, "Mr. President, please don't be alarmed. I am quite real, and I am communicating to you from the year 2010 by way of a science unknown in your time." Jefferson stared at me and gaped. Then the great man spoke: "Either I'm dreaming or this is one of the most momentous occurrences in the history of the universe. And, by the way, I haven't been the president for years now."

He had a slightly lilting, almost Irish-sounding accent. I should have known that, growing up in the eighteenth century, his English would have more in common with the Court of St. James's than the Grand Ole Opry. I just hadn't thought about it up to now.

"Yes, sir," I said, trying to be as respectful as I could. "I believe I am the first one to have done this. In my time, all former presidents are still addressed as Mr. President. You were always one of my favorite people from the early days of the United States."

"Why, thank you, my boy. That is very flattering. If you live in the year 2010, then to you, I must be history." Wow, the man didn't miss a trick. I had deliberately avoided using that expression.

"Well, yes sir, one could look at it that way."

"No other way to look at it," Jefferson replied. "Where are you located?"

"I'm in the vicinity of the city of Los Angeles, sir. It's in the southern part of California."

"Very impressive!" mused Jefferson—not the reaction I expected.

"How so?" I asked.

"You speak impeccable English for a Mexican," our third president replied. Oops. I forgot. It was a little intimidating for me to be suddenly talking to Thomas Jefferson. Gimme a break, I'm not Katie Couric.

"Mr. President, in 1850, California became a part of the United States. My name is Robert Packard."

"Brilliant!" exclaimed Jefferson. "Your speech pattern is, of course, unknown to me. Obviously, we will have developed a uniquely American sound to our English over the years, presumably with some marked regional differences."

Oh, more than "marked," I'd say. Obviously, people in Virginia were not yet saying "y'all," and people on Long Island were probably not saying "Noo Yawk" yet either, although I would never find out.

Thomas Jefferson continued, "You know, they laughed at me for the Louisiana Purchase, but I knew it would be a move that would prove prescient in the long run. In 1804, I sent Merriwether Lewis out west to find a passage to the Pacific coast. I guess you must know that."

I nodded. "The expedition of Lewis and Clark is very famous in the history books," I told him. He looked quite pleased with this.

"So, then, we have now bought California from Mexico as well, and less than half a century hence, the United States will have a Pacific coast. Bravo! I hope it cost less to buy California from the Mexicans than the Louisiana Territory cost me. It was very humbling, needing to borrow the funds from England to do that, but I'm still convinced we got it at a very low price."

"Oh, yes, the Louisiana Purchase is still considered one of the more fortuitous transactions the United States ever made," I told him. Jefferson beamed. I continued, "But, um, well, we didn't exactly buy California. It's more like we took it by force. We had a rather violent falling out with Mexico in the 1830s and 1840s."

Jefferson looked crestfallen. "Oh, no. Don't tell me the United States will become such a big power that we start to act like the very power from which we sought to separate? Doesn't anyone remember what George Washington said in his farewell address? I trust, at least, that you will have used your obviously impressive advances in science for good as well as conquest?"

"Oh, yes, sir, that we have. We can cross oceans in airborne public conveyances in a matter of hours now, have instant worldwide communication whenever we want, can cure a variety of diseases that were fatal in your day, all sorts of things that could only seem fantasy to people in your time." I wasn't about to tell him about the McCarthy Era, the atomic bomb or the Civil War. I knew that as part of his inspiration for the concept of the United States of America, Jefferson had spent time studying the Iroquois Confederacy, a solid alliance of Native American tribes that lasted some four centuries. No sense in telling him that his beloved project disintegrated into civil war, probably less than fifty-odd years (his time) after our little encounter. Why ruin his day?

"That's just amazing," he said, looking very much at peace with himself. "But you must realize something. You are putting yourself at great peril communicating with me like this. Make no mistake, I'm thrilled you did, but I can never speak of our encounter, and nor should you. Besides the fact that no one would ever believe either of us, it might cause something to happen that could affect the course of history and even negate your very existence. You just don't know, and I always say, he who knows best knows how little he knows." Did I mention that Thomas Jefferson was a brilliant man? Here, he figures out on the spot, all by himself, the very warnings I would be getting a couple of centuries into the future! Oh, yeah, speaking of which…

"I know that, Mr. President. That little saying of yours has actually become famous over the years. I couldn't resist the chance to speak to you, but I know I can't make a habit of it or tell anyone. It was pure chance that I even managed to find you. By the way, could you tell me the date—I mean for you?"

"Of course. I didn't realize that you couldn't determine that with your contraption. It's the twelfth of April in the year 1818. I'll be seventy-five tomorrow. You haven't met Ben Franklin, have you? He died almost thirty years ago. He was quite a tinkerer in his own right—nothing like this, obviously, but he would have loved it."

Wow, 1818! Jefferson was seventy-five years old, which was *very* old in those days. But his mental capacity was obviously undiminished.

"Thank you, sir, and happy birthday! No, I never met Benjamin Franklin, but there is one other matter, if you would indulge me."

"If I can, speak up," said Thomas Jefferson.

"We have something in common. We are both lovers of great French wine."

Jefferson smiled. "Why, yes I am. That is recorded in the year 2010? I'm very flattered. I learned about French wine while spending time there before my presidency, traveled extensively through the wine-producing area of France. Have you been to France? Do you speak the language?"

"Yes, sir, I do, and I've been there quite a number of times," I told him.

"Fascinating place, just delightful," he said, his thoughts visibly taking him back to times gone by. "I hope it still is. Communication and language are so important. I once went up to New York's Long Island with Madison—James Madison, you know?"

Madison. *James* Madison. President 004. Yes, I knew. I nodded.

Thomas Jefferson continued, "We went up there to try to list and preserve the vocabulary of one of the indigenous languages spoken there before it died out. Probably a futile effort, but we thought it a worthwhile pursuit at the time. I don't suppose you've ever heard of the Unkechaug language?"

I hadn't.

"Ah, well, that was over twenty-five years ago," he mused. Over twenty-five years ago to him meant before 1793! Here he was, telling me about hearing some Native American language that hadn't been spoken in two centuries.

"Tell me," he continued, getting back to the "here and now," such as it was, "is France indeed still the wonderful place it was in my time?"

"Oh, definitely," I replied. "As you might imagine, bottles of great French wine from your time are very scarce in my day. You are said to have had quite a cellar yourself."

"I most certainly do," said Jefferson. "Or, to be more accurate, I did at one time. But my finances aren't doing so well at the moment. It's not something I can actively pursue any longer."

"Maybe I can suggest something of mutual benefit," I said, hopefully.

"Oh?" he replied. "And what might that be?"

"I would very much like to purchase a few of your duplicate bottles from your cellar," I replied, "for which I could pay you in currency of your time."

"And you have access to such currency? Surely if the United States now stretches across the continent, the quantities of coinage we are minting now will seem miniscule by comparison to the quantities needed in your day. The coins of my day will have become items of some collector value, much as the coins of ancient Greece and Rome are collected in France in my time." This man missed nothing, I mean *nothing*! No wonder he wrote the Declaration of Independence at the age of thirty-three.

"Tell me, speaking of currency, do we still use the dollar as our unit of currency in your time?" he asked.

"Yes, we always have," I replied.

"Ah, that is reassuring," he said. "I had a long argument with Alexander Hamilton about that, did you know that?"

I told him that I was unfamiliar with that little detail of history.

"Oh, yes," he continued. "You know what happened to him in 1804, don't you?" I said that I did—the duel with Aaron Burr. Hamilton didn't survive it. Nor did Burr's career as Jefferson's vice president.

"Tragic, that was. But it's history now—even to me." He smiled to himself. "To return to the subject at hand, Hamilton wanted to institute something similar to the British pound as our unit of currency, where I favored a decimal system. Maybe a year after the Battle of Yorktown, I wrote a long document favoring the decimal system over the British system. It took something like eight years, but in 1792, we finally decided that the dollar would be our unit of currency, and that it would be decimal based. Hamilton wasn't pleased, but he was always more of an Anglophile, where I was the Francophile. I take it you have similar inclinations?"

"I have never even been to England," I confessed, "and I really don't know much about the place. As for access to currency of your time, I don't have access myself, as I never collected coins, but I know a merchant who specializes in such items." I didn't know if the word "dealer" was used in his day, so I used "merchant." He seemed to understand me, at any rate. "What sort of bottles would you be willing to part with, and for what price?"

"Well, now," the great man mused, "my stock has diminished somewhat since 1812. You know about our latest conflict with the British, I assume?" I did, and told him it was to be the last. "Ah, good. That rather interrupted the flow of fresh bottles to my cellar, I'm afraid. Nonetheless, I think I have a few worthwhile bottles left from my youthful years. Certainly a couple of bottles of Margaux and Yquem, probably a bottle of Rausan or two. The first two would be from 1784 and 1790. The Rausan would only be from 1790. I should have an odd Lafite or two as well—1785, if I recall correctly. You might care for a Brane-Mouton as well. It's not held in as high regard, but I find it quite pleasant. Same period, or possibly a year or two later. Are those vintages familiar to you?"

"Yquem, Lafite, and Margaux are well-known, but I'm not familiar with Rausan," I answered, "and Mouton has risen to be considered a top-tier wine in my day."

"Well, then, how about two bottles each of Yquem and Margaux, and of each of the two years, 1784 and 1790, and two bottles of the 1790 Rausan to make an even ten?" proposed Jefferson. "I'll check on the Lafite and the Mouton later on."

"Sounds good to me," I replied. "What would I owe you for them?"

"I'd like two dollars apiece, if it's all right with you," replied our third president. "I could actually use it right now."

"I'll check with the man who knows about such things and be back within two hours," I told him.

"Fine," said Jefferson. "I'll allow no one in here so no one sees this little phenomenon."

"Good idea!" I said, "I'll be back as soon as I can." With that, I ran to the car, hopped in, and drove back to California Coin.

14.

Twenty minutes later, I was back in "Ye Olde Coin Shoppe," otherwise known as California Coin. Before meeting Josh, my image of a "coin shop" was some crusty old brick building in New England somewhere or down some musty side street in Manhattan, with a wizened old man, age eighty-five or so, as the proprietor and an antiquated sign reading "Ye Olde Coin Shoppe" hanging outside. Instead, Josh's California Coin was a nondescript, clean, modern store like any one of a few dozen others in a mini-mall. Josh could just have easily passed for your neighborhood pharmacist. So much for stereotypes.

"More French gold for you?" asked Josh Crane.

"Nope," I came back. "Later on, for sure, but this time, I need $20 in face value Unites States money, and all dated before 1818."

"Curiouser and curiouser," mused Josh, but went to pull out an album. "The cheapest way to do that is with half dollars. Any other way will set you back way more than what bust halves would cost." *Bust* halves? What did *that* mean—half dollars that had been smashed into little bits? He explained that numismatists (accent on the second syllable; I got it on the third try) had their own slang, and half dollars from 1807 through 1839, with a few minor changes along the way as well as a big one in 1836, had a design with a capped woman's bust on them, and were therefore referred to as "bust halves." He explained that they were more expensive if unused, but relatively common in used condition. I asked, thinking I was being clever, if he had bust quarters and bust dimes, too. He said sure, but they were minted in much smaller quantities and were, therefore, much more expensive. Time for me to stop making wise cracks and pick out my bust halves.

He put the album in front of me and let me have my pick.
Sure enough, worn half dollars from 1809 through 1817 seemed to
be the cheapest of all silver denominations, although 1816 didn't
seem to exist and 1815 was way more expensive than the others.
One cent coins were cheaper on an individual basis, but fifty of
them would have cost way more than any one fifty cent piece.
The half dollars (*bust* halves! Do I catch on quick or what?) dated
after 1818 cost even less, but would have been useless to Thomas
Jefferson in the year 1818 and were, therefore, useless to me. As a
generic item, the ones before 1818 couldn't have been too rare, as
Josh had dozens and dozens of them, although they did indeed seem
to be a little worn. I had no trouble picking out forty coins at a $95
average price per coin. The price came to $3800 and Josh gave me
another $100 off the total. I didn't have anything like that much in
cash on me, my membership in the Saudi royal family having been
canceled sometime prior to this incarnation. But Josh said that if
I didn't mind his verifying my check with my bank, a personal check
would do. I had just put $20,000 from Aldous George in there, so I
knew it would be good. I said sure, go ahead. He called and my bank
gave their blessing. Josh even threw in a "Red Book" for free. Rather
than being an alphabetical listing of Josh's hottest girlfriends, the
"Red Book" is more coin insider slang for a catalog of American coins
that comes out every year. And here I thought just wine nuts had a
language all their own. Not only were there, indeed, bust quarters
and bust dimes, but also bust dollars and even bust *half dimes*!! I
would read through it and try not to make any more wise cracks
based on ignorance. I thanked him and drove home with my 40 pre-
1818 half dollars.

While in Josh's shop, I had seen some old American coins with
really high price tags on them. I knew nothing about old coins, but
saw a beat-up looking copper coin from 1793, a cent (but bigger
than a quarter and twice as thick), with a $10,000 price tag. It

occurred to me that I might be able to make even more money swapping "common" old coins for rarer ones of the same era, but I knew too little about them and didn't want to press my luck. Josh seemed like an OK guy, but might have started making inquiries I couldn't answer if I came up with expensive coin rarities I knew nothing about, and he might call the police, suspecting I was fencing a stolen collection. He had to know the local serious collectors of rare old coins, and had never seen me before, plus he could tell right away that I knew nothing about rare coins. In his place, I would have suspected the same thing, so I resisted the temptation to go into the rare coin business at the same time. A guy selling rare wine ought to be well-versed on the subject of what he had, and would have come across as suspicious if he weren't. I figured that the same would have applied to rare old coins. I hadn't forgotten that 1913 nickel sold by that auction house in Dallas for $3.74 million, but with items like that, there was no doubt a pedigree involved, and I could not credibly furnish such a thing. Stick with what you know.

It occurred to me that Aldo never demanded a pedigree for the bottle I sold him. He asked about my source, but didn't ask about a pedigree. Why? Maybe he thought I was fencing a stolen collection? If so, it didn't seem to bother him. *That,* in turn, bothered *me* plenty. A bottle (not to mention lots of them) of 1859 Lafite in a condition to indicate it had not been touched since being bottled, and had suffered none of the usual ravages of time, would have had to have practically come from the Château Lafite itself. Except for occasional feeble attempts to trick me into revealing the name of my source, Aldo never again asked me their name outright. Why not? Did he have something nefarious in mind? Oh, maybe. Oh, more than maybe, as I found out soon enough, though for now, before he had come up with some evil plan to get in on my action, he was content to make a hefty whack of profit on any bottle I brought him.

15.

By the time I got back, Thomas Jefferson had already searched
out the ten bottles of wine from his cellar and had them in his
sitting room. When I came back, he spoke first. "Robert, I usually
keep meticulous records about everything, but I think this is one
little transaction for which I will leave no account for posterity. I take
it that you are keeping still about your little device and will tell no
one that you got these bottles from me directly."

"Sir, I very much doubt anyone would believe me anyway."
Jefferson laughed, and said that no, he supposed not. I asked if
he had marked any of his bottles so that they could be pedigreed
to him. He replied that he had inked a cursive TJ on the bottles,
but had done so years ago, and that it was barely legible now. He
indicated to me where to look, and this was to prove helpful later on.
This was of particular interest, as bottles with a "Th. J." attributed
to him had been sold for fortunes, and the bottles he was giving
me had something else entirely on them. Too bad I couldn't come
out in some of the wine publications and say I now knew what
was what, and if anyone thought differently, they could ask Thomas
Jefferson themselves, right in my basement. Oh, yes, that little
declaration would surely remove all doubts—all doubts, that is, that
I should be carted off to the nearest loony bin ASAP.

I piled the half dollar coins onto my trusty ceramic spatula,
pushed it though, and Thomas Jefferson came over, took them
into his hands, and just stared at them for a minute, and nodded
silently in approval. "I was about to say that these coins had seen
better days," he commented, "but since they were close to 200 years
old when you got them, I would have to surmise that they have,
indeed." He then went over to his bottles, and we passed them via
the wooden box, one by one. These weren't as fresh in appearance

as the 1860 Lafite from Philippe—logical enough, as Jefferson had ordered them a quarter century earlier. However, they were in perfect shape for thirty-year-old bottles and, of course, unheard-of shape for bottles 220 years old. Un-friggin'-real. Aldo wasn't getting off so easily this time.

I thanked Thomas Jefferson, said it was a very singular honor to have met him, would tell no one, and asked if he might be willing to sell me another such parcel. Jefferson didn't take long to decide, and said that his financial situation was sadly such that he would welcome it, but that neither of us should risk messing up the fabric of history just for a couple of contemporary (if he only knew!) wine bottles—we both had to be very cautious. I also humbly asked if he would take some time and tell me some firsthand accounts of what it was like working with Franklin, Adams, Madison, Washington and the rest to create the United States. I wanted to know about how his contact with the Iroquois Confederacy influenced his ideas on how to form the government of the United States. I knew that his extensive contact with Native American tribes as a youth had influenced his thinking greatly on how a society could be organized, though I sure as hell had never heard of the Unkechaug. Maybe he would let me in on a few things that were sure to be absent from the history books. He couldn't know what was in our history books, but said he would be glad to take some time for me, albeit on the condition that they would go no further than me, as some things were not for baring for posterity. The thought of hearing some of the more intricate details (first hand!) of negotiating the Louisiana Purchase or chasing the Barbary pirates practically made me salivate. I didn't know if I could keep stuff that explosive to myself, but anyone questioning my source would get either silence or an answer they would never believe in the first place, so I promised. That is one promise I will keep as well. You just don't break promises to Thomas Jefferson, not that I suppose anyone reading this has a track record of how well they have kept their verbal promises to Thomas Jefferson. I could probably have explained the Internet to him—he was that open-minded—but I didn't want to get into blogs and stuff, so I never mentioned it, and I will not betray his confidence, even here. I apologize to any and all historians who would now like to waterboard me until I spill everything Jefferson told me. It ain't gonna happen. I'm spilling nothing, and you can't find me to waterboard me.

I moved the portal out of Jefferson's sitting room, and back out into the woods nearby, at treetop level, so that no one of his servants accidentally came in and thought they had to dust my basement. For similar reasons, I also moved the Lafite Portal into a similar position in the woods adjacent to the field where I had met the Boudreau family.

The bottles stood in a row on a table in my lab. Old, dark, uneven green glass with slightly (but only slightly!!) yellowing paper and that impressive old French script, still fresh, on all bottles, indicating their origin and year of production, seal near the top. Now I know what an art expert feels like the first time he gets to examine a Rembrandt up close. Each one had the faded, inked cursive "TJ" on the neck above the label. It took all the willpower I had not to open one of each and let them breathe and then sip them during the course of the afternoon. But my financial well-being took precedence here, if only just barely.

I carefully placed the ten Jefferson bottles in my wine cellar and contemplated how to present them to Aldous/Aldo. I couldn't just waltz into his shop with all 10 of them at once. Besides, I wanted him to try to pull the same stunt with me that he did with the first Lafite bottle. Make a fortune reselling the first Jefferson bottle, and whet his appetite before showing him others. I also had to figure out how much to ask him for each bottle. It had to be enough so he would think I knew the value of what I had, but not so much as to leave him too little margin to make a handsome profit for himself on each bottle. After all, I wanted him to be content enough so as not to get any ideas about sending any real-life Godfather cast members after me for an enforced discount (or worse). That turned out to be a rather naïve hope on my part, but I didn't yet know Aldo well enough to realize this.

16.

I had to be careful with how I explained the Jefferson wine to
don Aldo. There had been a big scandal recently about a guy in
Germany turning up bottles supposedly with a Jefferson provenance.
The bottles all turned out to have a cloud of doubt over them,
including one sold to a collector who was suing for outright fraud in
some huge, ongoing, high-profile case. I had a feeling that if Aldo
had the slightest impression I was selling him fakes, he would forego
the legal formalities and have me turned into prosciutto. Although
I knew my source was legitimate, I could hardly reveal *how* I knew.
The bottles would have to speak for themselves. Obviously, they
would stand up to any scrutiny of the physical aspects, but if really
sophisticated testing was done and the material proved genuine but
the age did not, I couldn't provide a credible explanation as to why no
deterioration had taken place. All I could say was that the bottles had
been preserved undisturbed under perfect atmospheric conditions,
etc., etc., and hope it would suffice. The cork would prove to have the
correct chemical composition, of course. However, if a lead-210 test
were conducted on the seal, I was in trouble. The seals almost always
contained a high percentage of lead. Lead-210 is a radioactive isotope
in freshly-mined lead that decays fully after 200 years. If any lead-
210 is found in something containing lead, then it can't be more
than 200 years old. We physics majors know about stuff like that.
The 18th century bottles I was getting from Thomas Jefferson were,
in effect, only about twenty-five to thirty years old. If their seals were
to be tested, their lead-210 content would be high, whereas the lead-
210 content of the seal of a bottle over 200 years old would be zero.
I had to hope that Aldo didn't have any nuclear physicists among his
elite clientele.

I called up Aldo/Aldous (I really had to be careful not to call him
Aldo to his face), and said that my friends with the incredible wine

cellar were pleased with his last purchase, and so decided to see if he could handle one of their oldest prizes, a 1784 Yquem given to their ancestor by "a family friend who had lived in Virginia." Knowing full well who the most famous American wine enthusiast in Virginia in the last part of eighteenth century was, the venerable Mr. George was quite interested indeed, and invited me to drop by at my earliest convenience. I think it had more of an effect on Aldo that I didn't elaborate on whether I even knew the identity of the unnamed Virginian. And now, no longer was I "Packer," the pest from the wine tastings, but his good buddy "Bob," who was welcome to drop by any time and get checks made out to him with his name spelled correctly.

The next morning, I drove down to Beverly Hills, trying my very best not to lose my patience with the choking traffic of West Los Angeles. This time, George's Wine Emporium had three or four customers, all competing for George's attention. But he saw I had a box with me, and promptly ushered me into a small waiting area, made *me* coffee (!!), and politely asked if I had twenty minutes or so. Why sure, Aldous, anything for my great pal from the local wine tastings—as long as your checkbook was well-stocked. It took half an hour, but I had nothing but time, and going off to blow $2750 on some $30 trinket just because it was in a shop on Rodeo Drive, Beverly Hills, was not on my agenda of things to do that morning. There was always that cool ice cream shop on Santa Monica Boulevard, just a block or two east of Rodeo, but I decided to wait. Besides, patience is a virtue, or so I had been told.

When he had "served" his last customer, Aldous George, all smiles, rejoined me and my cold, now-empty coffee cup, and said, "So, my boy, what have your friends decided to part with this time?" I explained that they had some big project or other that they had been contemplating for a while, and had decided to finance it by selling off some of their many duplicates from their most unique wine cellar. He again tried to get me to reveal some hints as to who my "friends" were and got nowhere, of course. The fact that they didn't exist was a great help in my being able to keep their identity a secret. I said that they had sworn me to secrecy long ago, and he would have to admit that I had never even hinted at their existence all the time I had known him. George nodded in approval at my discretion, acknowledged that I had never said a word about them (imagine that! Agent 008, that's me), and said that even he would have had a hard time keeping the knowledge of such a cellar secret. I said that the only reason they decided to let me sell their bottles for them is that they had verified that I had never said a word about them or their cellar to anyone. Now that they wished to raise some serious money, they had decided to let me be their agent. The expression "serious money" was not lost on Aldous D. George, and his interest was at fever pitch.

I opened my box, and took out a fairly fresh 1784 Château Yquem Sauterne. George took it carefully in his hands, examined the label, let the bottle reflect in the light of a nearby lamp, and he definitely did *not* miss the faded "TJ" inked onto the bottle. He had to have known about the scandal concerning the possibly phony "Th. J." on the bottles sold a few years back, and so would have also known that "TJ" was one of the monograms Jefferson *was* definitely known to have used. I didn't even have to bring up Jefferson's name. I had said "wine enthusiast in Virginia," and he *did* know the subject in and out, you had to give him that. He knew full well what he was looking at and was duly dumbstruck. Not taking his eyes off the bottle, he whispered, "How many more of these bottles are there?" I replied that I had no idea, as the owners had never given me a complete tour of their cellar, vast as it was. To embellish the mystery, I said, "If you think their wine collection is impressive, you should see the paintings they own." He nodded, and turned to me. "You know, I'm pretty sure I know who we're talking about here."

I thought, Sure you do, Aldo, and you're having dinner with the Easter Bunny and Little Miss Muffett at The Palm in West Hollywood tonight, too, but just said, "I guess it's not impossible. These *are* the kind of circles I hear you travel in, after all."

"True, true," he replied contemplatively, his ego satisfied, but his curiosity obviously not—like one of the answers in those multiple choice math logic tests: *necessary, but not sufficient.*

He asked, "So, what is the tariff on this little item?"

I said, "Not cheap. We're talking $50,000 for this one."

"That's way beyond 'not cheap.' That's outrageous for an Yquem," he said with a frown. "How could they be asking that kind of money for just a single bottle?"

I said, "Hey, don't go killing the messenger boy, here. These people have access to auction records, you know. I can take it back and say no sale, and you are under no obligation. I have a free hand in choosing to whom I offer their wine. I chose you first, since you're a friend {I promise, I kept a straight face}, but I haven't told them that you're the one I'm working with, so they shouldn't harbor the slightest of ill will toward you if you want to pass. Look, if you want, I'll just take it to Christie's, consign it to them for auction, and if it doesn't sell at their desired reserve, then they would have to come down in price, right?"

George thought for a moment, and said, "Look, if they consign it to an auction, it might bring their price, but it might not. You know that most wine auctioneers take a hefty percentage out of the hammer price before settling with their consignors, so even if it sells for $50,000, the consignor only nets at most $45,000, usually $40,000." I didn't know, actually. I didn't have the slightest idea. I had never been in the habit of consigning $50,000 wine bottles, or anything else, for that matter, to auctions at Christie's, Sotheby's, Heritage or whoever. But Aldo had been to plenty of wine auctions. He definitely *did* know, so I just nodded as if I had done nothing else all my professional life, if, indeed, my life up to now could have been considered to have been professional to any degree.

"Tell you what, why don't you ask your friends if they would consider $45,000 right now, and save them the wait and the paperwork?" he proposed.

I said, "I'll ask them anything you want me to. I can't reach the one who makes the decisions until this afternoon, but I'll get back to you as soon as I hear something."

"Umm, sure, that's fine," George said, "but would you mind leaving the bottle here? If any of my heavy hitters should chance by and want the bottle at a higher price, I can call you and we won't need to negotiate downward." I wasn't sure I could trust George, but I definitely trusted his desire to handle the rest of the "cellar," so I had no doubt the bottle would still be there when I returned, unless he sold it for a big profit in the meantime.

I was pretty sure the second I left that he would be on the phone to every high-brow wine collector in southern California, offering the bottle for $80,000 or more, but that wasn't my concern. All I cared about was his checks being good, and to keep him panting like a beagle, waiting for me to toss him his next bone. As long as he was sure there was more, and as long as he had no clue who my source was, I figured I was safe, and so were any bottles I left with him on a mere handshake.

17.

I drove home. Caro was nowhere to be found, but this was
not unusual. Our drift apart was still on an even keel, and if she was
seeing someone else at this point, I'm not even sure I cared any more,
sad as that was. I called into the office, and Juanita answered
the phone. "Everything OK with you?" I asked. She said she had
everything under control, and that I should enjoy my down time. I'm
not sure I would describe just having met Thomas Jefferson in person
an accurate description of "down time," but she'd have accompanied
the ambulance to my house herself if I had told her that, so I said it
was pretty nice and left it at that.

I went down to the basement to check on Bordeaux, 1860. I saw
Philippe in the distance, and he came over to say hi (or, rather,
bonjour). He said that had checked for me with people he knew who
worked at some of the other châteaux in the area, and could get
me some bottles of recent vintages, if I wanted, for the same price
I had paid for his first bottle. I said I was definitely interested and
would be glad to pay the same price per bottle. Philippe muttered
to himself, *"Qui l'aurait pensé?"* ("Whoda thunk it?" as we used to
say in high school). He said it was a shame I couldn't join them for
a meal some time. I said I might consider trying it, but had to make
sure I could pass through the portal myself with no adverse effects.
I hadn't tried putting any warm-blooded animals through, although I
had seen that one fly make the crossing with no discernable damage.
He said he had friends who worked at Mouton-Rothschild (until
"recently," i.e., 1853, Brane-Mouton), Margaux, Palmer, and some
of the smaller vineyards, Ducru-Beaucaillou and so on, and would
get me bottles from them as well. The stuff of which legend is made,
I tell you. He was certain he could get bottles from "older" years ,
as well as some larger sized bottles, such as the occasional magnum
(content of two bottles) or double magnum (four bottles). He said he

was sure he could get me a Jéroboam (six bottles) from his own Lafite, but that would cost me twenty francs. I didn't know what I could ask Aldo for a Brane-Mouton 1848 in mint condition, but I was fairly sure it would be plenty. After all, if a 1945 Mouton-Rothschild could bring $10,000, an 1848 in perfect (i.e., twelve-year-old) condition should be multiples of that. Normally, of course, not so, as cork damage, ullage (like I explained before, evaporation, sort of) would have meant a wine of that age would never be as good as one only a few decades old. But this was an exceptional cellar, right, Aldo? And who knew what kind of money I could get for a mint condition Lafite Jéroboam from 1858?

I read on the web page of the Heritage auction house in Dallas that there was one special stash of old collectible comic books in Colorado that had unfaded, unyellowed pages, due to the special mile-high conditions under which they had been stored, and they brought prices that were multiples of prices brought for comic books whose pages had yellowed. Well, then, this was the "mile-high" cellar of wine. Seeing (and, more important, tasting) was believing, and anyone who tasted any of the wine I would be providing would know immediately that this was a group of bottles like no other. A perfect Jéroboam from Lafite before 1860 would be a major prize.

I called up Josh Crane and said I could use 100 more of those French ten franc gold coins if they were around the same price. He said he didn't have that many of them, but knew the dealership in Texas that had sold that nickel for $3.74 million and that they had a big gold coin department with buying offices all over the world. I didn't tell him I had been getting information off their web site as well. He was confident he could get me what I wanted if he could have seventy-two hours. I said sure, that would work. He also said there was nothing to stop me from calling them directly, but he was a nice enough guy and seemed to have an easy working relationship with the guys from Dallas. I said no, it was fine, I didn't need to shave off his commission, and besides, the guys in Texas didn't know me from Adam. He was very happy with this and said he'd provide me with whatever he could as soon as I needed it. It also occurred to me that if I had ordered $12,000 in French gold directly from Dallas in my name, I would be taking a certain risk. This would have meant receiving a high-value shipment either at home where Caro might see it, or at the office, where someone might ask questions I didn't want to answer. Picking up the coins at Josh's shop could be done quietly and discreetly. To me, this was well worth whatever Josh was making off the deal.

At 3:00 p.m. that afternoon, I called back down to Aldous George in Beverly Hills. Before I even got a word in, he said that a serious collector had been by his shop and would be willing to buy the bottle I had left with him for "slightly over $50,000," and if I could let it go at $47,500, we had a deal. I was sure he had already sold it for $80,000 (I found out later that it was $82,500 with three, count 'em, three of his clients bidding for it—am I good or what?) but I kept a lid on it and said I'd call him back. At 3:45, I called back and said I had gotten the green light and so would be by to pick up the check. Traffic was starting to get really heavy—one of those days that turned "Wilshire Boulevard" into a worse profanity than anything with four letters. I didn't get to his shop until 5:00 p.m., but he was there, beaming and gushing and $35,000 richer, although I only found that out a few days later. I was $47,130 richer, if you back out the cost of the four 1814 half dollars I had needed to buy Jefferson's bottle, but I neglected to mention that little detail to good old uncle Aldo. He said he awaited with pleasure our next transaction. I said the pleasure was all mine, and left for home.

When I got back, it was close to 7:00. Caro was back and was actually in a good mood. She was starting to make herself some

dinner and asked if I wanted some as well. I said sure, mildly and
pleasantly surprised. She made some kind of chicken with rice
dish and a simple salad. Nothing that would have earned her a
Michelin star, but it was perfectly fine for an evening meal. I laid
down the check from George's Wine Emporium and started to look
at that morning's local newspaper. That's what you get for being
distracted and so caught up in yourself. It had been a while since
either of us much cared what the other was up to, so I hadn't given
a second thought to leaving something of mine around. Uh-oh.
Caro saw the check from the wine shop for $47,500 made out to me
with that day's date and her eyes grew wide in amazement. This was
something close to half what I made in a year, so she was curious
what it was for. As in, "What the (expletive deleted) was all that
money for? Did you sell an interest in some Napa Valley vineyard
I don't know about?"

"No," I replied, faking calm as best I could, which wasn't very good.
"I chanced upon a really rare wine bottle in an antique shop and the
guy had no idea what he had, so I bought it for a song and cashed in,
which is why I was out for so long this afternoon. Nice little deal,
huh?"

"Nice isn't the word for it," she came back, her voice almost tinged
with respect, something I hadn't heard from her in a long time.
"I didn't know your knowledge of wine was *that* extensive. Why
in the world are you working in that stupid office if you can pull
off deals like this? You could be making ten times as much as you
do now, maybe more!" Of course that office wasn't so "stupid" if you
happened to be one of the top lawyers pulling in a few million bucks
a year, but I let that one pass, since I wasn't one of them.

"Hold on here," I stopped her. "This was a one-time deal. It was a
nice little coup, but you can't just count on making $47,000 every

time you stop by your local antique shop. It was a fluke—a very profitable fluke, but a fluke, nonetheless."

"I guess!" she replied. "Even after taxes, that still leaves you with over $30,000 free and clear." I hadn't thought about that part. She was right, though. I was the CPA, I *should* have thought of this. It was all income, too, or at least 99% of it was. I couldn't even write off the money spent on my hobby lab in the basement. I don't think accidental time machines are on the approved list of deductible, depreciable assets. Not that I begrudged Uncle Sam his fair share. It wasn't the looming tax bill that made me suddenly very nervous. What made me nervous was the prospect of being asked where my sudden surge in income came from. I mean, my payments were all by check, so I wouldn't raise any immediate eyebrows from the DEA for large, inexplicable cash deposits, but at some point, the question might be raised as to how it was that I was suddenly getting all this money, for no apparent reason, and from a guy who was reputed to be Mafia-connected. Aldo might swallow the mythical wine cellar for a while, but the IRS might not, especially if they asked where it was. After all, my only cash out was a few thousand dollars to a local coin shop. Aldo wouldn't know that, but Uncle Sam would.

This might not be an immediate concern, but it would eventually be a concern, so I had to start thinking about this and soon. I had no desire to be accused of laundering money for the Mafia, especially as I was doing no such thing. On the other hand, if I were honest about declaring how much profit I was making and was willing to pay my taxes in full and if no illegal substances or stolen objects were involved, why should they give me a hard time? I decided that if they would play nice, then I certainly would.

Caro brought me back to the here and now (or, rather, there and then). "Hey, look, that's gonna be a nice boost to the bank account. We can start thinking about a nicer car, maybe a

Mercedes like your friends have." I didn't see why suddenly being able to afford a Mercedes meant we had to go right out and buy one just because our friends drove them. Caro definitely *did* see why, of course—she was always good at seeing things like that. And so, dinner was spent speculating on extras, like whether the navigation system should be built in or removable. This was not good. I thought I knew where this was going. As a matter of fact, at that point, I was close to the "clueless" end of the "knowing" scale, but I was on the right track, and I didn't like it.

18.

The next morning, I went to our bank and asked Tom Nakano, the bank officer who handled our joint account, if I could open another account, this new account being under my name only, not a joint account. Caro would see the earlier $20,000 on the next statement of our joint account, and she'd know that the $47,500 wasn't the first fluke and that I hadn't said a word to her about it. I had to deposit the $47,500 check into our joint account because she had already seen it. She'd also see the $3,700 check to California Coin for Thomas Jefferson's half dollars, as well as some other checks for the next batch of French ten franc gold coins. Although she wouldn't be able to figure out the connection, she was no idiot and would see that I had some interesting business sidelines I had deliberately neglected to inform her about. Potential storm clouds were gathering, and I needed to provide myself with some cover. I just didn't know where or how. I also didn't know just how close the storm was. I sold, at two-day intervals, the remaining seven Jefferson Yquem and Margaux bottles for $45,000 each, and the two Rausan bottles for $12,500 each, and deposited $340,000 into my new personal account.

I had bought a bunch more brand new 1848 through 1860 vintage local Bordeaux (Mouton and the like, as well as more Lafite) area bottles from Philippe Boudreau, and sold them for an average of $25,000 each to Aldous George. Philippe had even found me an occasional Jéroboam, which was the giant bottle that contained as much wine as six normal bottles. For these he wanted twenty francs apiece, as he had warned me, and they *were* huge (and heavy!), but still passed through the portal. They reminded me of the scene in Mel Brooks' "Silent Movie" where Brooks' character falls off the wagon to become King of the Winos. Aldo gave me $85,000 apiece for these babies—probably too little, as only a dozen or so were made per year, from what I understood. I would have loved to have gotten some contemporary Latour, as well, but in those days, it was mostly only sold in kegs. They didn't start putting it in their own individually labeled bottles in quantity until a few decades later, and I didn't think Aldo would have been as excited about an unlabeled keg, no matter what the vintage. There was also the minor detail of my portal not being wide enough to accommodate a large keg of wine. My bank account was growing by leaps and bounds. No reason to fool around with problem items.

Occasionally, I got to talk to Anne Boudreau alone, while Philippe was on his way with a bottle from Château this or that. Anne had had some home schooling, could read and write, and knew a little of history and the world, such as it was in 1860. Obviously, she was not aware of what was going on in South America or India or even the opening of Japan in 1854 by Commodore Perry. She had some knowledge about America, and knew that the situation between the North and the South was getting mean. She was well aware of local European goings on, didn't think much of their current monarch, Louis Napoléon Bonaparte, now Napoléon III. Everyone was sure that he would get France into some disastrous conflict with the Germans—"*les Prusses*"—at some point (good guess—in about ten years, as a matter of fact, but I didn't tell her). She was smart, but not sassy—sort of how actresses sometimes portrayed women in period films, but with a subtle self-assuredness that her social status mandated she keep under wraps for the most part. Oh, and she was stunningly beautiful, too—I *did* mention that, right? If you like Juliette Binoche types, that is. I *adore* Juliette Binoche types.

Call me what you will, but I was smitten, lost, a goner. I actually pined to talk with her, hear her voice, watch her face on the other side of the portal. She understood nothing of technology, of course, but accepted that the portal was real, it was accidental, probably unique, and possibly dangerous to living things. Marriage vows be damned, I wanted to reach out and touch her hand and just hold it if she'd let me. I didn't know if her smile meant she would, but I was ready to risk getting fried to find out—almost, anyway. I wasn't quite at the "life isn't worth living without her" stage, but I was well on the way, believe me. I even imagined what the local competition might be back in 1860 and started to feel pangs of jealousy—toward guys I didn't know for sure existed, and if they did, they were born around 1830, for Pete's sake!

I returned to work full-time, in part for the emotional distraction. I was going to go bonkers if I sat around the house and dreamed of Anne Boudreau in the cellar, just across a border that I could either just waltz across whenever I wanted to or be zapped out of existence by trying, and I didn't know which. My little complex had to be sucking up a lot of electricity, and I was thankful that our utility bills only came every quarter, the last one having been a very typical one back in late June, just after the lightning storm. If Caro had chanced upon a five-fold increase in our electricity consumption, she would have figured out in no time flat that my gadget in the basement had to be the cause and would have checked it out. "Oh, President Jefferson, I forgot to introduce you to my very irritable wife. I assure you, she wasn't always that way. Caro, I'd like you to meet Thomas Jefferson." Right. I don't think so.

After making himself a nice $35,000 profit on the 1784 Yquem, Aldo DiGiorgio let his hair down—figuratively, that is, as he was nearly bald. Probably the day after buying the last bottle out of the first group of Jefferson Margaux from me, he had called up Mercer Private Investigators and asked for Gordon Mercer. Gordon Mercer was no more Gordon Mercer than Aldo DiGiorgio was Aldous D. George. Gordon Mercer was, in fact, the former Guido Mauceri, but took his profession seriously and played by the rules. You know, as in "stayed within the law," tame stuff like that. There was enough divorce work in southern California that a competent private detective could make a decent living without threatening people with loss of limb or life, it seems. I wasn't an expert in the field. Blake and Brock had, of course, availed itself of the services of private detectives on numerous occasions, but all I ever saw was the bills and their inevitable approval from the attorney who had hired them. Whatever it was they actually did was covered by attorney-client privilege, I think. Whether so or not, I never knew what the "services rendered" were in detail, only that they had, indeed, been rendered. I logged in the bill, issued the check, case closed for the glorified office boy/accountant with the Guatemalan wonder-woman assistant.

Aldo must have asked his old friend Guido if he might have half an hour of his time. From what happened later, Guido had obviously said yes. It wasn't difficult to piece together what had transpired. Aldo was getting tired of buying these bottles from me and wanted to buy them from the "source" directly. After nearly a month of bottles from Philippe and family, as well as more from Thomas Jefferson's cellar than originally planned (he really needed the money, and Josh had the "bust" half dollars), Aldo had bought several million dollars' worth of rare wine from me and figured I was getting commissions from the seller that he wanted to be pocketing himself. This had gone beyond the point of small potatoes. Philippe had connections to quite a few other wine makers of the Bordeaux area and his bottles were always fresh and brand new. Aldo couldn't figure out how there could be such a stash of so perfectly preserved old French wine anywhere in North America that he had never heard of, and by this time, he must have at least suspected that my story about the family with the cellar was phony, which, of course, it was.

Still, despite the fact that Aldo had come to the point of "I know that you know that I know," he never confronted me with that directly. I assume he was afraid he would offend me and I would go elsewhere before he found out my real source for this rare, perfectly preserved wine. He was right, too. Had I suspected what he was up to, I would have severed diplomatic relations without a second thought.

Apparently, a few of his customers had opened and tasted their bottles and found them to be spectacularly fresh (surprise!), and said they'd buy more, even at a higher price. The fact that they found the taste to be remarkable didn't surprise me. Around 1870, a plague of phylloxera lice nearly devastated the Bordeaux area vineyards, and it is said that what was produced after that never had quite the same vibrant taste as the wine made from pre-plague grapes. So anyone opening a "fresh (if they only knew *how* fresh!)" pre-1860 bottle from Aldo would have had a taste experience unlike any available from a Médoc-area wine produced later on.

Aldo obviously saw a few hundred thousand dollars go into my pocket that he thought should have gone into his. If he only knew! My "modest" commission rate was hovering at around 100%. But even the idea that I might be earning an extra five percent or ten percent on what I sold him must have been grating on the esteemed Aldous D. George. Besides, I'm pretty sure it wasn't just the money. After all, as far as he knew, he was making far more off of this "cellar" than I was. I'll bet he just thought that the dispersal of any cellar this vast and prestigious should be handled by the likes of Aldous D. George and not by my lowly self. If his ego was enough to make him change his name to Aldous D. George, then it was certainly big enough to make him want to be the agent of choice for whoever it was who had chosen me instead.

19.

Gordon/Guido and his team were good at what they did, for
I wasn't the one who noticed I was being followed around, not that
I was looking for it or expecting it. One of the lawyers at the office
noticed it, however, and took down the license plate number of a car
that he saw on my tail enough times to not be coincidence. He called
a friend at the police department who searched the registration: The
Gordon Mercer Detective Agency. The B&B lawyer explained that
he knew about Guido/Gordon, and though they were known to have
some less-than-kosher acquaintances, they themselves were known
to be a legitimate outfit and were therefore probably tailing me as
some peripheral part of some above-board investigation. The partners
called me in for a brief meeting. Too bad Caro never called me during
that time. It would have been the only time anyone ever would have
said "he's in a meeting" about me, and the implied importance would
have thrilled her.

I was asked if I had any difficulties the firm should know about.
Since, at this point, I had no idea why anyone should be following
me around, I said, truthfully, that I knew nothing about it and could
only assume that someone was looking to exploit a possible weak
point at the firm through me as their most visible non-attorney.
The firm's attorneys liked that idea, said it made perfect sense, that
I should have been a lawyer myself, and they would put a tail on
the tailers. It didn't take me long, though, to wonder if Gordon/Guido
was another Aldous/Aldo. Richie Genovese, B&B's resident ethnic
Italian attorney, said I had better watch out or I would end up in
a supporting role in Godfather XVII. Very funny, Richie. Like
he would know, anyway. He had never even been to Italy, and his
family had been in the States for so long, his preferred beverage
was Guinness beer. He had long ago abandoned any vestige of *in
vino veritas."* Richie was a very competent attorney and his motto, had

he had one in the first place, would have been more like "In sworn testimony veritas, except in case of perjury."

B&B's own private investigators determined in short order that Mercer's tailing me was not connected with any of their cases, and so the partners called me in again to ask if there was *really* nothing I should be telling them. I repeated that I had no clue as to what a private detective would want with me and maybe they should send someone there to ask them straight out. They said they'd think about that. I didn't appreciate the seed of doubt being tossed into what had been an unassailable rep I had at the firm. A law firm needs to get rid of any seeming liabilities before they become liabilities, and I knew they'd toss me out on my ear the second I looked to them to be trouble. Wonderful— more than ten years now in this great job, and my position was in peril for being tailed by some private eye for reasons I could only guess at and could never reveal even if I was right—*especially* if I was right. I was no longer completely financially dependent on the job, of course, but they didn't know that.

My guess was correct, of course—it was Aldo. I can imagine his frustration at Mercer's reports. Aldo wanted to know where I was getting my wine. He didn't want me to disappear before telling him, so he wasn't (yet) about to threaten me directly, but he wanted to cut me out of the equation for sure. This had to be the mother of all wine cellars, and I was getting to be an expensive middle man. It's a good thing for me that he never found out HOW expensive! I can imagine the scene in Aldo's shop. Mercer goes in there, says they have tailed me everywhere and I have visited no place at all where there could conceivably be an immense wine cellar. They had cased my house from the outside, and it was far too new and small to house a wine cellar of any serious magnitude. The only place I had visited that they couldn't figure was a coin shop called California Coin, and the owner's level of wine knowledge stopped with Ernest and

Julio Gallo. They didn't ask about me directly, and once they established the owner had no clue, didn't bring up my name, so as not to alert me (or so they thought—Josh mentioned the funny P.I. types who stopped in and wanted to talk more about wine than coins, so I figured out what was going on). The esteemed Mr. George obviously didn't think I was conjuring these fabulous bottles out of thin air, although he would have ironically been closest to the truth with that guess. Nor could he figure out where or when I was acquiring them, and it must have been driving him crazy with frustration. I'm sure he had people watch the firm to see if some elegantly dressed types were coming in periodically, carrying wine bottle-sized packages, but of course, he struck out there, too— for now, anyway, and it was still five months or so before Christmas. I hadn't had any sham delivery scenario set up yet, but I did make it a point from then on that every trip to Aldo's shop was preceded by a stop at the office, even on weekends, and with me carrying out packages to my car that might well have had wine bottles in them. I did not relish the thought of waking up at 3:00 a.m. with a gun at my head and an unfriendly voice telling me, "Take me to your cellar."

I imagine they had tailed Caro around as well, but she wouldn't have noticed and she didn't have the slightest interest in my hobbies. She hadn't set foot in my part of the basement in two years. Good thing, too. She would probably have told Thomas Jefferson what a second-rate Declaration of Independence he had written (or some such criticism). But she could not have told the Mercer Detective Agency about the source of my wine, as she hadn't the slightest clue beyond my nebulous, nameless antique shop where I had supposedly found that one bottle, for which I got the $47,500 check that I carelessly let her see. Even if some of their guys had engaged her in casual conversation while waiting in a supermarket checkout line, she would have been of no use to them. Like Hogan's Sgt. Schultz, Caro knew nossssssink.

I don't know if there were screaming sessions in the office of Gordon Mercer, but Aldous/Aldo obviously got no satisfaction from the results of the very thorough, and no doubt very expensive, inquiries of the Mercer Detective Agency, because after ten days or so, they stopped following me around. This was noticed by the guys my firm had hired to tail the tailers (and, not incidentally, determine in the process if I was indeed as clean as I had been so loudly proclaiming, which, they were happy to inform me afterward, I was). My visits to George's Wine Emporium wouldn't have raised an eyebrow, as my wine hobby had been explained to the firm when they had first hired me, and George carried $20 bottles as well as the rare stuff. My private bank account was at the same bank where our joint account was, so my visits there to deposit George's checks wouldn't have sounded any alarms with anyone, either. This is why I risked having it at the same branch, something I would have preferred not to do, so as not to risk Caro's discovering that I had, in short order, become the multi-millionaire she had always wished to be married to.

Around the time my private bank account was zooming beyond the $7 million mark, some new players entered the scene. None of them was very welcome.

The first one was Naomi Roganov. She pronounced it "ro-GAH-nov," not like the beef dish with an "St" in front of it. She was with one of those three-letter agencies whose attention you would rather not attract. Not the KGB, or their successor FSB, as you might think from her name, but rather the IRS. Apparently, with all the financial scandals, as well as suspicion of money-laundering and financing of "terrrrists," as some southern politicians always seemed to put it, many banks, including mine, reported unusual surges in private citizens' balances to the government as a matter of routine.

Naomi called ahead and asked if she could have a minute of my time at the office when it was convenient.

When she arrived, she asked if I wished to have an attorney present, seeing as how I worked at a law firm. My confusion was genuine when I asked why in the world I should need an attorney. She mentioned the opening of my private bank account and the sudden huge amount of money it in, all from an individual "of interest" to the government. I replied that if she was referring to the illustrious Mr. George, I had no idea why he would have been of interest to them if he had paid his taxes on time. I further explained to her that Mr. George was of interest to me, as I had found him to be a wonderful outlet for some rare wine bottles I had found cheaply, and that I had been able to turn a remarkable profit on them in a short period of time, as her agency had no doubt seen.

Naomi Roganov made some notes, her oversized glasses slipping several times down her Michael Jackson (post-surgery) thin nose. She had to keep pushing them up, and did so subconsciously. Her brown hair was up in a Sarah Palin-style bun, and she had a scratchy voice that the late Gilda Radner would have killed to have been able to imitate. In her early forties, I estimated, she was the very caricature of the unpleasant IRS agent, the female equivalent of the Rick Moranis character in "Ghostbusters," but minus the nerdiness. She had chosen her calling well. She asked if I was aware that I would owe some considerable estimated taxes on September 15, which was some six or seven weeks from then. I said yes, of course I was (I was lying; no, I wasn't, I had forgotten completely, but maybe it wasn't the best time to admit that to an IRS agent), and that was one of the reasons I hadn't invested much of my money yet, beyond a few coins (she looked at her notes and nodded) so as to have plenty in the account when the time came to remit my estimated tax payment (I'm *such* a patriot). Hey, I could still think fast. Instead of lauding my fiscal conservatism, she remarked that she certainly hoped so (cynical b.....). She made a few more notes, but I hadn't told her anything her own information didn't confirm. When she apparently couldn't find anything else to catch me on, she stood up and proclaimed that she would "find my way out." Seeing as how we were in an unenclosed alcove about twelve feet from the front door of the Blake and Brock ground floor reception area, I refrained from lavishing praise upon her exceptional navigational skills.

I thought that would be the last I saw of Naomi Roganov, and for all I know, it may have been. At least, it was the last time I ever spoke to her. I think my eardrums still have scars from her scratchy, nasal voice.

20.

A few days after the visit of the prim Ms. Roganov, I found out that I had had a bit of lousy luck at my bank. An "account executive" that I didn't even know worked there had apparently struck up a friendship with Caro a year or two back. Her name was Wendy Etxeverría (notice the spelling), and she was—figured it out yet?—a Basque from Elko, Nevada. *This* was Caro's friend, Wendy—not good for me. Recently divorced from a local, she had retaken her maiden name and decided to remain in the area. I guess we can't all be sand moguls. On a visit to the bank to deposit some checks from Aldo, I caught a glimpse of Wendy, and she and Caro actually did look somewhat similar, but had never met in Elko. I was under the mistaken impression that every Basque in Elko must know every other Basque in Elko, but this was apparently not the case. Before striking up a conversation at our bank branch, they had never met. I can imagine how their first meeting must have gone:

"I'm not from around here, originally."

"Neither am I. I'm from Nevada."

"So am I! What part are you from?"

"I'm from Elko, out in the desert, how about you?"

"You gotta be kidding! I'm from Elko, too! *Zazpiak Bat?*"

"*Zazpiak Bat!* Arregui."

"Etxeverría! This calls for a celebration. I get off at 4:30 today. What do you say?"

"Absolutely! I'll meet you right here out front."

Caro must have been hanging out with Wendy Etxeverría quite a bit, and they must have become really good pals, because what Wendy did was *so* against bank rules (and, probably, the law) that she could have gotten into deep, boiling water if her action ever got traced back to her and prosecuted. I'll never find out now, but I hope it eventually does if someone ever reads this. Caro obviously must have mentioned the $20,000 and $47,500 checks from the Aldous D. George Wine Emporium. Wendy must have taken a look and then noticed my own individual account as well. She had no business telling Caro anything she had seen that didn't have to do with Caro's own personal stuff, but at some point she must have been unable to hold it in any longer—wronged women sticking together and all. I can pretty much pinpoint when it must have happened. It was in mid-August. From one day to the next, Caro, who had been actually somewhat civil to me since the $47,500 check, turned into an Antarctic glacier, pre-global warming.

I hadn't made any plans for the money, and so hadn't said anything to Caro about it. She, in retrospect, must have thought I was planning to divorce her without telling her I had the money. No such thought had entered my head, I'm now almost ashamed to say. I'm such a nerd, I swear. But it obviously entered hers. In fairness, I guess I should have known that if she ever got wind of my new wealth and I hadn't said a word to her about it, the obvious conclusion for her would have been that I never intended to. The truth was, our communication was so sparse by now that the subject never came up. I admit that I made an effort to conceal the money from her by putting it in an account of my own, but that was more because I feared that she would want to go out and immediately spend the whole wad on a Rolls Royce with platinum siding, enhancing our other material belongings, and figuring there was always more where that came from. Her reaction to the $47,500 check had really rattled me. Here we got this nice infusion of cash and the first and only thing she can think of is how much trophy car it would buy. Had her life with me really been that deprived? I must have been off in a world of my own not to have noticed, not that she had really made an effort to have a serious talk with me since I lost my parents, and that had been five years ago. I guess this was the stuff of which soap operas were made. Apparently, it was also the stuff of which divorces were made.

Wendy had gotten a decent divorce settlement. My firm wasn't the only one in southern California with gifted attorneys. She lived in a nice, spacious house a mile and a half or so from ours. I know this because about three days after the new Ice Age set in, Caro moved out and in with Wendy. She left me a note saying she just didn't see any sense in pretending we were a couple any more, we didn't share the same values, the same interests, weren't even really friends any more. I'm sure you can figure out the rest without me quoting verbatim. I chuckled at our not being friends any more. When she saw the check for $47,500 made out to me, we were certainly friends. Maybe even on the way to becoming good friends again. Therefore, the big money had to be the cause of the big chill. This got confirmed the day after she moved out.

At work, I received a visit from a crew-cut, pinstriped attorney named Stanley Chase from another firm (Caro being no idiot), presenting me with documents saying that Caro was filing for divorce. He warned me not to fiddle around with any major assets, including "any eventual bank accounts in my name only." Do tell. There is no way Caro, and therefore Stanley Chase, could have known about my private account without its being illegally divulged by someone at our branch. I could have lodged a complaint, but I didn't see any point in it. A complaint would just have given the impression that I really did plan to hide it from Caro and keep it all for myself, and besides, there was no way to push the oak tree back inside the acorn. I told Stan Chase I had no plans at all for any assets, minor or major. I must have looked so baffled by his warning that he may have started to wonder if his client was wrong the part about me suddenly being worth millions. I certainly hadn't done anything to overtly indicate that I was some $10 million wealthier than I had been two months ago, and he knew full well he could not admit to knowing about any kind of amount like that in my name without admitting to having been part of an illegal act.

Now, with all these years working for a law firm, you think I'd know all about legalities, including, especially including, divorce. After all, this was southern California, the divorce Mecca of the western world (Reno was only an administrative capital). But the fact is, despite our failure of a marriage, I had gotten so used to Caro that I had never considered divorce. I promise, it had never occurred to me. My raging hormonal drives of my early twenties must have been dulled by all the wine tastings or something, but I had never sought an outside relationship. I'd have to admit, too, that no outside relationship ever sought me, either. Sad, so sad. Where were all these desperate housewives, anyhow? I didn't even merit getting hit on by desperate singles. Anyway, the visit from Stan Chase did catch me off guard, and I reminded myself to be on the lookout for other possible ramifications from my new sideline.

Caro and I had never discussed a pre-nuptial agreement, of course. My parents had such a great marriage that I never even considered it a topic for discussion. Besides, my financial prospects at the time we got married were such that I was positive the subject would never come up in the first place. The thought of trying to fleece her family in case of a falling out had never entered my mind, either.

I asked Jim Hernández if I could see him for a minute. I had the presence of mind to invoke an attorney-client privilege right away, just in case I said anything that I might regret later on. That put him on red alert in a hurry. I told him to relax, I was not about to be indicted for being the next Bernie Madoff. I basically laid out that Caro was divorcing me, that it might get nasty, and I needed him to recommend to me the firm's best divorce lawyer. He said right away that Steve Clark was the man, but he didn't come cheap. I said that I had come into some money by pure accident and could afford him. That raised Jim's eyebrow a little, but I reassured him that it was by purely legal means, and that the firm would not be covering up any illegal actions on my part. I reminded him that their little investigation of me after seeing Mercer's team tailing me had reinforced that. I had done tasks for Steve Clark, booked trips, hotel rooms, paid bills of private detectives he had hired, and so on, but I had obviously never needed his services personally. I had never been divorced, or even contemplated it, so I hadn't the faintest idea of what to do in such a situation. Jim got me half an hour with Steve that same afternoon.

Steve Clark was about forty, a tall tennis-player-looking type, very relaxed, and he put me at ease as well. He had obviously been here a thousand times, so I probably wasn't going to tell him anything he hadn't heard before. He had probably *not* heard, "I was just talking to Thomas Jefferson, as well as some people working at Château Lafite in 1860" before, and he wasn't about to hear it from me, either. I wanted his professional help, not weekly visits from him in my padded cell. Our conversation centered on my situation, not that of the man who negotiated the Louisiana Purchase in 1803. I told him about our marriage from the first, Caro's family situation, the fact that I had come into a lot of money recently due to a discovery of an old wine cellar. I figured I might as well tell him where all the money came from. The checks from Aldo's wine business would be on record anyway. I told him the truth about why I set up the separate account, and he nodded in understanding. I got the feeling that talking to a divorce lawyer was sort of like visiting a psychiatrist. They nodded in understanding, but you never really knew if they were nodding in agreement with your situation or nodding so you didn't freak out at how badly off you were. I surprised myself at how much of a babe in the woods I was here, having worked for a law firm all these years. A quick look at my tax liability told me where I stood. I had, after all, been a licensed CPA for a while now. But divorce? I knew as much about that as I knew about Basque grammar, and that is so complicated that even most Basques can't explain it.

Steve explained to me that California was a "community property state," and that in such states, all property acquired during the marriage was to be divided equally between the two parties. External factors, such as the fact that my ex-to-be's family was filthy rich already, played no role whatsoever in the considerations. My heart sank when I heard this, as this meant that Caro, despite coming from a rich family, would have claim to half of my newfound fortune, as well as half of the house. This scared the living you-know-what out of me, because it would mean that when the time came, the house would be inventoried and my little secret would be out permanently. This was something I was not about to let happen under any circumstances. I had not thought out a long-term strategy as to what to do with my little windows to the past, but having them as featured items on the Discovery Channel was definitely not part of my plan. Let them go interview Thomas Jefferson on their own time. Besides, if Caro found out that I been in touch with Thomas Jefferson for real, then she might have assumed he gave me an autographed original copy of the Declaration of Independence and she would try to take me for $20 million more than I really had. Come to think of it, I should have asked—he might even have sold me one, and those guys in Dallas did have a department that auctioned off stuff like that. Oh, well, can't think of everything, and besides, they wouldn't have put a lot of credence into my story as to where I had gotten it, either.

"Well, you see, Jefferson and I had gotten to be friends, and he gave it to me in 1818 as a token of his friendship while I was visiting him at Monticello." Right. "Yes, sir. Excuse me, could you please tell me again which mental institution you are calling from?"

21.

I subconsciously knew that my portals to the nineteenth century probably wouldn't last forever. Either some other storm would come up, or the portals would become unstable, or mice would gnaw through the power cable, or something. But it was a prospect I hadn't really come to terms with at that point. When a child gets a new toy, the only thing on his mind at the moment is to play with it and enjoy it, not what he'll do when it's broken and in need of repair ("Bill's Time Machine repair, may I help you?"). But with this new situation, I was now forced to see the portals as a finite phenomenon. I was OK with taking my leave of Thomas Jefferson, as he himself had pretty much said that our encounters would have to be finite as a matter of security and history. I was *not* OK with it being the end of my contact with Château Lafite. I neglected to tell Steve that I had met "someone else," as we had not yet even physically touched at that point. Besides, if he were to ask where she lived and how often we saw each other, I could hardly explain, "Steve, it's like this. She was born in 1832; she's a gorgeous twenty-eight-year-old and I'd really like to start something with her in earnest." I was a CPA. Steve knew that my math skills were in perfectly good shape and so, by definition, my sanity would not have been.

He said that he'd be glad to take my case, but that I would have to deal with the prospect of having to give up half of my wine earnings. He said that he had heard of my visit from the IRS, and so presumed that he didn't have to warn me about tax liability as well. I said I had that covered. I guess it depends on what you mean by covered.

It was slowly dawning on me that except for Jim Hernández, Steve Clark and Juanita Chang, I didn't really have a lot of friends right now—at least not ones I could depend on for help in my current situation. Aldo had obviously been trying to go behind my back and cut me off, and Caro was now definitely an enemy combatant—at least on a legal and emotional level. Well, I did have one new friend I could talk to, if not for long.

In my second visit with Thomas Jefferson, we did have a long chat about his life. He asked a few details about what happened "after my time," but asked surprisingly little. He said that he didn't want it to influence his correspondence with his contemporaries, and it might be dangerous if he let slip something he couldn't possibly have known. He mentioned that he kept in close touch by letter with John Adams, his immediate predecessor as president, and that their "epistolary intellectual discourse," as he put it, might be conserved by one party or the other (were they ever! Just ask any autograph dealer). Even his little offhand comments displayed little flashes of brilliance. Here's a partial list of what we talked about: his thought process while composing the Declaration of Independence, his weighing the risks of taking on the debt needed to finance the Louisiana Purchase, his ceding most of the writing of the Constitution to James Madison ("an extraordinary fellow in his own right, you know,") his pride in what he had accomplished, his dismay at not accomplishing more, especially in the area of abolishing slavery, his regrets that he had not managed to get a better handle on his finances, his regret at having to settle debts by giving up most of his library to form the core collection of the Library of Congress in 1815, his pride in the fact that it was nonetheless *his* collection that now was enshrined there for posterity, his joy that wine was still very much appreciated, and, not least, that his own love for wine was documented in history. There were many details of our conversation that he asked that I not reveal, as I mentioned before, and I won't. But any C student in American History in any high school in America would have figured out what themes an educated twenty-first century person would bring up with Thomas Jefferson if he had the chance, so I don't think I'm letting any cats out of any proverbial bags here.

My portals seemed to be running on sort of a parallel time with the present, and so I was able to estimate what time of day was convenient for me to visit both with Jefferson and the Boudreau family at Château Lafite. The time difference at the opening of the portals did not respect the spatial differences of real-time geography, and it seemed that both Bordeaux and Monticello were within a few hours of my PDT in California. The huge infusion of electrical energy from the storm seemed to have fixed the parallel times as ongoing from the moment of the establishment of the portals. I was able to pinpoint it better with Jefferson, actually, meticulous as he was about details like that. He was about an hour behind me, where Virginia was three hours ahead of me at the present. Bordeaux, 1860, was about an hour ahead, whereas France is really nine hours ahead in the present. Jefferson was in April 1818, and Bordeaux, 1860, was in early June, only a few weeks behind "my" calendar. Needless to say, I tried to take off from work a couple of hours earlier than my usual 6:00 p.m., so that I could visit with Anne. Juanita said she would be glad to cover for me. She was a one-woman argument against any restrictions on immigration, let me tell you.

22.

During all these goings on, I did my best to visit with Anne
by herself, especially after Philippe, her father, got more comfortable
with our improbable arrangement. The Boudreaus quickly came
to accept the lucrative (for them, as well as for me) arrangement
as a nice sideline to their work, and since I had never crossed to
their side of the portal and I had never tried to entice any of them
to mine, they obviously figured Anne was in no need of a chaperone.
Philippe became comfortable letting Anne deliver the various local
wine bottles to me on her own, and collect the ten franc coins I was
using to pay for them. We did get to talk—more and more as time
went on, and when my situation started getting a little precarious,
a *lot* more. She could tell that I was under some kind of stress,
but I could hardly explain to her what it meant to be harassed by
private detectives, California divorce lawyers, or the IRS. She seemed
to be at ease with me, and I could tell that I held some kind of minor
fascination for her as well. I guess talking to someone 150 years in
the future holds a different meaning if you are not the science buff
that Jefferson was. But she was genuinely interested in what I had
to say and understood about my disintegrating marriage. I got up
the courage to tell her that I found her to be beautiful, just to see
her reaction, and her immediate blush and lowered eyelids, along
with her softly uttered, *"Non, non, sûrement pas moi,"* told me that
if she had been told this before, it couldn't have been too often by
someone she cared about. I asked her about her own boyfriends, and
she said that there had been one young man she cared about a few
years ago, but he had run off with some Spanish woman and left to
live in Andalucía somewhere near Sevilla. It had hurt her deeply, but
that had been some five years ago and she was over it. How anyone
could decide in favor of another woman over Anne was a complete
mystery to me, but I was glad someone did.

After Caro left to stay with Wendy, I told Anne what had happened, though not all the details as to why. Anne seemed to show more than just a casual interest in what I had to say about my separation, and if I say it got my heart to racing, I would be understating things. I told her flat out that in a few weeks, the portal might be in jeopardy and I didn't want to lose contact with her before telling her how much I appreciated her company. Not knowing the etiquette of her era, I said I hoped it was all right to be this straightforward and honest with her. She smiled her wide Juliette Binoche smile and said that I was fortunate we had the barrier between us or else she would kiss me. *Au secours!*

I was lost, gone, hooked, you name it. But still, I wouldn't get to kiss her if I got scattered to the four winds the second I went through the portal. I said I didn't know how to test it without risking killing myself. Anne thought about this, and asked, *"Je te passe Minou?"*

Minou? Here I thought I was talking to this wonderful, civilized French woman, and she suddenly would risk the life of some poor, unsuspecting village idiot? *"Qui est Minou?"* (Who is Minou?) I asked as nonchalantly as I could.

"Il se promène toujours ici quelque part," (He's always walking around here somewhere,) she replied and looked around, as if checking on the whereabouts of a cat. Funny thing about that. She continued, *"C'est un chat."* (He's a cat.)

Minou was nowhere to be found, but she kept an eye out, just in case. I guess I could rationalize the loss of a cat, although even that would have bothered me if I had made some animal suffer a horrible death just to satisfy my own personal, romantic whims. I tried to justify Minou's impending potential demise in my mind, saying, well, if the cat gets fried, he won't know what hit him—like

I had a way to know that in advance. Anyway, that evening, Minou wasn't around, so he got a reprieve from being that evening's guinea cat. I heard Philippe call Anne from a distance, and figured that it was curfew time, or dinner time, or whatever time it was that meant that Anne had to leave me. I almost stuck my arm through the portal to try to reach for her hand, but still didn't dare. Call me a wuss, but at least I was a live wuss with both arms still attached. Anne, for the first time, put her hands to her lips and blew me a kiss, and I returned the gesture. She turned and left. If Minou didn't show up in the next day or two, I would go to the local animal shelter and get my own Minou, and tell him/her that he/she was about to make a great contribution to science. Cats appreciate being told that sort of thing prior to being disintegrated.

The first two months of my little promotion from wine nerd to wine mogul went by as sort of a blur. All these changes in my life were happening so fast, I neglected to write them down at the time so as to remember exactly the sequence in which everything had occurred. It's not like I ever expected this to happen, and I sure as hell did not expect events to have such an effect on me as to cause me to practically scream from frustration and pressure. After all, a wife who didn't love me had just left, I had come into more money than I had ever dreamed of, and I had just had a long heart-to-heart talk with Thomas Jefferson. What the hell was I complaining about, right? Besides, an absolutely gorgeous woman had just (well, kinda, sorta) declared that my affection for her was returned in kind. If you leave out the part that I was terrified to initiate physical contact with her, my life should have been swell. Well, the missing physical contact was more than just a minor detail. Although my sex life had pretty much died with Caro, the desire never disappeared, just the consciousness that it was there. In short, I wanted to touch Anne in the worst way (and every way—dormant hormones are not disabled hormones).

111

I also had three major problems weighing on me. When the third one made its unwelcome entrance into my life, the point was reached where I felt I had to do something more than just contemplate my options and consult with lawyers. It was bad enough that in a few weeks, I was supposed to cough up a few million dollars as my September estimated tax payment to the IRS. But that was the easy part, unpleasant as their agent had been in reminding me. All I had to do to keep them happy was to write them a check and not forget to put my social security number on it. Getting a visit from Caro's divorce lawyer was far less pleasant, although I now had Steve intervening on my part. But with two strikes against you, you're still not out. What threatened to be the third strike also threatened to put me out. Worse, this was not for an inning or by implication, but permanently and in so many words.

23.

When you imagine the Mafia, you imagine guys with dark complexions, two days' worth of beard growth, Mediterranean features, black ties and barely concealed weapons under cheap, pinstriped jackets.

Not even close.

I was approached as I stopped for a rare visit to a Starbucks on the way home from work and some light grocery shopping. The visit wasn't even long enough for my smoked salmon to go bad or for me to be terrified until after my "guests" had left. Three ordinary-looking guys in casual suits waltzed in and joined me at my table. The fact that they didn't order anything disconcerted me somewhat, but they were blondish crew-cut types, and I figured the IRS decided to send me a second reminder about my upcoming estimated tax payment. I had read that they had harassed some poor soul up in Sacramento for a difference of four cents on a tax bill, so nothing would have surprised me. Besides, they smiled and said, "Hi Bob," as if they had worked in my building for the last five years and we had regularly met for lunch on Tuesdays at PF Chang's. I had never seen them before in my life.

The guy obviously in charge sat across from me, and said, "We just need a minute or so of your time. You're not in any rush, are you?" I said I wasn't. He said, "That's good. We don't want to keep you." I didn't want them to keep me either. So far, our interests were mutual. I got the distinct impression that this would not remain the status quo for long.

"You can call me Stef." Stef? I asked out loud, "Stef?" He smiled. "Well, that's short for Stefano, but I prefer the short form."

I preferred neither the short form nor the long form. I would have preferred that he and his friends, who, upon reassessment, didn't look so ordinary or friendly after all, disappear from my life now and forever. "Stef" got right to the point.

"A mutual acquaintance of ours has heard of a rather fabulous wine cellar you have access to," said Stef.

"Well," I said, drawing it out to gather my thoughts and say as few stupid things as necessary, "your acquaintance has good sources. I thought that it was rather a private matter."

"Oh, don't get me wrong, Bob," continued "Stef." "We very much want to keep it a private matter. As a matter of fact, we want to keep it so private that we want you to put us in touch with the owners of that cellar and have no further contact with them yourself. You'll have our solemn promise that you'll get a fair commission on all transactions resulting from any contact we have with the owners of the wine cellar. We'd just prefer that the transactions be conducted by us from now on. Is that a problem for you?"

Oh, just ever so slightly. Like the biggest problem in the world, you smiling jackass, if you overlook the IRS and Caro's lawyer breathing down my neck. But, as I was neither armed nor dangerous, and they were probably both, I formulated my answer somewhat differently.

"Of course it's a problem. You don't need to bother to explain who you are. I get what's going on. But, you realize, I can't just call these people up and say there's new management," I said. "They have property all over the place, and their own security will clamp their cellar up tighter than Fort Knox if they have the slightest impression that something unfamiliar to them is in the neighborhood. It took me a decade to gain their confidence, and if I just show up with new, shall we say, 'representatives' without a plausible explanation, not only will you get nothing out of them, but I won't get anything more, either."

By now, it was obvious to me who I was dealing with, and I made no pretense of not realizing it. "However much firepower you may wish to use as persuasion, I promise you they have more of it."

I don't think Stef was prepared for a line of conversation quite this direct. Obviously, he knew from Aldo that my source for the rare wine was not easily identified. Just as obviously, Aldo was not satisfied with Gordon Mercer's failure to find out the source of my wine, and had opted for more drastic measures. What a greedy, low-life, son of a bitch. He was making a fortune off what I was selling him and that wasn't enough for him. He wanted it all. Or else, he wanted the prestige of representing the "owners" himself. Whatever. He wanted Aldous D. George in and Robert Packard out. I'm not sure he even still gave any credence at all to my yarn about the old family acquaintances with the extensive wine cellar. After all, he had to have known from Gordon Mercer that during the time he had me shadowed, I hadn't been anywhere that could have housed such a cellar.

I figured I might as well not pretend I didn't know what was going on here. I told Stef that I assumed I would come to grievous bodily harm if I was not able to persuade my source to deal with him and his friends in my stead. Aldo's name, of course, was never mentioned in the course of this conversation. Aldo(us) who? Stef smiled, and dropped all pretense as well.

"I'm glad we understand each other. But we're not unreasonable, and we certainly don't want to get to that stage. We won't need you to complete arrangements tonight. We've checked your house, as you might imagine, and its dimensions don't allow for a wine cellar of the magnitude required for such a collection as you've been selling out of, so it's clear you do have a contact, although you have to be some kind of magician to have kept your contacts so discreet all this time. I'll admit, we still have no clue as to where you get your wine, and that's saying something. But you're also correct as to what methods we'll use, if necessary, to find out what we want to know. Since you seem to know as well, I take it no such methods will be necessary, right?"

I figured playing along would be healthier at this point. "Look, as long as your word is good that I'll continue to participate in the action, I guess I can live with that arrangement. But you have to understand that I can't spring this on them overnight. We're talking about the owners of thousands of bottles, and a change like this will have to be introduced gently, or they'll cut me off and you'll never get in. These people have their own resources and are not exactly easily intimidated, you know? I'll need three or four weeks, and even then, I'll have to ask you to let me give you a progress report on when I can make the introduction, OK?"

Stef thought about that a moment. "We were hoping for quicker action than that."

"Look," I said, "it took me ten years to gain entry here. *Ten years!* You can ask your contact that sent you to me. Three months ago, I was nobody to him. Your employer couldn't even pronounce my name right, I mattered that little. In the meantime, I've sold him well over $10 million worth of fabulous old wine, and that barely scratches the surface of what is in this cellar. People like that are every bit as cautious as you are, and they'll cut us both off the second they think something isn't right. You can't tell me you or your friend is willing to risk that. This is very old money, and old money buys a lot of good security. You don't break in to places like theirs. You get invited, or they send a messenger. I don't want to lose this deal. When is a guy like me ever going to get a shot at something like this again? Go about this right, and I keep on walking without crutches, and you get what you want. Go about this wrong, and no matter what you do to me, you go away empty-handed and so does the party that's paying your bill."

He thought for a moment, his face immobile. He then broke out into his best-buddy grin, and said, "Sure, Bob, we don't want to endanger anything here. You obviously didn't inherit this stuff, so you have to be getting it from somewhere. You're not going anywhere, either, from what we understand." I confirmed that I had no travel plans. "Good. OK, let's say you have a few heart-to-heart talks with your source, and in a month or so, you make the introduction. We'll leave it to you as to how you wish to introduce us. But no longer than that, OK? Let's say that by the end of September, you'll be getting your commissions from us, and we'll be handling the transactions directly with the owners."

I sensed that by agreeing too readily, I would give the impression that I intended to do no such thing, so I made what I thought to be some reasonable objections. "Look, I'll try, OK? You don't know these people. If my parents hadn't taken me on those trips to France when I was a kid and met the family branch still in France, I wouldn't even have known these people existed. They're not the kind of people who get a kick out of seeing their names in the papers, you know? Let me broach the subject slowly, figure out a plausible reason why I won't be doing this myself any longer—impending divorce requiring my full attention, I'll think of something. In the meantime, cook up a good story for yourself and be ready to be very conversant on the subject of old wine. If they sense a phony, their own security will be on all of us faster than you can say 'Bordeaux.' I'm sure you can find someone who can teach you the basics." Someone named Aldo, for example. "I'd also be interested in knowing just what my commission scale is, once I'm out of the picture. It's not like I'm looking at some golden parachute at my day job, you know?"

The smile disappeared, and the real Stefano started talking. "Hey, we have our instructions, too, you know. We can't let this thing drag on forever. We have other projects we work on besides just you. We don't know what your future pay scale will be; we don't decide that. We can tell you that you *will* be alive to receive it if all goes well. That little benefit alone should count real high in priority." One last phony friendly grin. "Hey, man, we'll be in touch in four weeks or so!"

He stood up, and like some electronic signal sent by his movement, so did his two silent "friends" at exactly the same moment. I didn't really put much faith in his promise of residual commissions. I figured they would not shoot me in the back of the head and leave my remains in some car at the long-term parking garage at LAX, but I wouldn't put a "freak accident" beyond them, once a certain amount of time had passed. But they also knew that I worked with a bunch of lawyers and could very well leave a detailed "in case of my death" letter with one of the attorneys, so maybe they wouldn't hurt me after all. I knew full well what, if not exactly who, they were, and it was clear to all parties concerned who had put them up to this, but it would do me no good to swear out a complaint. These guys were contract "labor" brought in from outside and it was obvious that the contract was not written down anywhere. They didn't care one bit who liked what vintage of wine, and they didn't seem the types to know the difference between red and rosé (or care). They did what they were paid to do and were concerned that the man paying them was happy. Nothing else was of any concern. I had a concern, though.

24.

I didn't know to what extent Aldo was doing his homework. He obviously knew I was getting a cut off the top, but as he had known me for years as a nobody, he would have figured that, even if what I had told him about my source of the wine bottles was a fantasy, I was indeed getting them from *somewhere*. This meant that I was, indeed, fronting for someone. If he had been talking to Wendy or Caro, he would have known that just about all the money I had gotten from him was sitting in a local bank account in my name. If he had known *that*, the house would have been raided by Stefano and friends before now. After all, if I had kept all the money, the wine had to be all mine, so a thorough search of my house might yield a clue as to where it was coming from. Also, luckily, I had not given in to Caro's fantasies about a big, fancy, new car or any other ostentatious displays of new wealth, so he had no reason to suspect that I was anything more than an errand boy for someone with an unimaginable wine cellar, being paid a modest commission for my services and for keeping the owners' name a secret. Stefano and friends obviously worked on a pay scale rather higher than minimum wage, so Aldo wouldn't have brought them in unless he expected a big payoff for their efforts, and I'm sure they weren't used to failing in those efforts. Though I was sure they would be keeping a close watch on me, I didn't think they'd initiate another direct, face-to-face contact unless they thought it would be productive for them (or my month's grace was up). In this, I was correct.

The next time I would actually see any of Stefano's "delegation," it would be very briefly and definitely for the last time. He would be "in touch," though. I actually went out of my way to make sure he would be. I figured that with these guys, the bite, so to speak would be a lot worse than the bark. I had to be careful that I wasn't the one being bitten, chewed, and spit out like a stick of gum that had lost its flavor and, with it, its use to humanity. Or something. I never chewed gum.

The meeting with Stefano and his pals was on August 24, 2010. You don't forget visits like that. It was on a Tuesday afternoon (no connection to Moody Blues lyrics). I have a pretty vivid memory of the timeline after that, and will try to stick to it.

Before getting in my car to drive home, I took out my cell phone and called in to Juanita. I asked if it was OK if I came in at 10:00 the next day instead of at 8:00. She said sure, you go ahead. It came out as "choo, djoo go ahé," but I knew what she meant. Her written English was so eloquent, I sometimes forgot that her spoken English would have embarrassed Bill Dana's José Jiménez. I also made one other call. Josh was in his shop. I asked him if he had a few minutes for me the next morning. He said he normally opened at 10:00, but could be there at 9:00 if I couldn't be there during normal hours. Ah, service with a smile. I said I'd be there. I had started to formulate a plan, but its chances of success depended in no small part on Josh and his friends in Dallas, as well as Minou liking smoked salmon. If he didn't, I'd probably be calling Josh up in the morning to cancel our appointment.

I got home and the smoked salmon I had bought was still good. I had bought more than I wanted for myself, but then I wasn't planning on eating it all. I made myself a light dinner with the smoked salmon, some salad I had thrown together, and sprinkled some olive oil and some balsamico on it. That, some mineral water, and a glass of a decent red and I was happy. I didn't drink any of the expensive collector wines I had acquired, wanting to use as many of them as possible to pad my burgeoning bank account as quickly as possible. I was anxious to get downstairs and ate quickly.

I put aside the screen door and saw Anne. She said she hoped she might see me there. I said the feeling was mutual, but then she threw me a curve (not that she had the slightest idea of what a curve ball was). She said she had brought along someone she wanted me to meet. I didn't know what this was supposed to mean. Had she been engaged all this time and not had the heart to tell me? Was she going to introduce me, as a consolation prize, to her best girlfriend who had buck teeth and weighed 300 pounds? Or her new fiancé, René, who looked like Alain Delon in his prime? I couldn't stand the suspense, so I just asked straight out, *"Qui est-ce?"* (Who is it?) She must have read my thoughts on my face, for she laughed from pure amused delight. *"Tu me fais rire. J'aime ça. Ça m'a trop manqué."* (You make me laugh. I like that. I've missed it too much.)

She looked down, and called softly, *"Minou, Minou, Minou, viens!"* A nondescript tabby cat came cautiously trotting up and she took the animal up in her arms. She pointed to me and purred to the cat, *"Voilà Robert! Il est sympa, non?"* Oh, yes, that's me. *Très sympa*, especially if you're a 160-year-old cat. And Garfield thought *he* was old! She kept cooing to the cat. *"Tu veux aller voir mon ami Robert, oui?"* This was it. Anne wanted to touch me as well, and she was willing to risk disintegrating her pet to find out if we would ever be able to do it. I had been hoping for this. I hadn't bought that extra salmon for me, but to entice her cat to pay me a visit. Never mind what a girl *tells* you. It's when she proves she's willing to vaporize her cat for you that you know she's serious.

She held Minou up to the portal and I held a plate with the salmon up to the portal as well. The cat must have smelled the fish, a good sign. I set the plate down on a table I had brought into the room for this purpose. I patted my hands in the salmon to give them the right smell, and Anne held the cat up as close to the portal as she dared. I held out my hands and the cat, smelling the salmon, sensing no danger and hungry for dinner, made the small jump to me. I held my breath.

25.

What I *should* have held was my nose. The cat smelled like he had played in cow manure all day, and he needed a good dose of feline Listerine, if there was such a thing. But, other than that, and the fact that he nearly knocked the plate with the fish off the table in his haste to get at it, Garfield *à la bordelaise* had made the jump as if there had been no portal at all. No snap, crackle, or any other kind of sounds of electrical discontent. Minou was in cat heaven and purred contentedly as he demolished the rest of my smoked salmon. Despite the smell, I patted him and stroked him as he ate, and his tail switched from side to side as if to say, "Mister, you *do* know how to show a cat a good time." When he was done with the salmon, I picked him up, which he let me do without resistance, in my experience not typical for a cat when being handled by a stranger. Anne marveled, *"Il a l'air de bien t'aimer."* (He seems to like you.) I smiled back at her and concurred, *"En effêt!"* (Indeed.)

I brought a contentedly purring Minou back close to the portal and Anne held out her arms. Minou positioned himself and jumped back across to Anne. Anne caught him, let him down on the ground, then turned back to me, cocked her head, and said, *"Alors?"* I knew perfectly well what she meant, but was still a little apprehensive. I stalled with *"Alors, quoi?"* (Well, what?) She held her hand out, palm up and curling her index finger upwards, and made me that proverbial offer a man can't refuse. *"Tu viens me dire bonsoir, ou quoi?"* (Are you coming to say good evening or what?)

The moment of truth. I was totally infatuated with this woman, there was no use in denying it. But although we had chatted about this and that, we hadn't really spent a lot of time talking, learning to really know each other. How come she was being so forward? A good Catholic French country girl acting like this? But I guess living in a somewhat rural area, with arranged marriages still a standard way to get couples together, maybe she figured she would test the waters elsewhere? Or maybe she was just a woman with more of a mind of her own than was deemed appropriate for her time? Or maybe twenty-eight was considered past a woman's prime in mid-nineteenth century rural France and her family was getting desperate to marry her off? I couldn't figure out an answer there on the spot, but I *did* sense that an important moment was at hand.

Some quick calculations of my options told me that whatever else may occur, I wanted Anne to be a part of it. Maybe I was being too optimistic, or maybe I was reading her vibes wrong. I had certainly become adept at doing *that* over the years. But the little birdie that shows up on a person's shoulder every lifetime or so told me that this was it. This was my moment to reroute my life, even if it meant taking me to unchartered territory. All my life, I had always had to settle for what circumstances had offered me. So it seemed, anyway. I never got to be the one who decided, OK, now we're going to do it *my* way, and spare me the Sinatra jokes. But this time, I was offered a chance to step outside the path that fate had chosen for me and go for the grand prize. The guy who was known for being a bunt artist trying for a grand slam home run, if you will. Once, in some Chinese restaurant, I got a fortune in my fortune cookie that said, "The great pleasure in life is doing what people say you cannot do." It was time for some "great pleasure" in my life.

I positioned myself so that I could step through the portal by stepping across sideways, ducking slightly, and then pulling my other leg through. I didn't dare touch the sides of the portal. I was scared that I might accidentally change the settings and my right leg would be standing in front of Anne, while my left leg might become an uninvited guest at a planning session of Abraham Lincoln's presidential campaign committee. I may not have been a track star, but I managed to slip though without touching anything.

The first thing I noticed about the grounds of Château Lafite, 1860, was the smell. I had been out in the country before, of course, but this was a smell I had never before encountered. A fresh, earthy—how do you describe this?—nature smell. No diesel motors, no plastic, no chemicals, it was almost a primeval kind of sensation. I took a deep breath and looked at Anne standing before me. I guessed she was about five-foot-eight, which may or may not have been tall for a nineteenth century French woman (I suspected it was). She also had a very pleasant "earthy" smell to her, which I got to experience immediately as she came up to me and kissed me on both cheeks. She stood back and looked at my clothes. She stared in curiosity at my pants, which seemed a little forward until I remembered that in her time they had buttons, not zippers. She had never seen such a thing. I looked down and laughed. I told her that it was normal in my time. She said she had somewhat come to accept that I was, indeed, from another time, but seeing me here in front of her made it real. I had a quick sense of panic and looked behind me, but there, through the portal, was my lab and the empty plate that used to have a slab of smoked salmon on it.

Seeing Anne there, a few inches from me, was overwhelming. I didn't know to what extent the two kisses on my cheeks were meant as a friendly greeting, or maybe more. I couldn't know what she had said about me to her parents, of course. I didn't even know if she was here alone with me with Philippe's blessing, but there was no one else around. It had to be about 7:00 in the evening where she was. I reached up with my hand and touched her cheek, let my hand linger there, and said softly, *"C'est un plaisir de te sentir."* (It's a pleasure to feel you.) She put her hand over mine, keeping my hand on her cheek. She smiled and replied, *"C'est un plaisir de l'entendre."*

(It's a pleasure to hear it.) Her skin had a kind of soft, smooth feel to it, sort of like what you expect a child's skin to feel like. I remembered—these were rural people. They probably didn't use much in the way of make-up or cosmetics. Heavy vegetable diet, probably, too. In case you're wondering if we ripped off our clothes and looked for the nearest soft pile of hay, I have to disappoint you. If you are or were a Billy Joel fan, one of his songs was called "Leave a Tender Moment Alone." That was more like it. We held hands, talked, strolled a little, although I was still too nervous to let the portal out of sight. Even so, I got a sense of where I was. This was at the edge of the grounds of Château Lafite. Anne told me that she and her family had been gathering mushrooms in the woods when I first appeared. Usually, no one spent any time at that spot. With the woods in back of me, I took in the (to me) idyllic scene. Some simple dwellings could be seen in the distance. The edge of the château was visible, just beyond the edge of the woods, with the vineyards taking up much of the land around it. A photo of the scene might well have been taken for a contemporary, well-executed landscape painting.

I got up the courage to ask her about her love life. She blushed but laughed a little, and said she had "been with a man," but it had been years ago, and though she had a few men in the area express interest, it was not mutual and she was in no rush, although her parents were alarmed at her single status at her "advanced" age of twenty-eight. She asked about me, and I told her the truth. I was married, in the process of divorce, and should have never gotten married in the first place, except that I despaired of ever finding the perfect girl.

"Et maintenant?" (And now?) she asked. Why be less than honest? I kept nothing back. I told her that although we had not known each other long, and there were some obvious barriers to us becoming anything permanent, that I had never been so totally lost in the

thought of one particular woman as I was now and that I hadn't been able to stop thinking about her since the moment I saw her. I was going to explain about Juliette Binoche, but I remembered that I would have had a hard time explaining movies to her, let alone who Juliette Binoche was (or would be, as the case may be). She smiled and said that my sentiments were reciprocated on her part, although she, too, was nervous about losing her heart to a fantasy. I assured her this was no fantasy. Improbable as the whole thing was, it was also the first time in my life I had ever felt myself truly falling in love, and I would not let it go. She asked me point blank if I could imagine myself living out the rest of my life in her world, foregoing all the wondrous, unimaginable things I took for granted in my time. I admitted that there would be much for me to sacrifice if I came to stay with her, but that I would gain something that all the wondrous technology of my day had not been able to give me. She nodded and asked me what I would do if I came to live with her.

Another moment of truth: I told her that if she wanted me, I would have no problem finding something to do and that I would start preparing for such a move, but only if she was sure she wanted me. She looked into my eyes in one of those moments you only see in the movies, and just smiled and said, *"Oui."* I stared at her and then kissed her—not on the cheeks this time. This was what I had been waiting for all my life, and it was all G-rated. I didn't even have to worry about the rest. Like they said in those Astérix comics, *"Alea iacta est."* (The die is cast.) I was committed. Time to start thinking about putting Plan A into motion and making sure it would work, because there would be no Plan B.

She had a thousand questions, of course. Would evil people from my time follow me? Would I be able to occupy my time enough to not get bored? How would I support myself? I said that if I came to stay with her forever, I would take care of those problems. I begged her to trust me on that point. She nodded again and remarked that she inferred from what I had just said that I would be going back "home" this evening? I said, yes, I had to think about many things before I could consider coming to stay with her forever. There would be arrangements I had to make.

She asked me about what life was like in 2010. How do you answer a question like that? I said the world had changed beyond what she could possibly ever recognize. Medicine had made incredible progress, technology had made things possible she could never even imagine (my time portals were a fluke, and unique). I explained about airplane travel, which she thought fabulous. I also explained about the Internet, which she also found fabulous. I told her about nuclear weapons, which horrified her utterly. She asked why in the world would anyone want to build such a weapon? Um, yes, why indeed? Under the circumstances, it seemed like such a reasonable question.

I didn't even mention the world wars of the twentieth century. France was still fighting wars with Prussia and was about to fight another one in 1870, and I sure as hell wasn't going to tell her about the extermination camps at Auschwitz and Birkenau. If the French had the slightest inkling that their neighbors to the northeast were capable of such things, the whole of France might have emigrated to Tahiti before even getting around to sending us the Statue of Liberty in the mid 1880s. I told her the world in my time was changed, but not necessarily for the better. She nodded. If she had gotten the implication that I would not like to show her around Los Angeles, 2010, I was glad of it. I also explained that we only spoke English there, which she did not. It probably would have been overkill to explain that, depending on where you were in L.A., Spanish, Korean, Farsi or Amharic would have stood you in equally good stead. I had told her how it was that I spoke French long before now. She remarked that my French seemed somewhat strange to her, but that I had no doubt been accustomed to using expressions that were not yet part of everyday speech in her day. She may not have known much of the world, but she was no idiot. Anne surmised that her speech must seem somewhat antiquated to me the way her grandmother's speech had seemed antiquated to her. She seemed to be content to let her imagination fill in the blanks for her about my world, for which I was very grateful.

I told her I would start making arrangements as soon as I got back to my side of the portal so that I could come stay with her. I asked her again if she was really sure she wanted me, and she nodded. I then cautioned her not to say a word about any of what we had discussed to anyone. She agreed. I think her intuition told her that it might jeopardize our future together. We headed back toward the portal, which seemed a little less daunting than it had before I had used it myself. I wished I had dared to use the other one to visit with Thomas Jefferson and stroll the grounds of Monticello with him, but he had servants all over the place, and I didn't want to risk my visit being recorded by someone for posterity. I was already playing with enough fire as it was.

I held Anne close to me, felt her thick, dark brown, silky hair, kissed her again for a long time, and got ready to step back through to my lab, noting with no small pleasure that she was in no hurry to let me go. I made the hop back with no trouble and a lot less apprehension than on the way over. Lincoln's campaign committee would not be burdened with any of my stray limbs tonight.

On the other side, Anne softly said, *"Bonne nuit, et à bientôt, mon cher Robert,"* and turned to go back to the house where her family lived. Reality vertigo was starting to hit me with an 8.0 on the Richter scale. Had I really been with my Juliette Binoche look-alike in a classic G-rated love scene at Château Lafite in the year 1860? Or was I just out of my friggin' mind and wanted desperately to think so, due to my thoroughly messed up situation back in *"Chèrmanne Auxe"* (as Anne pronounced it), California, 2010? I turned to the portal once more before going upstairs and was able to catch a glimpse of Anne before she disappeared from view. No, señor. This was for real. Use it or lose it. Here's a hint: I did not intend to lose it.

Once Anne was out of sight, I went upstairs and checked my bank balance online—$12,675,000 plus a few weeks' worth of interest income. Not a bad haul for a little over two months' worth of wine trading, if I do say so myself. Even if Aldo figured I was getting only 5% off the top, this was more than half a million dollars, and he definitely wanted the next few years' installments to go into his own bank account. Hell, I'll bet he wouldn't even cheat on his taxes. Well, come to think of it, no, I would NOT bet on that, but I'm sure he wouldn't try to get out of them entirely. Maybe a little creative accounting to soften the bite? I had yet to worry about such matters, although Naomi Roganov would no doubt be there on September 16 to remind me, probably armed with a court order to freeze my account, in case I hadn't made my estimated payment the day before and Caro's lawyer hadn't beat the IRS to the punch. I decided to keep up the sham of my business relationship with Aldo, so as not to give him the impression I had been thinking how to end our little business relationship in a manner other than the one that he had in mind. He was decidedly less friendly than he had been before he decided to get nasty, but as none of us—not me, not Aldo, and not Stefano—had ever come out with naming names, no one officially knew who was behind my impending retirement from the rare wine business. So he wasn't really mean to me, just went through the motions, kept buying my bottles, figuring that in a month or so, he would be in the driver's seat, and I would be either walking or thrown under the bus altogether. Nice, huh? Aldo had to have made profits of somewhere between $4 and $6 million on the bottles I had sold him—money he would never have made if I had gone to someone else—and this wasn't enough for him? Maybe this was small change if you're Bill Gates or Oprah Winfrey, but to mere mortals like me, it was real wealth.

26.
Wednesday, August 25

This morning, after slapping myself awake and reminding myself that my close-up scene with Anne was real and not some dream to be filed in the "wishful thinking" category of Freudian dream interpretations, I got up and drove to California Coin. Josh was there at 9:00, as promised, and I thought, *there are some people who are decent in my era; they are not all divorce lawyers, crooked wine merchants, well-spoken thugs or eager IRS agents.*

Josh asked, "So, what's on your mind this morning? Need some Kruger Ponds to go play high stakes poker with Cecil Rhodes?"

Luckily, I had no idea what a "Kruger Pond" was, because I freaked right out upon hearing that one offhand remark, with which he had pretty much nailed perfectly what I was doing with all these coins I had been buying off him. He had taken what must have been a very disoriented look on my face to be perplexity as to his coin reference. I wasn't about to discourage his misconception, and said, "OK, gimme a break. What's a Kruger Pond? I know what a Krugerrand is, but I've never heard of a Kruger Pond, and I get the distinct impression you're not about to tell me it's a small biotope in South Africa where Boers used to fish for smallmouth bass."

Josh laughed, and said, "Good guess. It's a gold coin that circulated in South Africa in the last decade of the nineteenth century, about the size of our $5 gold piece. The portrait of Paul Kruger on the Kruger Pond is practically identical to the likeness of him later used on the Krugerrand. I take it that's *not* why you wanted to see me at this hour?"

"Not exactly," I said, trying to sound very serious. He immediately sensed that this was not going to be a visit like the others. "How much face value in French gold dated before 1860 could I buy for $12 million?" That stopped him in his tracks.

"All these other times, you were just testing me to see if I'd treat you fairly to see if you wanted to give me this one big investment order, right?"

Wrong! "You got it," I said. I couldn't exactly explain that my situation had changed, or the how or the why of it, could I? I figured it would be better to let him draw his own conclusion and then confirm it for him, if it made any kind of sense. Since he knew none of the background, his interpretation sounded perfectly plausible.

Josh told me that he might be able to put such an order together, but he'd have to do it through that big coin dealership in Dallas. I said, go ahead. "Now?" he asked. "Now," I confirmed. He said he'd have to make a phone call. I told him to go ahead and make his phone call. He went into the back room, and evidently got who he needed on the line in Texas. After a few minutes, he came back. He said, "OK, look, that's a tall order, since you only want one specific type. But the type you want is the most common type, so they're pretty confident they can fill your order. However, no one in North America keeps that kind of a stock of those coins lying around the house. They'll have to import it from Swiss banks, and they won't even know until tomorrow if the kind of quantity you're looking for is available right now. He thought so, but refused to confirm such an order until he knew he could get them."

"That's reasonable enough," I replied, and continued, "What would I be able to get for the money?" He turned to his computer and started punching in some numbers.

He explained, "Here's the deal. French twenty franc bare head (I knew by now what this meant) coins have a basal bullion value of $229.64 based on today's price of $1230 for an ounce for gold. This fluctuates, as you know. Assuming you were to fix the deal based on $1230 gold, the coins would cost them $235.50 a coin plus shipping and insurance, figure maybe an extra half dollar a coin. They'd want $240 from me, and I'd charge you $5 a coin, and pick up the cost of delivery from Los Angeles to any local address you want delivery to—presumably your bank, right?"

I said that I hadn't yet decided where I wanted delivery. I asked if that could be determined at the last minute. "Hold on," he said. He made another phone call, came back and said yes, all he had to do was to give Brinks the delivery address. At a net $245 to me, my money would be enough for around 50,000 coins, or a million francs in face value of that time. I had no idea what a franc bought in 1860. I was pretty sure Philippe was gouging me mercilessly by his standards at ten francs a bottle, but I definitely wanted to keep him happy, and so never tried negotiating his ten francs per bottle downward. A million francs would have been about $200,000 at contemporary exchange rates. I knew that because of the Red Book that Josh gave me when I bought my first "bust halves" for Thomas Jefferson. I hadn't studied it much, but there was one part where it said that from 1879 to 1880, the USA was considering striking a $4 gold coin to have an exact counterpart to the French 20 franc coin. The U.S. Mint had struck a few pattern coins, known as "Stellas," as trials, but never went ahead with the project. Still, the information in the book was enough. Twenty francs was $4 (i.e., a franc was 20% of a dollar). Therefore, 50,000 gold 20 franc coins (i.e., a million francs) was $200,000 in 1860 money. I also knew that $200,000 was a bloody fortune in America in 1860, and figured it had to be the case in France as well. I said I was cool with the price, and if he could place the order successfully, he could consider it a done deal.

"Hold on, it's not that simple," said Josh. Uh-oh, I should have known. He said that the guys in Dallas could never order that much gold without them paying up front, and consequently Josh would have to pay up front, and since he didn't have that kind of money lying around, that I would have to pay up front. I said, sure, no problem. He stared at me.

"Just like that? It's no problem? Twelve million dollars is no problem? Who the hell ARE you anyway?" I said that I had never pretended to be anything other than what he saw, that I had come into some money, and due to certain family considerations that I didn't care to elaborate upon, I wanted my investment in gold in this form. He asked if I had gotten my inspiration from TV ads. I said I didn't even know there had been TV ads for these coins. Josh said that one channel had been promoting them rather heavily. I said I guessed I didn't watch that channel, as I had never seen any such ad. He shrugged and said OK, whatever, and promised to call me the next day when his Dallas contacts had talked with their bank contact in Switzerland. He said that from the looks of it, gold was on a fast track to hit and exceed $1300 an ounce this fall, and soar past $1400, maybe even $1500 next year, so my purchase was probably not a moment too soon. I thanked him and drove to the bank.

From my cell phone in my car, I asked to speak to Tom Nakano, the account exec who had set up my private account. I asked him to come meet me outside the bank, as the last thing I wanted was to give Wendy Etxeverría a reason to go monitoring movements in my account and running to Caro to tell her about it. Seeing me talking to the guy who handled my private account would have been grounds for more curiosity on her part than I wished to arouse. Tom came down, met me in the Starbucks across the street, and asked what was up. I told him that someone in the bank was telling private third parties about movements in my personal bank account.

His face went a little pale (no small feat for a full-blooded Japanese) and he said he presumed I had concrete information about this. I said not only did I have concrete information about it, but had been confronted with it personally, and by someone with accurate information as to my balance. This was the reason I had asked him to meet me outside of the bank's building, as I feared that merely being seen talking to Tom inside the bank could set off a new round of prying. He said that the bank did cooperate with the IRS when large movements occurred, and I said this was not a problem, and that I had already been in touch with them, getting information on estimated tax payments. I left out the part that the contact had been their idea, not mine. I explained to Tom that it was definitely someone inside the bank doing what they perceived to be favors for parties unfriendly to me, and that although I could not prove it, I had been confronted with the information and wanted him to know that I knew.

Tom asked what I wanted him to do about it. I said there was nothing he could do except to keep our meeting secret, and to divulge any big movements in my account only to those parties who were authorized to know, and even then, only if they asked. I told him flat out that I intended to make a large investment with some of the money, so he should not get alarmed if a big check or two should come through. I said that I was keeping a close eye on all my tax obligations and that he needed not worry about that. He knew that I was a CPA and he accepted what I told him. He said he would keep a watch on anyone he heard or saw trying to monitor movements in my account. As a bank officer, he could trace any other bank employees looking at my account, and if he saw the electronic footprint of anyone else looking at my account, he would confront them as to why. I said he should definitely *not* do that, but just make a note of who it was and call me. I said if I knew who in the bank was peeking, then I would know who their contact was outside the bank. Tom saw the wisdom of this approach and said he would call me before doing anything. It took all of half an hour before he called me to tell me that Wendy Etxeverría had been poking around in my account a few weeks back, carelessly leaving her electronic footprint (easy to trace by any bank officer). Tom asked if there was any reason I knew of why that should be so? I said I had my suspicions, but that I would check into it, and he was to please not say anything to her or his superiors yet. He said OK and commented that one thing he could do would be to put a flag on my account so that any future peeking by another bank employee would trigger a notification to Tom. He said that that might deter Wendy from looking again if she knew that doing so would mean possibly losing her job. I liked this plenty, and told Tom he was the best, etc., etc., and thanked him for his initiative.

I then drove on in to the office. Juanita was the first one I saw, and she grinned from ear to ear when she saw me. "What?" I asked, not recalling having worn a Santa Claus suit to work that day. "Djoo gotta noo gerFREHN!" she trilled. If she had put this to paper, it would have come out something like, "Sir, you have won the heart of a new damsel, 'tis plain to see!" But the gap between her written English and her command of the spoken language remained as large as ever, which is to say, somewhere on the order of the Grand Canyon. "You got a new girlfriend," would have been the translation into contemporary English, for those not used to the cadences of English à la Guatemalteca.

"This is not fair," I told her. "Mind readers need a law degree to work here!" Juanita said it was as plain to read on my face as if I had painted signs and hung them like placards on my front and back. I'll spare you her version of how she said it. I hoped her ability to see through me was superior to that of the rest of the firm. I could get myself into really hot water by having a new "gerFREHN" during a divorce proceeding. Although, come to think of it, no one would ever have seen us together (no one alive in this century, anyway), and aside from Juanita's intuition, no one could possibly guess what was going on, not even if they confiscated my computers and read all of the e-mails I had ever written. The name Anne Boudreau appears, at least in connection with me, for the first time in this narrative, and I'm not posting it until I'm positive neither of us will suffer any consequences from my having done so.

The rest of the twenty-fifth of August was routine—to the extent that what I did was "routine." I was doing accounting stuff in between juggling appointments for the partners and the attorneys and the travel schedules all over the place, drawing up reminders that September fifteenth was the day estimated tax payments were due, in case anyone had any to make. I didn't need to be reminded on my own behalf, needless to say. Caro's lawyer got in touch with Steve Clark about something or other, but it wasn't anything that raised a red flag that was cause for immediate, drastic action. If Wendy had taken a peek at my current balance, I'm pretty sure Caro's lawyer would have shown up at our bank with all sorts of court orders and injunctions freezing the assets of my account. Maybe Tom Nakano's little electronic "do not enter" sign on my account had deterred Wendy from further snooping, but maybe she just hadn't thought to snoop of late. Either way, I got no news that indicated danger on that front.

I did notice cars that *seemed* to be following me at times, and at this point, I couldn't begin to guess if they really were or who they belonged to. The IRS? Caro's lawyer? Aldo's thugs? Of the three possibilities, I guess I feared the IRS most and Aldo's thugs least, odd as that may seem. But think about it. For the IRS, I was a sitting duck, as my account was there for the taking (or freezing by court order) any time they felt like it. Therefore, if *they* were watching me closely, it might have been because that's exactly what they were planning. Aldo's thugs, on the other hand, wanted to find something out that they could never find out by tailing me, so they were the least of my worries in the short term. If Caro's lawyer was looking for some sign I was spending money lavishly or seeing another woman, he'd draw a blank as well. Since Caro had never shown any interest at all in my basement hobbies, she had no reason to ask her lawyer to check into the house, either. But whoever it was that was tailing me had to be coming up empty-handed and, while that would have continued to perplex Aldo's hired help, it would have set both the IRS and Caro's attorney at ease. Let them follow me all they wanted, as long as the basement was my briar patch.

27.

I had no reason to swing by California Coin again, and had no bottles for Aldo today, so I stopped for some food, including some more salmon for Minou and was almost tempted to bring something for Anne. I thought better of it. If I were to pass the rest of my days with her in her world, it would have been a bad idea to bring anything with me that indicated I had come from a time 150 years in the future. It would have been bad enough knowing all the things that were going to happen, both good and bad. Even an empty bag of nachos could have had unforeseeable consequences if someone found and examined the cellophane wrapping a few decades before the invention of cellophane.

Among the many parts of Plan A I had to think of was medicine. In France of 1860, I would certainly not be able to walk up to the local pharmacist (if there even was one!) and ask for Excedrin. Certain items I could purchase without a prescription, of course. Aspirin, water purifier tablets, that kind of thing. But certain things were just not to be had without a prescription. This sounded like a job for Juanita. Before leaving that day, I pulled her aside. "Juanita," I started, "you know about my personal problems, and you're right about my new girlfriend. I'm telling you this in the strictest of confidence because I need your help." Her face grew serious and focused. "Choo, Bobby (Sure, Bobby)." When an issue grew really serious, Juanita addressed me as "Bobby" instead of "Señor Roberto," just the opposite of what you'd expect—as usual with Juanita.

"I'm planning an extended vacation," I continued, "maybe two months, maybe a little longer, and it's to a tropical destination that doesn't have a lot of modern medical care. I don't want to arouse anyone's suspicions, so as to give a clue where I'm going.

You follow me?" She nodded that she did, understanding the need for me to keep my new *girFREHN* quiet for now. "I need a big supply of antibiotics, both penicillin and amoxicillin, and any other medication a doctor might recommend for a stay of that length in a place like that."

"Djoo not goin' to Guatemala?" she asked. I said no, much farther away. Otherwise I would have asked her to contact family members. There was no way she had any family where I was going. "OK, I gotcha." She nodded, and said the magic words (allow me to translate): "I know exactly what you need and who will give it to me. I can even pick up the prescriptions. Do you mind giving me some money in advance to pay for it? That stuff gets expensive." I kissed her on both cheeks and gave her $1500 in cash I had withdrawn from the bank in smaller amounts over the last week. She winked, said she knew a doctor and a pharmacist who would "help" and I could count on her. I hugged her and almost told her that if she were fifteen years younger and looked like Juliette Binoche, I'd forget the whole thing. But then she'd ask *what* whole thing and who in the world was Juliette Binoche anyway? So I kept my mouth shut.

At least for rest of the day, I had no further visits from people who were paid to make me uncomfortable or nervous. That evening, before going downstairs to see Anne, I got on the Internet and did some research of a kind I never thought I'd be doing. I used to think only farmers or really, *really* evil people did this kind of research. I learned that another sort of person also did this kind of research—someone desperately in love and feeling himself surrounded on all sides by nasty people who were paid to make his life unpleasant. I know I had friends, too, but they were in no position to offer me much more than some sympathy and some legal counsel. I started in by typing the key words into a search engine, and I was mildly upset to see how easy it was to find everything I was looking for. I am NOT going to go into details, as I don't want to encourage this kind of thing. I was in a situation like no one else has ever been in, nor will they ever be, in all likelihood. I took some notes, took a quick walk through the listings for places where I might get what I needed, put it all in an encrypted file, and closed up the computer. I went outside and saw with some satisfaction that the grass needed mowing and that Caro's garden needed some tending. I got out the mower, and mowed the lawn myself for the first time in I don't know how long. I also did a little weeding and made a visible fuss over some flowers and other exotic plants, even though I didn't know what the hell I was doing. But this was not for the flowers' benefit, but rather for the benefit of anyone who might have been watching. This was all part of Plan A, in case you hadn't figured that out by now.

I went down to see Anne. She was there and alone again. This was the first time I had seen her alone twice in a row. Either someone saw us the night before—someone with an approving eye—or else there was a bug going around in the Boudreau family and Anne was the only one who hadn't caught it. It didn't matter to me either way. All I cared about was being able to be with her alone again. The memory of the night before seemed way too surreal already. I wouldn't say that crossing over to be with her again a day later made it seem routine, but it was less traumatic a decision to jump across, as you might imagine. I don't mean to imitate the language of drug store romance novels—hell, I've never read one, so I'm just making assumptions here anyway—but my heart was pumping like a Ginger Baker solo by the time I held her again. She greeted me with a soft, *"Bon soir, cher ami,"* and one of those kisses you usually roll your eyes at in 1950s westerns. She pressed up close against me, and if I had any intentions of concealing my joy at seeing her, she left me no room to hide it. She knew what she was doing. But she made no indication that she was looking for further intimacy than that, and though I was close to "bursting at the seams," so to speak, I made no effort to initiate anything beyond what she did. I didn't know if this was just her speed of doing things, or if the rules of etiquette of her time demanded it, but I wasn't about to break any rules. I knew that this was it—a real romantic encounter of the Hollywood kind. Did things like this ever last? Hollywood films seldom ran beyond two hours, and I was clearly looking for something more permanent.

We strolled, this time leaving the portal behind, and just walked around. She pointed out where she and her family lived—very modest residences a short distance from the castle grounds. I asked her what a nice, big house would cost. She shook her head and said it was nothing "we" could afford (I loved that she already said "we"). She said it would take between 50,000 and 100,000 francs in gold to buy a big, fancy house, and that most people couldn't even afford a tenth of that. I nodded, and must have smiled a little smile to myself, because she looked at me with a mixture of awe and disbelief. She quickly caught herself, but like I said before, she was not stupid. Without saying a word, and just by (correctly) interpreting my body language, she saw that I could easily manage the price of a big, fancy residence. I always was an open book anyway, and intelligent women can read me like a third grader laughs at his Dick and Jane textbooks from two years earlier. It's fortunate for me that Caro had long since stopped caring what I felt about most anything. She was bright enough and might have caught on, had she been the slightest bit interested. Juanita, of course, knew about my new "gerFREHN" the second she saw me that morning, even though I hadn't given the slightest indication about Anne.

Anne never mentioned money again until I was in the final stages of Plan A and needed her assistance. But without either of us saying a word, I had let on that finances wouldn't be a problem, and she let on that she was in no great hurry to find out why. We discussed philosophy, life in general, all the sort of things that I now realized couples can freely discuss after they know they are in love but are still in the discovery stages of each other's thoughts. This is not easy for me to put into words, because I am still steeped in my twentieth century southern California cynicism about such things. As corny as it sounds, you know it when you feel it, and if you've never felt it, you can't understand it. But I could listen to her forever and I couldn't take my eyes off of her. She was worth every bit of risk that Plan A entailed, and I just hoped that Plan A didn't end up with me getting my legs broken, or in jail, or both.

When it started to get dark, I said it looked like it was time for me to get back home. After requesting her to get six more bottles of *"quelque chose de bien"* (something good) from her father for the next evening, I told her I needed to ask her two things. *"Vas-y,"* (go ahead,) she said. I asked her if she could get me some locally made clothes and shoes that would fit me, and if she had access to a horse-drawn cart that could handle some weight. She asked me if I had some large dinners on my schedule back in the year 2010, and I laughed. I said I'd explain in about ten days. She cocked her head as if expecting a more detailed explanation, but I just stood there smiling at her. She put her hands on her hips, and just said, *"Je peux m'en occuper."* (I can take care of that.)

I grinned and said, *"Je n'ai aucun doute."* (I have no doubt.)

She smiled and said, *"Bon, tu me diras quand c'est le moment."* (OK, you'll tell me when it's time.)

I nodded and we strolled back to the portal. My youthful hormones were raging back as if awakened like Rip van Winkle, but I held them in check. If there were ever an oxymoron more ridiculous than "military intelligence," let me tell you, it's "delicious anticipation."

There's nothing delicious about it. More like Chinese water torture. As if reading my thoughts, Anne pressed up against me again when I was about to cross back to my lab and whispered, *"J'attends avec impatience le jour où tu resteras avec moi."* (I'm impatiently awaiting the day when you'll be staying with me.)

I have news for Shakespeare. Parting is *not* "such sweet sorrow." In the case of Caro, it was not sorrow, and in the case of Anne, it was not sweet. I don't mean to make Caro out to seem like some kind of Harpy; she wasn't. But she was a product of her time and upbringing, and we were just not the right fit. I was also a product of my time and upbringing, and while my desperate desire for feminine companionship obscured that for a while, the rose-colored glasses did eventually fade. When the "thrill was gone," there was nothing left. Caro just wasn't Mrs. Me, and I wasn't the man she was looking for (or the man her parents were looking for). No, no, no, it ain't me, babe. I was sad for the lost time. Caro was furious for the lost time and, on top of that, she was now probably convinced that I had been concealing some huge aspect of my life from her for many years. In fact, it had been for less than two months, but if I had tried to explain to her what had happened—well, you can imagine the scene. There we are in some room with a judge and our two attorneys, and Caro's lawyer wants me deprived of any legal say in any assets because I have gone stark raving insane. The arbitrating judge asks me if I feel in full possession of my faculties. I say, "Yes, your honor, and my new friends, the Boudreau family of Bordeaux, 1860, and Thomas Jefferson, third president of the United States, will be happy to vouch for me." How many judges will accept that as proof enough that I am sane? For that matter, how many judges do we *want* that would accept that as proof someone is sane? There's poor Steve Clark, shaking his head in despair and pity as I am led away in a straitjacket. Probably only my assistant at the office would have intuitively perceived that there might have been something to my story, no matter how outrageous it might have sounded. A whole lot of good that would have done me. What judge is going to listen to someone named Juanita Chang, whose IQ was probably 50% higher than his, but whose verbal prowess was imprisoned in the voice of a cartoon character who was the epitome of an ethnic insult? No, it would not be wise for me to let it come to that.

Anne and I said our "adieus" for the evening, and I won't give a play-by-play rundown of the physical aspects. Suffice it to say that we were still G-rated, and that if she had invited me to the nearest barn with a clean stack of hay, we would have been G-rated no longer. I crossed back into my lab, we blew each other our goodnight kisses, and I went up to get ready for bed. Juanita called around 10:00 to ask if I would be at work tomorrow. I said sure, why wouldn't I be? She said that she had been to the "farmacia." I said, *"Está bien,"* (That's good,) and we both knew that nothing further needed be said. Plan A was advancing. One detail down, about 999 to go.

28.

Thursday, August 26

The day started with me at work a little earlier than usual, and Juanita was there even before I was. She pressed $227 into my hand and said that the rest had gone for my little "order." If we could meet for coffee after work, she had a "present" for me. I said I'd be glad to invite her for coffee after work. Let the office tongues wag at that one. Josh Crane called me on my cell phone and said that his friends at the big coin firm in Dallas had found 30,000 of the 50,000 coins I wanted, and thought they could scrape up the rest from their European contacts by tomorrow. The gold price had actually dipped by $12.50 per ounce that day, and if it didn't go up again the next morning, then I had saved myself more than $100,000 on what my total order would have cost had I fixed the price this morning. I said cool beans, and to confirm the 30,000. Josh said he had already done that, but would need a check from me for $7,350,000 by this evening to cover it, and it needed to be good. I said I'd bring it over on my lunch break.

When lunchtime came, I first called Tom Nakano at the bank and asked him to meet me again at the Starbucks across the street. He was there before me, sipping on some concoction with an Italian-sounding name completely unknown in Italy. I told him that the first part of my big investment was being made today, and told him the amount of the check. As my account now held well over $12.5 million in good funds and no lien had been placed on it, he said there was no problem. He said that it looked like someone had made a tentative try to look at my account, but as soon as they saw that they'd be leaving a trace with their name, they backed off and the inquiry was never made. This meant that he couldn't tell who it was that made the tentative poke, but we both knew who it was anyway. Wendy now knew that if she pried, she would leave her name and could get into big trouble if she passed any more information on to Caro, possibly lose her job, and never get a job at another bank as long as she lived. Her friendship to Caro obviously didn't extend that far, and so she had decided not to cross that line. I told Tom again not to approach Wendy about it. He was pretty upset about her doing something illegal like that, but if he had gotten her into trouble, then Caro might have tried to get her lawyer to petition a judge to freeze my account, and I definitely did *not* want that. Tom said he'd keep an eye on my account and call me if there were any rumblings, but so far there had been none, and frankly, he didn't see why there should be any unless Wendy was willing to risk her job to check my account. It would have been disastrous if Caro had found out about a $7 million dollar withdrawal, so it was a good thing Wendy had a healthy fear of waiting on tables for the rest of her life.

I had not made any ostentatious expenditures, not visited any real estate agents, Mercedes dealerships, or travel agencies, so even if Caro or her lawyer was having me followed all over the place, there was nothing to give them cause to suspect that I had plans for any of the money in my account. Caro had always taken me for such a plodding, unambitious type anyway, it would have been completely out of character for me to spend $1 million on anything, let alone $8 or $9 million, or whatever the amount was the last time Wendy took a peek. Caro had every reason to think I would be a creature of habit and take forever to decide to do something with the money, by which time she would have grabbed half of it. Had it not been for Anne and Aldo's elegant goons, she probably would have been right, too. But there was no way she knew about either, so I figured that her getting a court-ordered Denver boot on my account was not a danger. She didn't credit me with enough creativity to warrant the gesture. Sorry, dear. Everybody makes mistakes.

Tom and I shook hands, and I left him to finish his *Stupendissimo Caffè con Carne,* or whatever it was he was drinking (it looked big and mean), and drove over to California Coin to hand Josh his check. He said delivery to L.A. would be in about ten days, and I said this was fine, but I didn't want to take delivery myself until all 50,000 coins were there. I told him that after checking my finances, I would be able to take another 21,000 coins instead of 20,000, especially after what he had saved me with the dip in the gold price. At $5 per coin as his commission, that meant he made an extra $5,000 in commission off the deal. He smiled and said I was *the man.* I was definitely not used to being "the man." I was more used to being Bob, the criminally unambitious husband, or "Packer," the useless wine wannabe. This would be a very brief period of my life, but I was enjoying it all the same. Josh said he'd try to confirm the last 20,000, er, no, make that 21,000 coins the next day. If all went well, he'd be able to make physical delivery on September 8 or 9 at the latest, maybe before. I said that would be perfect. He said that if he could confirm the next and final group of gold 20 franc coins the next day, he would need to deposit another check by the close of banking hours. I said I'd bring the check by at lunchtime again. I also bought six more 10 franc coins for six bottles Philippe had secured for me for that evening. Josh asked why I was still fiddling with them when I had "come out" about the big investment I had really been planning. I said that they really were for some special friends of mine who had a personal connection to the era and they liked to put them away for their kids, which was only a slight exaggeration. "Aha!" he said. "So that's why you wanted all your 20 franc coins to be bare heads." I smiled and said, "You got it."

I didn't know if I was being followed by any one or combination of my three nemeses, but I just figured I was. Josh and I did our big deal in a space behind his counter, and I seriously doubted that his phone had been tapped, as there had never been any big transactions (yet) to warrant that. If Stef and friends weren't tapping his phone, then it was even less likely they had some CIA-issued, sophisticated, directional microphone that could follow our conversation through the shop entrance. When I met Tom Nakano at Starbucks, it was so noisy at lunchtime that even a directional listening mic would have only picked up an unintelligible babble of chatter. I doubted the IRS was following me, as September 15th was not yet there. I figured that Stefano and his pals could be tailing me at any time in case I got "careless," but as my "friends" with the mythical wine cellar didn't exist, Stef and Co. would have had a difficult time tailing me to their residence or, if located elsewhere, their wine cellar. If Caro's lawyer was having me watched, his watchers might have picked up on my meeting with Tom at the Starbucks, but as no documents were being passed around or bags of cash were being loaded into a car trunk, he wouldn't have had grounds for anything more than mild curiosity. I paid Josh for the big orders of French gold by check instead of wire to allow for a few days of "float," to leave a day or two more of limbo in which the activity on my account would not show up.

I met with Steve Clark briefly, but so far there were only preliminary formalities that were involved in setting a date for a hearing, or whatever you call it when you start divorce proceedings. What did I know about divorce? Although, it could be just as legitimately asked what, if anything, I knew about marriage? Precious little, I had to admit. There was a lot to do for the rest of the afternoon, distractions for which I was grateful. I had a few things to do before going home that evening to see Anne, too.

So, after about fifteen flights to book, along with as many hotel rooms around the country and getting bills paid that were due on that date, I called it a day and went to the local Starbucks, the one nearest the office, not the one near the bank where I met with

Tom Nakano. After ten minutes of sipping on a small-sized tea (I do not do *Stupendissimo Caffè con Carne*), Juanita came in. She had her briefcase and took out some official-looking papers and what looked like a large-sized thick legal envelope, sort of a manila version of the packages of 500 sheets of copier paper. She went through the motions of discussing some of the documents with me, and then shoved the whole batch in my direction, as if to say, "It's your ball to run with now." I opened my briefcase, put the loose papers on top of the manila envelope, which was far too light to be full of paper, and closed it again. Juanita didn't even ask where my trip was going to lead me, for which I was grateful. She knew full well that France was not considered a destination that required a battery of medical defenses. She did get me everything I wanted, though, as listed on a sheet she had provided. Besides water purifiers, which were not prescription, there were antibiotics of all kinds and flavors, as well as various other prescription preventatives, like antibiotic ear drops, strong nose spray, i.e. medication that you just can't get over-the-counter. I thanked her profusely, for which she refused to take any kind of praise at all. She just said it was her pleasure and she was proud to be able to do me a favor that was out of the ordinary. I think she figured I was planning to elope with my new girlfriend. I would have had a hard time explaining that my new girlfriend was already "there" and, indeed, had never been "here."

Juanita took off in her Honda, and I went to a gardening center for some tools and some fertilizer. I had been spending some token time in the garden and mowing the lawn now that Caro was not around to attend to it, so this wouldn't (I hoped) arouse any suspicion on the part of any of my secret "admirers." I made sure that the questions I asked would lead to a recommendation to buy ammonium nitrate fertilizer. I said I had fruit trees and needed something that wouldn't evaporate too quickly. When told that ammonium nitrate was probably best suited for my purposes, I asked in feigned horror if the stuff would not blow up on me, and the sales girl laughed and said no, only nut cases even bothered to learn how to do that, and if used properly, it was harmless. I said that was a relief. I bought a modest bag of the stuff, and then repeated the procedure at two other garden centers in the area. I didn't want to buy such a large quantity in one place as to arouse fears that I did, indeed, want to make something blow up. I love a country where shops are open late.

It was dark by the time I got home, and loading the "documents" (i.e., medical supplies) from Juanita and the gardening accessories into the house only took five minutes. I didn't see anyone watching, but anyone good at watching wouldn't have been easy for me to spot anyway. I left the gardening paraphernalia alone for the moment. The ammonium nitrate was flammable, but I didn't smoke and there was no real danger of it igniting unless the house burned down. I took out the medicine Juanita had secured for me and carefully removed each pill from its metal foil, then resealed each pill in wax paper. I put each category of pill into its own sturdy (but biodegradable) paper sack, labeled in black magic marker, and when I had the whole batch of medical supplies packaged that way, I put the whole package into a cotton pillow case, brought it downstairs to the lab, and packed it into a small trunk near the Bordeaux portal. I then put the large pile of foil packing in which the pills had come into a trash bag, which I made sure would be dumped far from the house and collected soon. As long as Juanita kept her mouth shut, no one would ever make the connection, and I was fairly sure I could count on her to do just that.

I then made some quick, nondescript dinner. No smoked salmon was necessary this time, so I won't bore you with the details of my culinary artistry for this evening.

29.

At the portal, Anne was there at the appointed time, even though it was a little late this time. Philippe had given her the six bottles for which I had gotten the six 10 franc coins from Josh that afternoon. Philippe was going out of his way to get me some variety, that's for sure. There was a perfectly preserved Brane-Mouton of 1848 this time! Aldo would be frothing at the mouth. I put them carefully into six boxes in my lab. I was planning to see Aldo tomorrow. I couldn't very well vary my routine or he'd suspect that I was up to something. I was, of course, up to something, so I just played my "lamb being fattened for the slaughter" role as best as I could (Caro was the drama major, not me), collecting my big checks at periodic intervals, with Aldo getting more and more smug as the appointed time for the "transfer" drew near.

I then crossed over. She had found some kind of perfume to put on this evening, and I noticed it right away. *"Tu aimes?"* (You like?) she asked coyly. *"J'aime!"* (I like!) I answered without hesitation. I had no idea if it was special for a woman of her social status to use perfume, but I suspected it had not been cheap for her. Her family was not exactly of serf or slave level, but they were obviously not of the moneyed nobility either, and I guessed that for a woman to do this for her beau was a strong statement of affection. Not that her statements of affection prior to now had been less than strong, to my way of thinking, but wow, nonetheless. She had told me that she had "been with a man" before, but I didn't know what she meant by this and I was reluctant to ask. For all our mutually declared affection, I was playing by an unknown rulebook here, and did not want to be disqualified at this stage for an inadvertent violation. Still, I immediately caressed her cheek and hair and took in her exquisite smile as she looked up at me, and I wondered if there was some kind of good karma rewarding me for some past benevolence. So far, I could think of nothing. I was a conscientious worker at my job, but I was a lousy husband and was about to become a cheating husband the moment the woman of my dreams said the word. OK, it was my wife who left me first, but who's keeping score? I had already realized, without admitting it to myself, that the divorce would just be a paper formality. We had been a divorced couple long before now. My problem was that I was looking for something far more fundamental, an emotion uncomplicated by how many horsepower my car had, where it was imported from, or how many square feet my house had compared to those of my friends. I knew instinctively that this elemental simplicity had to exist, but at age twenty-two, I had just been too impatient to go out into the world and look for it.

The folk singer Pete Seeger once said, when talking about Woody Guthrie, "Any damn fool can get complicated. It takes genius to achieve simplicity." I was looking for the simplicity and had been too impatient to wade through the "complicated" to get there. Now, due to this impossible bit of science fiction humming in my basement, I had finally cut through all the "complicated" and found the genius of simplicity. Anne knew nothing of fancy cars or how many square feet (or meters) a fancy house was supposed to have. She just knew that if you were good, you had a chance of that goodness being reciprocated, and that if you worked, you got paid and had maybe even enough to live on. It was a joy to talk to her precisely because there *was* no ritual I had to go through to convince her I was "cool." She didn't know what "cool" was. She was only interested in "nice," and that I could handle. I had hit the jackpot in the lottery. All I had to do now is not screw up before it was time to collect. Of her, all I requested was that she get me some sets of contemporary clothes made up and have access to a horse-drawn cart when I needed it, and she had said she'd take care of it. I said the day was not far off. She wouldn't accept the money I offered her to get the clothes made. *"On parlera de ça quand tu les porteras,"* (We'll talk about that when you start wearing them,) she said with a mischievous little smile.

While I walked with her, we talked little of the politics of the day (hers or mine), but rather of matters that concerned the two of us. Did she want children (*oui, mais pas avec n'importe qui*—yes, but not with just anybody), did she want to travel (*un peu*), did wealth matter (only if it didn't corrupt your *ésprit*), was religion important (*pas vraiment*—not really). Her great desire was to find *un équilibre* in her life, a situation that, while not immune to disease, natural disaster or war, would be emotionally fulfilling, as that was a goal she thought she could aspire to—indeed, had a right to aspire to. I remembered my parents and my bewilderment as to how they managed exactly that, and why I had so utterly failed at it up to now. This is what Caro had never craved, even while she had craved so many other things. To be envied should be an accidental side effect, not a goal. Anne had summed up the whole ball of wax in the space of about ninety seconds.

The great awakening of my dormant romantic fantasies was at hand, because she had enunciated exactly what I had been searching for, even before I knew myself that I had been so desperate to find it. Anne had the advantage of being unencumbered by all the fringe benefits, because in her time, at her social status, there were no fringe benefits, just the basics. In her day, except for a distant moneyed caste, almost everybody spent his or her life as a member of the lowest common denominator, so the people around you *really* mattered. While she talked, she perceived, quite correctly and with no small surprise, that *she* was the one who was bestowing a new great revelation on *me*, whereas she had expected there was nothing whatsoever that a man from 150 years hence could possibly have to learn from the likes of her. How was I to explain to her that she could teach simplicity to someone used to only (and suddenly

very tired of) complication? She had obviously never heard of
Pete Seeger. Umm, yes, well, seeing as how he wouldn't even be
born until fifty-nine years in the future, I guess that was reasonable.
I would hold off explaining the musical and lyrical philosophies
of "Pierre Siguère" for now. I also asked her something I had never
asked Caro. I asked her if there was anything she was really afraid of.
There was a reason for this. Caro, with the passage of time, seemed
to fear living out her life with no crowds of people wishing they
were her. Like I said before, she craved envy. As I found this to be
a very unpleasant character trait to have to deal with, and as Anne
was obviously far from well off, I wanted to know if Anne had any
of the same demons lurking. I needn't have worried. Her main
fears were disease and loneliness. The disease I could understand,
as in that day, people of her social standing didn't stand much of
a chance of surviving a serious illness. I asked her what she meant
by loneliness. She said that *"franchement ,"* (frankly,) she didn't want
to grow old without a husband with whom she could have long and
uninhibited talks like the one we were having now. The thought of
that terrified her, and she hadn't found such a man yet. She looked me
in the eyes. *"Jusqu'à maintenant."* (Until now.) She smiled. I can take
a hint—especially if it's delivered with a sledge hammer.

I don't mean to be portraying some kind of "Dances With Wolves"
or "Avatar" scenario here, where the protagonist of the story finds
more truth and substance (as well as love) in a hostile culture closer
to nature than his own. It's not like southern California was ever in
a territorial conflict with nineteenth century France, and we never
really considered the French to be more primitive than ourselves
unless one was a member of the Bush administration when France
declined to join us in invading Iraq. Besides, I'm sure that not all
French women were just like Anne, even in 1860, and Philippe had
certainly taken advantage of me with the price he was charging me
for the bottles of wine (or so he and his family had thought)—not

exactly the "noble savage." I was not looking to "get back to nature" in any pure sense. I knew that living the life of a mid-nineteenth century Frenchman would not be one long, fun camping trip with the Boy Scouts. I was just looking to get into a harmonious union with a woman I thought was not only stunningly beautiful, but also one whose personality seemed perfectly suited to my own. There would be occurrences that I knew would happen in the world, but of which I could never speak. I would practically have to materialize out of nowhere and try to be accepted without suspicion or jealousy in a society whose rules I barely understood. But I knew—not just felt intuitively, but *knew*—that with Anne, I had found that great missing link to what I had been hoping to feel about a woman and have reciprocated. For this, I was willing to risk much—no, make that risk *everything*. This was Last Chance Gulch.

Love does not necessarily mean "never having to say you're sorry." It means being willing to change the course of the river that is your life, and do it unhesitatingly and without recourse, even if you find downstream that the going is far rougher than anticipated. It's the willingness to take the risk that determines whether or not you've found the real thing. That's where I was with Anne. It had happened in a relatively short period of time. The physical attraction had certainly hastened my actions like a chemical catalyst, no two ways about that. But while I found that physical attraction is a vital part of the equation, it's not enough, as I know from personal experience. Caro is certainly attractive enough in her own way. But Anne just radiated in my eyes, and to have a partner who evokes *that* kind of reaction in you tell you the feeling is mutual, well, if that is not the loudest wake-up call you can get, then you have the emotional makeup of an eggplant.

I won't go into detail about our parting scene at the portal that night, but suffice it to say that it was still G-rated (well, maybe progressing to PG-rated, but still somewhat tame), and that I was flying by the time I got back into my basement. I had asked Anne one small favor before returning to the house, and she had agreed. I couldn't wait for tomorrow night. I somehow got my clothes off and brushed my teeth, but I must have been on autopilot, because my thoughts were anywhere but with dental hygiene. I managed to drift off to sleep, but not right away by any means. Visions of something were dancing in my head, and they were not sugar plums. I did get an idea for some diversions for the next week, and made a mental note to put them into action.

30.

Friday, August 27

The next morning, I got up a little early and went online looking
for courier services. Not DHL or FedEx, but the kind that employs
college students and cyclists who didn't make the last round of choices
to compete in the Tour de France. It's not like there was any lack
of them. Jobs in August 2010 might not have been as scarce as they
were two years before, but they weren't exactly reaching out of the
ground and grabbing at the heels of passersby, either. I noted the phone
numbers of six of these services and made sure they were well spread
apart geographically. I planned out a sequence that would send Stefano
and his vigilante pals a signal to back off if they were watching me, and
if they were, that they weren't doing it unobserved by others. I only
needed them off balance for maybe two weeks, but that was, if Josh's
gold brokers in Dallas came through, all the time I needed.

I got to work and checked in with Steve Clark. Nothing new
from Caro's attorney today, maybe next week, was I in any rush? Um,
no. He said that divorces moved slowly. I was rooting for a glacial pace,
but I kept that one to myself. There were a few tax questions I
answered for some of the attorneys, some tricky plane connections
to arrange so that one of the partners could get from Shanghai
to Sheboygan, Wisconsin, in the space of thirty hours (yes, Virginia,
they do have hotels in Sheboygan!), checking out scenic routes on the
SNCF for some of our guys who wanted a four-hour meeting with some
French counterparts on a train so they couldn't be interrupted between
Nice and Paris, stuff like that. I was ready at lunch and had my cell
phone charged to the max. It was time to give some hungry courier
service cyclists some welcome business.

I'm not going to actually put down the names of the courier services.
They didn't know what I was putting them up to, and I don't

want Stefano and friends to go harass them any more than they might have already. The cyclists hadn't the slightest idea what I was paying them to do, and neither did their dispatchers. Hell, they wouldn't even know it was me. All they knew was that they had some business with someone who paid up front and without complaint or any haste. What I did was basically this. I had Juanita go out and buy two cases of quart-sized bottles of generic ginger ale. I then asked our mailing department to get me some cardboard boxes made up that could accommodate two to three quart-sized ginger ale bottles. After packing a few boxes with two or three bottles of ginger ale, I then made up a some computer-printed sheets of paper, and printed on them, "**Stef, I'd really appreciate your maintaining a little distance and letting me try to convince my people to do what you asked without you and your friends breathing down my neck the whole time. They are watching you watching me, and you have obviously not noticed their people. They have certainly noticed you. Their description of you was pretty accurate. This was news to me, as I had no clue that either of you was watching me that closely. You didn't exactly leave me a cell phone number, so I figured if my people are correct about your following me, knowing how eager you seemed, you'll get my message this way. If you are reading this, then the wine cellar owners are correct and you are putting your own project in serious jeopardy. Do us both a favor and back off. I had hoped to be able to give you some news you'll like in a week or two, but if you do not back off immediately, there will be no news except bad news for us both. Feel free to call and discuss this anytime.**"

I then set up a round-robin sequence where, starting the following Monday, the boxes of ginger ale would leave the office inconspicuously, and then two days later, return to the office, addressed to me, having been forwarded via a circular maze of various courier services. Each courier service (except the last ones) would only know they had received a package and were supposed to forward it on to the next courier service. This way, if a package was intercepted by Stef and his pals, he would automatically reveal his surveillance, whether he wanted to or not.

I couldn't be seen sending the packages out, however, or checking on them en route. I needed help. I asked Juanita if she knew of anyone and told her it was for a security test.

Juanita told me that her brother was visiting from Guatemala and was getting a little bored waiting for her to come back from work every day, so he would probably have fun doing this. Perfect, I thought. If Stef's goons were really tracing my every step, and if they got onto this, they wouldn't be able to find Juanita's brother in the phone book or in any Internet listing.

I told Juanita this would be perfect, but to keep it our little secret. She thought it sounded like great fun, and said no sweat. I asked if her brother spoke English. She said his spoken English was as good as hers. Oh, great. I hoped the courier services were all Hispanic owned.

I went down to the mail room and packed the ginger ale into four various-sized boxes and laid one of my printed sheets for Stef in each one. In case Stef was really *not* following my every move, the worst thing that could happen would be that I was out a couple of hundred bucks in courier fees, and the office would have a small surplus of ginger ale for a week.

Before lunch break was over, I checked with Josh at California Coin, and he said that the guys in Dallas had come through and he had confirmed the last 21,000 20 franc bare head gold coins. I would have to bring in a check for $5,040,000, and soon. Friday evening traffic being what it is in Los Angeles, I asked if Saturday morning was soon enough. He said OK, but he needed to put it into his account ASAP to guarantee the money to Dallas. I said OK and reserved time on Saturday morning. I also called Tom Nakano at the bank to let him know that another big check to California Coin would be coming through and would he please clear it. I told him that my account would slowly start filling again, and that I planned no more withdrawals of anywhere near that size. Account execs at banks get brownie points from above for bringing in big deposits and frowns when big accounts go empty, so he was happy to hear it. I just explained that I wanted to diversify some of what I had into hard assets. As he had seen that the beneficiary of my other big check was "California Coin" and would see that this new check was to the same entity, my explanation would seem plausible enough. I told him the amount of the big check that would hit next week, and he made a note of it, reminding me that I had "only" $530,000 or so left in my account after that. I told him that more would be coming in soon and that most of it was not going anywhere. I left out the "not right away, at least."

Most of my life had been a mixture of partial, yet never total, satisfaction and Murphy's Law. Still, so far, Plan A was coming along. More important by far was the fact that I was getting to spend my evenings with Anne, although I wasn't yet to the point where I felt comfortable staying "over there" overnight, even if I would have been welcome. The portals had now been stable for three months, but the longer they lasted, the more nervous I became that they might disappear in an instant. I could think of no reason why they should, but then, I could think of no reason why they should exist in the first place, either. While I would have reluctantly risked staying with Anne before Plan A was completed, the rest of my life would be made vastly more tolerable if Plan A were a done deal.

31.

August 27, 2010, was to be a monumental date for me. I was going
to do something I had never done before, something that I knew
would cost me a whole lot of money. I didn't care. I had a different
perspective about money now. To hell with the money. I brought a 10
franc gold coin with me when I went to visit Anne that evening, and
she came through with the small favor I asked of her the night before.
All this time, I had been cashing in the big bucks from Aldo for all
these fabulous wine bottles, but had never opened one for myself. I
had wanted to, of course. It was a test of will power above and beyond
anything I thought I had in me, but tens of thousands of dollars a
pop were just not to be sneezed at. It was time for a sneeze. Anne
brought a five-year-old bottle of Château Lafite 1855 from Philippe.
Just to satisfy the famous French avarice, I had brought her another
ten francs in gold for her father, but I suspect that I would have
gotten this one "on the château" if I had asked. But I didn't want
to start making requests of Philippe just yet. I didn't know just
how much pull he had with his employers, the château's owners,
who were, of all things, from the Netherlands. I didn't know if the
Dutch of the mid-nineteenth century had the reputation for penny-
pinching that they have in the early twenty-first century, but
I didn't want to press my luck. Besides, I'm sure Philippe's day's
wages weren't anything like the ten francs I was forking over for
each bottle, and I didn't want him to think that I was using Anne to
bargain his price down.

Anne had brought a corkscrew (*plus ça change*), two glasses and a
sort of picnic blanket. She was wearing just a simple skirt with an
almost simple blouse that had a little decorative embroidering. She
looked stunning. She definitely seemed to be enjoying my attention,
and I found myself wondering if by any chance she did *not* embody
her era's ideal of extreme beauty. I was no art student and hadn't

made a note of the portraits of the time. But either the men of her region were functionally blind, or they just had an idea of what constituted a knockout that was completely different from my own. It did occur to me that Anne and I must have looked like the preliminary setup for a movie shooting: Anne in her nineteenth century (and so *very* authentic, too—kudos to the costume guys, ha ha) getup and me in my twenty-first century nondescript L.A. duds. Now, even though I had lived all my life in southern California, I had never been anywhere near the set of a movie shooting that I was aware of. But I must have looked so totally out of place there, I was glad that it was such a rural area, with no onlookers other than the occasional member of her family. I hadn't had the tour of the château or its grounds, but it was clear that the portal was on the edge of it, in some corner not in the middle of things.

We found ourselves a suitable patch of grass and opened the bottle. It may have been 155 years old by my reckoning, but it was only five years old as far as taste went. Let me tell you, that was plenty far. Even Aunt Murgatroid would have been impressed. This was a fresh, five-year-old pre-phylloxera Lafite, and no one alive in the year 2010 had ever tasted such a wine, at least not as a five-year-old bottle. Anne had no idea what the big deal was, as she had grown up drinking this stuff (ah, cherie, if you only knew!). She looked a little startled when she saw me sipping this stuff, which was about as exotic to her as a can of Dr. Pepper would be to a kid at a Dallas vending machine. My face must have looked like I had just chewed on some psychedelic mushroom. I was in seventh heaven. I don't mean to go on like some of those pompous asses at the L.A. tastings, but this was something like I had never tasted before. When they talk of a wine's bouquet, they usually have a standard stock of fruits and aromas to describe it. But this was beyond all the usual clichés heard at snotty wine tastings. This bouquet had more different fruits than a Hawaiian buffet breakfast. This was what it was all about,

Alfie. The flavors just swirled around my head and massaged my senses until I was off in la-la land. Getting kind of pompous, myself, I guess. Sorry about that. This was a sensation of the sort we all dream about, but never get to experience, at least not in the year 2010. I saw I had better reassure Anne that nothing was wrong. She was staring at me as if I had just taken a large dose of some illegal hallucinogen and was tripping somewhere in the general vicinity of the asteroid belt. I returned to earth, smiled, and told her that the wine was beyond excellent, and that I found it to be a rare pleasure to enjoy it with her. She remarked that I seemed to be enjoying it quite well all on my own, without a whole lot of notice as to whether she was there or not, but she laughed when she said it. She wasn't angry, just amused. I'm such an open book. I had to watch it very carefully for the next ten days or so.

I didn't want to get too tipsy, so we didn't finish the bottle. I figured there would be time (no pun intended) enough to finish that bottle, as well as many others, so we walked together. It was strange to walk around in a place with unpaved roads, no noise of cars or airplanes. Birds and insects were the only background noise we had. Anne caught me listening to the...um, well, the nothing. She asked what I was listening to. I tried to explain the constant noise that accompanied my world. How do you explain constant street traffic and airplane noise to someone who has never even heard the sound of a motor? She said it was difficult to imagine what I meant, but it sounded awful. I guess it did, if you have never grown up with it. The term "noise pollution" was definitely not in use in the nineteenth century in rural France. Her words got me to thinking. She would never hear the sound of digitally recorded music, but most people in southern California, 2010, would never get to spend time in a place without the noise of engines either. Who was the poorer? I wondered if I could discuss this with Thomas Jefferson? I planned to visit with him one last time anyway. He would have understood and accepted the idea of the internal combustion engine, even if he had never seen one operate, heard the sound of one, or tolerated the noxious fumes they emit.

When it started getting dark, Anne and I headed back to the portal. I repeated what I had told her every day for the last few days now, that I would come to stay with her, and that it would not be much longer. At the portal she hung onto my hands tightly and pressed into me. My determination not to bring her with me to California for the night was crumbling, but I stuck to it. If I brought her and, for some reason, the portal should disappear before I was ready, she would be completely lost in California in 2010. The bureaucratic mess would be a nightmare in itself, even if I didn't live in Arizona. America in 2010 was just not set up for the sudden appearance of a woman speaking only French for whom there was absolutely no documentation anywhere. No passport, no entry into the country, and no record of her even in France, except for maybe some obscure birth notice from the year 1832. France might be known for their great cosmetics, but I couldn't see trying to convince a bunch of stiff bureaucrats in 2010 that the gorgeous young woman in front of them had no papers because she was 178 years old and just "looked younger." That one was probably more than even Obi-Wan Kenobi would have wanted to attempt with his "you don't need to see their identification." It was definitely more than I was prepared to attempt. I told her I would be back the next day.

That night, I started the initial preparations for my grand finale. This involved doing something I never thought I would do. I opened the file I had encrypted the day I bought the fertilizer and started to go through the process of learning how to become dangerous. I had to be careful, but what I had in mind was easily doable, and it was a snap to acquire all the necessary ingredients for the soup I had in mind. I memorized most of what I had to know and closed up

166

the file, encrypting it anew. I doubted anyone would be sneaking into my house to run through my computer, but better safe than sorry.

32.

Saturday, August 28

I went to see Aldo, brought some bottles, collected a big fat check, and told him with what I hoped was sincere resignation that I might be soon retiring from the rare wine business. Aldo just gave me a small smile, a smaller shrug, and a fake-friendly clap on the shoulder, saying that I had had a pretty good run up to this point and maybe I'd be keeping my hand in on a smaller scale. Not even a phony "How come? What happened?" Still, it was nice to know that he at least was keeping up the pretense of there being something in it for me after the changing of the guard. Of course, I had no way of knowing if he meant it, or if he was just placating me until he had taken over the "account" completely. At least he was no longer playing this game of having a good idea of who it was I was dealing with. If he had had the slightest idea who my "secret supplier" was, he would have approached them long ago. The fact that the secret cellar didn't even exist had never occurred to him. I couldn't blame him for that. I think half of his frustration was at admitting to himself that I might be sneakier than he was. To have figured out what was really going on, he would have had to consult with Stan Lee for real, because unless he was still reading Marvel Comics (or maybe Robert Heinlein?), he wasn't going to come close to guessing the true story. I even wonder if he was starting to feel a little sorry for me, and that his greed and ego just wouldn't permit us to continue on the way we had been. Ah, the tragic flaw of a Greek tragedy! It was hard to figure out. He was a phony, pompous ass, that's for sure, but he *did* respect the fact that I and no other had delivered to him the greatest stash of old wine he had ever seen, and that if it hadn't been for me, he wouldn't have gotten anywhere near it. Not that I think he was experiencing pangs of remorse—more like a prison warden having to sign an execution order for a prisoner he had grown to like and respect as a person over the course of the guy's years of appeals. But like the warden who dutifully gave the execution order all the same, Aldo had obviously not cancelled Stef's contract. So, whether it was his greed, his ego, or both, he was determined to have this incredible "cellar" all to himself and sideline me one way or the other. My appearance of resignation to my fate apparently woke some stirrings of sympathy of which I (and presumably he as well) had not thought him capable of. He knew that this was my only source of income outside of my day job salary, and he only knew what I had told him about my receiving a tiny commission off the top. If he had had the slightest inkling that I was pocketing 100% of the money from the checks he had written out to me, I think he would have had me hanging upside down by my toes long before now, watching with glee while Stef cut off my fingers, joint by joint, until I told them all they wanted to know.

When I got back to the house, there was a letter from the IRS. Great. I opened it, but it was nothing more than a form for submitting my estimated income tax, due September 15, as well as a form for the next installment on January 15, 2011. Ms. Roganov was not about to give me the impression she had forgotten me, not that I expected her to. If she had taken the trouble to pay me a personal visit at work, and she had been monitoring my bank activity, then she was expecting to show her immediate superior what a good girl she was, and how she had brought in an unexpected $3 million or so. Oh, dear, if only she had asked me nicely.....(yeah, right, you can put that one on the same page with the offers of oceanfront property in Nebraska). But you know what? That, it occurred to me, was one of my main complaints about my three would-be creditors. No one asked nicely. No one even asked. Not the nasal-voiced Naomi Roganov, not Aldo and his Rodeo Drive Mafiosi, and not Caro. Just, "You got something? Gimme!" The only people who weren't like that were the ones who hadn't the slightest idea of the small fortune I had amassed—Juanita and the others at B&B, the simple vineyard workers at Château Lafite, especially Anne, although I had by now given her a hint when I asked about the price of a house. I guess I'd have to include Josh Crane from the coin shop in this group as well, as he didn't know until a week ago how much money I had—for that matter, when I first met him, I didn't have a cent of it. And yet Josh had treated me with patience and good humor. I'm sure not all in his profession would have. I'd have to include Thomas Jefferson, too. What a shame about him. If I had told anyone in Los Angeles in 2010 that I had been talking with Thomas Jefferson, they would have had me arrested for doing illegal drugs. If I told the vineyard workers at Château Lafite, they probably would have, at best, a faint idea who I was talking about, since Jefferson's visit there had been some seventy-five years earlier. So now, I'm posting it on an Internet blog, and no one will believe me anyway. Dem's da breaks.

That afternoon, I got a call from Caro, much to my surprise. At first, all small talk. Was I doing OK? Yes, I was. Was I looking after her garden? Yes, I was. Was the house OK? Yes, it was. Had I been looking at new cars? Aha. *Now* I knew why she was calling. Here I thought some small remnant of the old affection had caused her to wonder how well I was dealing with our separation. Fat chance. She wanted to know if I had been doing anything with the (i.e., soon to be her) money, now that Wendy had been put on notice to keep her prying nose out of my financial affairs. Apparently thinking she had all the time in the world, Caro had not yet thought to ask her lawyer for a subpoena or a freeze on my account. No, I hadn't been looking at any new cars, houses or plasma TVs. I told her that I hadn't been contemplating any of that kind of stuff. I wasn't lying. New cars, bigger California real estate and plasma TVs were not even on my radar. I wasn't even going to think about cars or plasma TVs *after* "our matter" had been settled, but I didn't want to invite questions from her, so I just kept my answers to a bare minimum. She seemed satisfied with my apparently phlegmatic responses. I had been learning in the course of all these complications that if someone wishes you ill, one of the best defenses is to give them the impression that things are exactly as they wish them to be. If Caro would be placated by me being my usual (in her eyes, anyway) unambitious, undynamic, underachieving self, then that's exactly what I would give her. So, that's just what I did, and after a short conversation, she seemed happy and hung up after dismissing me with a quick, "See ya," which, in fact, she would not.

I don't know if she went by the house to check on the garden while I was at work, but she never came to the house when I was most likely to be there. She was content to let her lawyer work things out, take me for whatever she could, and then write me off. Had I been *that* big a disappointment to her? We were definitely mismatched, that's for sure. We should have listened to her parents, but these days, who does that outside of South Waziristan? Well, maybe people in North Waziristan. But in Elko, Nevada, they don't stone you to death for disobeying your parents' advice on whom to marry. They just tell you, "I told you so," and cheer you on for the best divorce settlement you can get.

Caro's call left me feeling something I hadn't felt in a while —namely, depressed. For the first time in months, I started to have doubts like I hadn't had since the days before I landed the job at B&B. Had I really been *that* inadequate as a partner? Useless and worth nothing to any woman who had the misfortune to be tied to me? What was my big defect? Now I was being taken all the way back to my high school days. Not an athlete, not Brad Pitt and not rich (not that anyone knew, anyway). But hell, is that all there is to being a desirable mate? What about compassion, interest, affection, humor? None of that counts? This was getting to be one very depressing train of thought.

But hold on here. Snap out of it, *"Ro-BAIR."* My parents had an absolutely great partnership, and it lasted for nearly forty years, right up until they got smashed into the side of some Greek mountain. I didn't recall *People* magazine coming to interview them as the world's unique and only happy couple, either. So cut the crap. This may have been my fault, too, but I was not a total washout as a person, or even as a potential partner. The marriage of Bob and Caro was a washout, granted, but it takes two to tango, and we were both too slow to catch on to the fact that we just were never going to be dancing to the same rhythm. That's not a good reason to never dance again. It *is* a good reason to find a new dance partner. Well *merde*, I knew a great new dance partner, and she was waiting for me on the other side of a nominally impossible portal in my basement right now. I looked at the phone. Hung up. Conversation over (and out). *Konyets svyazy* (an ex-U.S. Air Force intelligence guy I once met told me that Soviet air force pilots used to end their transmissions that way—trivia lesson for today). There was my beautiful Juliette Binoche reincarnation, well, no, make that *pre*incarnation (OK, smartass, so how would *you* put it?) waiting for me downstairs, and a mere 150 years ago. No sweat. I left thoughts of Caro upstairs and headed for the basement. Caro never went down there anyway.

33.

I was expecting to see Anne alone. I saw someone alone all right, but it wasn't Anne. It was her father, Philippe, carrying a pitchfork (though not menacingly) with a grim "we gotta talk, you and me" expression on his face. Uh-oh. This was not turning out to be my day. I know Anne and I hadn't done anything that could possibly have offended the "family values" morals even of Catholic France of 1860. So what was this all about? I thought quickly. Anne had to have told her father when to expect me, and if she wasn't there, this meant Philippe meant to have a serious talk with me. Now, the USA had not yet even gotten the Statue of Liberty, we had not yet saved France from Kaiser Wilhelm II or the Nazis, De Gaulle had not yet pulled France out of the military structure of NATO, and France had not yet declined Bush's "invitation" to join the invasion of Iraq. So this was not to discuss politics. It was personal. The subject he had on his mind probably was not wine, either. So it had to be Anne. I suppose I should have been expecting this sooner or later. As usual, I was caught completely off guard.

Philippe was no Paul Arregui. He wouldn't be here to take me down a notch for not having made the UCLA varsity football team, and he sure as hell wasn't about to give me a hard time for not driving Anne around in a Mercedes (unless he had a horse cart named "Mercedes"). He didn't keep me guessing, either. I don't remember how it went word for word, so I'll just translate directly.

"Anne is falling in love with you. You are married. This cannot happen. What are you doing with her?"

I explained that Caro had left me, not the other way around, and that she was divorcing me. Typical France. The idea of a mistress, especially if it was *not* his daughter, was just fine, but divorce was not? I said that divorce was perfectly normal in America.

Buzzzzz! Wrong choice of words. The only part of my foot you could actually still see was the top half of my ankle just visible outside my mouth. After his face started to lose some of its menace and his fists uncurled, I said, well, not normal in the sense that all marriages ended in divorce, and nor did we all routinely change spouses on a periodic basis. It's a good thing he had never heard of Hollywood. I remarked that even in France of his time, there had to be marriages that went sour. This, at least, he agreed with. But in his day, that was an obstacle to be worked around, not one to be resolved by divorce. His natural reaction was to ask me what I would do with Anne if I no longer cared for her like Caro now no longer cared for me? Would I just walk away from her then and go find some new woman in some other century?

Ah! *This* I could deal with. Philippe had seen that I could come up with money of his era, appear and disappear at will, and thought I was some kind of leisurely time traveler who went where I wanted and when I wanted. He probably thought I was having a similar affair with Cleopatra during my lunch breaks, while Cæsar was off checking to see if all Gaul was still neatly divided into three parts. I tried my best to explain the very random, accidental nature of the portal. I also told him something I had not spelled out even to Anne. I told him that when I had completed certain "arrangements financiers," I intended to destroy the portal and stay with Anne forever. I had some difficulty making him believe that the portal was a complete accident and that I hadn't the faintest idea how it had come to exist, how long it would last, or if it could ever be duplicated. I asked him if he had ever had any other visitors from another era. He said no and that he was still having a hard time believing that I was from another era, although the zipper in my pants certainly indicated I came from a weird place far, far away. Ah, oui, le zee-PAIR. If he thought zippers were weird, it's a good thing he never saw a tongue piercing, Mr. T or Lady Gaga. I tried to be

174

very convincing when I promised that no one would be following me with exotic, horrible weapons or evil intentions.

I told him straight out that I had, indeed, fallen in love with Anne, that I really intended to come stay with her, and was not afraid to do so in a land and time where divorce was not a solution to marital difficulty. I also asked him if he thought I would have a hard time showing up out of nowhere and joining their society. He thought about that for a moment, and then said he supposed he could start a rumor that a friend of a distant cousin, whose family had been in Canada for generations, would be coming to France to live. It would help explain my "odd" (to them) speech until I could learn to speak as they did.

I think I had him convinced of my honorable intentions as far as his daughter was concerned. He then broached the subject all potential fathers-in-law ask of their future sons-in-law: Could I provide for Anne if I came to live among them? I wasn't yet comfortable mentioning my ongoing project to buy a million francs in gold from Josh. But I did come up with an answer that spoke to him in a language a Frenchman understood. I said, "Mon cher Philippe, why do you think I agreed to keep paying you ten francs in gold for contemporary bottles of wine all this time?" He grinned and spread out his hands in a "ya got me, pal" gesture. I don't know to what extent he had been overcharging me, but it had to be exorbitant by the standards of the day. I'll bet even the occasional Jéroboam, for which Aldo had paid me nearly six figures each, didn't really cost ten francs in gold in 1860, and Philippe had charged me twenty francs for them.

But Philippe was no fool. He said he was positive I was selling his wine bottles for much more than I was paying for them or else I would have never agreed to keep paying his inflated price. This was no time to lie. I said of course I was doing that, and that it was helping me finance my move. He nodded.

"*Nous en avons tous tiré profit, alors,*" (So we all profited,) he remarked.

"*Exact,*" I replied. I thought it prudent not to say to what extent I had profited.

"*Tant mieux pour tout le monde.*" (So much the better for everyone.) He smiled. He looked at me long and hard and asked me if I knew all along that ten francs apiece in gold was a very stiff price to be paying for these bottles. I said sure, I knew. He asked if they were worth so very much more to me in my time that I could pay such an exorbitant price without complaint. I told him that they were worth plenty, and that in a short time, I would explain to him just how much. He said I didn't have to, as over the past ten weeks, his family had accumulated a small fortune selling these bottles to me. He almost looked a little ashamed when he said it, and admitted he would have never asked me for so much in the beginning if he had at all suspected that I would pay the price, not just for one bottle, but for hundreds of them. I told him that I suspected as much, and was happy for him that it had turned out so well. I said that he could rest assured that I had done very well with them as well and would not only prove it, but share the results with his family when I joined Anne.

He held out his hand. I had passed the test. I took it and gripped it firmly. It was the leathery, calloused hand of a working man. "*Elle y sera demain,*" (She'll be here tomorrow,) he reassured me. Before he left, he made sure I knew the reason for this little encounter. "*Il fallait que je sache. Vous comprenez, oui?*" (I had to know. You understand, right?) I would have preferred to spend the evening with Anne, but if this was necessary to pave the way for future harmony, it was a small sacrifice. Philippe would not be measuring my character by the square footage of the house I lived in. It was a refreshing change of climate.

I smiled and said I was very happy to hear that Anne would be back tomorrow, and by the way, did he by any chance have some more bottles for me? He grinned: *"Bien sûr, qu'est-ce que vous croyez?"*(Of course, what do you think?) I told him I could use a nice assortment of maybe fifteen bottles. He said he would put together an assortment of bottles from the last ten years and from around the region. I said I'd bring the same number of 10 franc coins to Anne tomorrow.

Philippe turned to go. I didn't even know what kind of place he lived in. There was a lot I had yet to learn. I went back to the portal and went upstairs to get ready for bed. Only a thousand or so different thoughts were dancing around in my head, but I somehow drifted off to sleep eventually.

One down; the IRS, Caro's lawyer and the Mafia to go.

34.

Sunday, August 29

I had a minimal breakfast, read the paper, got ill over the Gulf of Mexico oil spill situation (even if they had capped it, I didn't believe a word about the fish being safe to eat, and the fact that a group of Mississippi fishermen had said, in effect, they'd rather go broke than sell poisoned fish to their customers pretty much proved it), and decided to pay Thomas Jefferson a last visit.

He wasn't there. His sitting room was empty. It looked like a gorgeous day in southern Virginia from what I could see through the window, so I went back upstairs to read some more of the Sunday papers. I thought I saw the tail end of an evil-looking black limousine pass by the front of the house, but I couldn't be sure, and at any rate couldn't be sure that it was watching me. Maybe I was getting paranoid in my old age. But maybe I wasn't, either. By the end of the week at the latest, I figured I'd know. It did occur to me that I didn't really have anything to do with myself on a Sunday morning, and found that a little disturbing. It also occurred to me that this was one unique set of events that was happening to me, and I should leave an accounting of it somewhere, whether or not my endeavors were crowned with success. This was going to end either with me gloating from someplace where my nemeses would never be able to get at me, or with Aldo toasting my unfortunate demise, and Caro and the IRS battling it out over my estate.

So, I started writing all this down, with a brief explanation of who I am/was/will be (depending on how this all was to turn out). I don't know why I suddenly thought it was important for me to do this, but I wanted to leave behind something more comprehensive than "On the whole, I'd rather be in Philadelphia," and didn't know how else to go about it. Even then, I didn't know if anyone would ever see it. Maybe if Caro or Aldo tried putting my name in a search engine on the Internet, they'd stumble across it. Or maybe someone with no connection to me at all would stumble upon it? I translated a lot of the French in case it got discovered by someone whose only foreign language was Hungarian and the closest they'd gotten to France was a package of Brie in the deli section of the local supermarket.

After a couple of hours of writing my blog-to-be (i.e. this thing you're now reading), I felt better and went downstairs again to see if President 003 was in his sitting room. Better luck this time. There he was.

"Good afternoon, Mr. President," I said.

"Well, good afternoon to you, sir," replied Thomas Jefferson. "It has been a while, although I have detected the presence of your portal even when you weren't around."

"Yes, sir," I explained, "I told you that it was a completely accidental phenomenon, and I'm scared that if I were to extinguish it, that I wouldn't be able to recall it at will. Actually, that's what I came to talk to you about."

"Ah, so this is to be our final chat?" he inquired. "It's probably just as well. I've very much enjoyed meeting you and chatting with you about my life and times, not to mention your own. Your purchases from my wine cellar have been appreciated as well. Did you try any of them?"

I confessed that I hadn't, but had to sell them for financial reasons. Jefferson nodded.

"So, you are to some degree in the same boat as myself, I see. Well, I actually suspected as much and had set aside something for you, in case you decided to pay me another visit. But this, you have to promise me, you will enjoy for yourself. That is a requirement."

"In that case, I promise to respect your condition to the best of my ability," I answered, "but now you really have me curious."

"Please, give me a minute," he asked, and disappeared for about three minutes. When he reappeared, he had a wine bottle with him. It was a Margaux from 1787. "This is yours for nothing, but only if you promise me you will drink it yourself." I gulped at drinking what might have been a $100,000 bottle of wine, but I couldn't very well explain to him the reason why. This bottle was thirty-one years old in terms of condition and real age—perfect for drinking. To hell with it. I said I would keep his promise, and I meant it. He handed it to me through the portal, and I thanked him profusely. He said it was in appreciation for not only having helped him out financially to a small degree, but also for giving him optimism about the future of the experiment he and his contemporaries had created in the United States of America. I accepted it with gratitude and humility, let me tell you! I probably should have told him about the Civil War, nuclear bombs, oil spills ruining the Gulf of Mexico, religious fanatics trying to undo all he had done for the separation of church and state, etc., etc., etc. He probably would have had better insight as to some solutions than many of our best think tanks of the day. But who would have listened? What was I going to do, walk into the local studios of CNN, say I'd been talking with Thomas Jefferson, who happened to be in my basement temporarily, and here's what he suggested to solve our current bout of crises? Somehow, I don't think that would have gotten me on their Sunday talk shows.

I had to ask him one thing, though, as he was the only one I could talk to about this.

"Mr. President, there is one thing I would like to ask you, and I can't ask anyone in my own time. There is one other portal besides this one. It leads to the Bordeaux region of France in the year 1860."

"My, my," mused Jefferson, "I hope the wine is as good that far in the future as it was when I was there." That far in the future. The concept of the year 1860 being "far in the future" was, needless to say, rather novel to me.

"Oh, it is," I assured him. "I have tried it. A huge plague befell, er, or rather, will befall the region in 1870, and most of the vines will perish. Only a very few will survive, but Bordeaux wine will live on, not only at home, but in California, Australia, South Africa, Chile, many places."

"Fascinating, but please leave it at that," Jefferson cut me off. "Remember, Robert, I can't know any of this, and it would risk much if I were to let on by casual error that I did."

"Sorry, sir," I said. "I got carried away by the moment. About what I wanted to ask you…"

"Go on," he prodded.

"There's a woman there. In Bordeaux, I mean. I've fallen hopelessly in love with her. She speaks no English, and I can't bring her to my world. To be with her, I would have to abandon my own world, with no recourse of return should I regret my decision, go to an era where creature comforts I take for granted do not exist, and I would have to gnash my teeth and keep silent about everything I know that is going to happen, every armed conflict, every cataclysmic world event. But I have waited all my life to feel this way about a woman, and I feel it is worth the risk. Am I crazy to contemplate this? Should I abandon the thought?"

Jefferson pondered. "I had only ten years with my Martha. She died before her thirty-fourth birthday. I was devastated. I must have spent three weeks inside a room in utter despair. Much later, I took up with someone that was completely illicit, at least in my day."

"It's all right, Mr. President, we all know about Sally Hemings, and don't consider it a stain on your legacy at all."

Jefferson looked stunned. "Really? You *all* know about Sally? Please don't even tell me how. I don't want to know. You can't imagine what a scandalous thing this is in my time. Our country, then, has truly become the beacon of enlightenment we hoped-- Franklin, Madison, the others."

"Well, not entirely, I'm afraid," I answered. "There are still strong, even violent forces of reaction that would bring the country back to the days when people were burned at the stake for such things. But they are a distinct minority, to be sure." I didn't want to get into the Texas School Board. "We even abolished slavery entirely in 1865."

"It took *that* long? I failed in my efforts to get slavery abolished over the years, although I still hold some slaves myself to this day. Ironic, isn't it? Many of us who were part of the beginning of this country envisioned abolishing slavery altogether by 1808. As president, I even signed a law back in 1808 banning the slave trade with Africa. Some of us had hoped to have slavery abolished by then, but we underestimated the resistance from the southern states, whose economies depended upon its continued existence. From what you say, it took far longer than any of us thought it would. I *am* glad to hear that it was finally done away with, although I imagine it had enormous economic consequences for the southern states. I'm sure some of them must have had a few objections."

Oh, just a few, yeah. I didn't comment on that.

He went on, "There will always be a conflict between the forces of free thought and enlightenment against those of glorified ignorance, control and darkness, I suppose," Jefferson said. "But as long as they are beaten back by the forces of light and truth, they can be a tolerable evil—indeed, perhaps a useful one, so as to point out by example what is *not* worthy of aspiration and is to be avoided. I gather from what you're leading up to that you want my opinion as to whether you're right to consider abandoning your present life for what, to you, would be the more simple life in an era you would find, superficially, at least, to be primitive?"

"That is basically it in a nutshell," I admitted.

"In a nutshell," Jefferson repeated. "Nice little expression. You got that from Hamlet?"

"Umm, no, it's a common phrase in my day. Is it from Hamlet?"

"Originally, yes. It is very apt. The evolution of language is never-ending. I'm glad you've given me a glimpse into what's become of English in America. It certainly has evolved beyond anything we recognize as contemporary, which is only natural. But back to your question. You've said you're married, but that your wife has left you and has petitioned for a legal dissolution of your marriage, correct?"

"Quite correct," I confirmed.

"This is feasible in your day, and you have lost whatever affection you had for her long before this little marvel here occurred, correct?"

"Correct again."

"Well, then, I'll tell you what I think. But let me preface this by saying that I tell you this as one who has taken reckless risks in life.

My affair with Sally may not raise eyebrows in your era, but in mine, it would be grounds for shunning me completely or even worse. This doesn't even take into account the risk we all took in taking up arms to separate from Britain so many years ago. It cost years of hardship, and many lives were either lost or disrupted forever. The human cost was incalculable. What we call the American Revolution is still called the War of Rebellion in England. But the end result was a miraculous political experiment the likes of which has never been seen on this earth, at least not since the age of Pericles. From what you tell me, it has turned out far from perfect, and so is still a work in progress. But it is a never-ending path, the course of human events. Actually, I used that phrase…"

"In the Declaration of Independence," I completed. "We all learn your words in school: 'When, in the course of human events, it becomes necessary for one people to dissolve the political bands which have connected them with another…'"

A smile formed on his face, spreading to a wide beaming. "*That* is one of the most pleasing things I've learned from you, Robert. Thank you. You've truly made my day."

I managed—just barely—to keep from chuckling and telling him that "make my day" was a familiar phrase, too, but not because of him. I think I would have had a difficult time explaining Dirty Harry to Thomas Jefferson.

Jefferson went on: "Robert, I can't possibly put myself in your shoes any more than you could put yourself in mine, either now or back in 1776, when we all put our names to that most dangerous of documents. But I will tell you this: if you feel with all your heart that you've found personal happiness with this woman and that you think you can manage to disappear fully into her world for her sake and your own, then I'd say that your destiny has called upon you as surely as mine did to me. If *your* course of human events, if I may make the extrapolation, calls for you to dissolve your bonds to your present for an unknown jump to another world, then by all means do so.

"You must travel a different path from my own. Where I rose to prominence, you must inevitably remain in the background for the rest of your natural life. But you can aspire to happiness and productivity without the harsh glare of history recording your every word and move. I believe you to be sincere. Go where your heart leads you. I would. I like to think I did. That's what I have to say to you on that subject."

I'm usually ready with a sarcastic quip on most any occasion, but not now. The man who had written my country's Declaration of Independence had just advised me to make my own personal declaration of independence. I was deeply moved by Jefferson's words, and the force behind them. I faced him across the portal and struggled for words that wouldn't sound too trite.

"Mr. Jefferson, I thank you for your companionship, your sincerity and your wisdom. The story of our encounter will never be recorded in any history book, but I will never forget it. I'll tell you that I *have* crossed the other portal to the year 1860, and know that there's no physical danger. Your home remains a national monument to this day, and I'll not walk your halls for fear of wanting to stay for months and, therefore, risk being seen. Still, may I reach through and shake your hand before bidding farewell?"

Jefferson stood and approached the portal. "It would be my pleasure, Robert." I reached through the portal and grasped the hand that wrote the Declaration of Independence. His grip was, as I expected, warm and firm. I halfway expected him to say, "May the Force be with you," but all he said was, "May you find what you seek."

I just nodded, and said, "Thank you, Mister President, I intend to do just that." He smiled, released my hand, and turned to leave the room. I just stood there, wishing I had a video of the whole encounter so I could play it over and over again. I made sure I wrote it all down while it was fresh in my memory. Anne Boudreau and Thomas Jefferson—two people whose paths would never cross except in my own meager consciousness. Both of them changed my life forever due to some quirky effect of a lightning storm a few months back, an effect no one would ever know of or believe. I think I'm starting to get ever so slightly melodramatic here. Time to float down to earth, "Ro-Bair." You're not out of the soup yet.

I moved the Monticello portal back out of Jefferson's residence and up and back into the forest about treetop level, then replaced the screen door so no bugs or birds would get through. It would be just my luck for some 200-year-old squirrel to jump through, gnaw through a power cord, and zap my connection to Anne forever. When the screen door was firmly in place, Igot ready for my visit through the other portal. It was about 6:00 p.m. at Château Lafite and Anne would be there soon.

35.

Anne was dressed in the same outfit she had on two days ago. I guess my little heart-to-heart talk with Philippe had gone OK, as he wasn't here tonight. I wanted to talk about practicalities—where we would live, what kind of medical facilities (if any!) were nearby, what I would do with myself to occupy my time, and so on. Anne must have been thinking about that as well, but she had been way ahead of me. She said not to worry, that there would be a place for me in her world, and that there was always something to do around the château. I didn't see myself as plucking grapes for the rest of my life, but I got the impression she already knew that and had something in mind. I didn't know what, but then, I hadn't told her that I'd be bringing some money of my own to ease the transit, let alone how much. I would have to do some serious research into how far a million francs would go in 1860. I hadn't the faintest idea, of course, but the information had to be out there somewhere.

There was (well, would be) a man in France I very much wanted to meet, but there would be plenty of time for that. I could finally make use of my B.A. in physics, but not for twenty years or so. The man was only one year old in 1860, a little young for an academic tête-à tête, even for a prodigy of his caliber. Besides, he was up in Paris, or would be. I would make it a point to search him out in fifteen or twenty years. It might be fun to contribute in some small way to the "discovery" of radium and polonium (his wife would be from Poland), as long as I could keep my name out of it. I'd also have to keep my mouth shut about his future, as he would die at age forty-six in a stupid street accident. He would slip on a slick cobblestone in Paris in 1906 and get his head run over by a horse-drawn carriage—rather an ignoble end to a guy who had just received the Nobel Prize in physics just three years earlier. But that was for much later. As long as Pierre Curie was still in diapers, I would have plenty of other things to occupy my thoughts.

After a silent walk in the approaching dusk, Anne's grip on my hand tightened and she asked if my impending move was to be soon. I told her that I expected it to be in less than two weeks. She nodded and said, *"Même si c'est demain, ce n'est pas trop tôt."* (Even if it's tomorrow, that's not too soon.)

This was not a moment of "be still, my raging heart," but more of a "calm down, my raging hormone level" moment. After a year (damn, had it been that long?) since Caro had come to my side of the bed, I was more than ready. Caro hadn't so much as patted my shoulder since the day she saw the $47,000 check from Aldo. If I had some steamy sex scene with Anne to recount here, I might even have done so, just to satisfy your expectations. But I didn't dare upset my standing with her family. I still didn't know the social mores here, and the last thing I wanted was to mess up my relationship with Philippe at this point. I told her flat out that I couldn't wait to spend the night with her, and she just raised her eyebrows with one of those unmistakable expressions of "then what are you waiting for?" Unmistakable to me, anyway. I have been known to misinterpret a woman's sentiments in the past—as in "usually."

She pressed herself up against me and said, *"Je connais un endroit où on nous dérangera pas."* (I know a place where no one will disturb us.) Uh-oh. Turn up those hormones a notch, why don't you? My twenty-first-century zipper was being given one of its tougher tests for metal fatigue.

"Est-ce que c'est loin d'ici?" (Is it far from here?) I asked slowly.

She breathed out a sigh. *"Ce n'est pas tout près,"* (It's not next door,) she admitted.

"Combien de temps faut-il pour y aller?" (How long to get there?)
I asked.

"Une petite demi-heure," (Close to half an hour,) she admitted.

Off the menu for tonight, anyway. *"Trop tard pour ce soir,"* (Too late for this evening,) I said, but I would try to visit a lot before the ten days were up. She brightened up.

"Je t'attends." (I'm waiting for you.) I was being made an offer I in no way wanted to refuse, and Philippe would be getting used to the idea sooner or later anyway. OK, I'd see about getting off work early some day this week, although I had a lot on my plate if Plan A was to be completed on schedule.

It's not like I had become the world's biggest prude or anything. I was definitely not looking to play hard to get or imitate Henry Fielding's "Joseph Andrews." I did still have this overpowering terror of upsetting my status in a world where I had no system of support in place or refuge if something went wrong.

Before we parted for the night, Anne told me, *"Avant que j'oublie, j'ai tes vêtements."* (Before I forget, I have your clothes.) Ah, my ticket to not standing out like an ostrich in a chicken coop. I asked her how she knew if they would fit or not? She gave me a sly smile and said, *"On verra bien."* (We shall see.) Not that I was overly concerned. If they were close to fitting, I was happy. It's not like I expected her to have gone to the nearest Ralph Lauren outlet for mid- nineteenth century men's furnishings.

Anne arranged the fifteen bottles Philippe had given her to deliver to me. She had dragged them over in sort of a wooden precursor to the roller carry-on suitcase everyone has at airports. I gave her fifteen more 10 franc coins (a deal is still a deal, after all) to take back to Philippe. I took the first five bottles across to my basement, and then returned for the next five. She returned to press up against me again and we just stood there for a minute, our arms around each other in one of those perfect moments you only see in the movies. The sun slowly setting, the château in the background, and my hand running through her thick, dark brown hair, I was almost driven to tears because this was a scene I had fantasized about for the last twenty-odd years. She gave me one of those kisses whose meaning cannot be misinterpreted and turned to go home. I took the last five bottles across to my basement and looked back across. She had turned to watch me and gave me a look that spoke a thousand words, all of them ones I wanted to hear. She then turned for a final time and slowly disappeared into the deepening tranquil Bordeaux evening.

36.

Monday, August 30

At the office, Juanita introduced me to a wiry, diminutive man with decidedly Asian features. This was her brother, Miguel. His Mayan features were even more pronounced than Juanita's, and if you had told me he was Han Chinese, I would have believed it. I said, *"Buenos días,"* and his face broke into a big smile.

"¿Hablas español? Djoo espeak espanis?" he asked, hopefully. Juanita wasn't kidding about his spoken English being as good as her own.

"Not really," I answered, "just a few words."

"No problem. I espeak inglis."

So I noticed. I said, "So tell me, what do you do for a living in Guatemala?"

"I am instructor (een-strook-TOR) in *maa shalats*!" he explained proudly.

I had no idea what "maa shalats" was. Some long-lost Mayan herbal medicine treatment, maybe? I nodded, not wanting my ignorance of "maa shalats" to show. Miguel was no fool, though, as I should have figured, seeing as how his sister's IQ was probably tops in the whole firm. He saw I didn't understand him. "Djoo know maa shalats?" he asked carefully. "Like dis, I show you." I wanted to be polite, but I didn't really want to chew on some magic herb that would transform me into a chicken. However, he didn't pull out some pouch full of crushed leaves from behind his back. Instead, he casually came up to me and twitched his arm. In half a second, I was looking up at his smiling face from a prone position on the floor.

After helping me up, he said, "Not juss jujitsu. I know kung fu, karate an' Thai kickboxing, too!"

"Maa shalats." Martial arts. Took me long enough, didn't it? Who knew they had martial arts instructors in Guatemala?

I asked him where he had learned all that, as I doubted there were too many dojos in Guatemala City. He said he'd spent half his life in Los Angeles. He didn't offer any details, and I didn't ask, but I suspected that *"carta verde"* was neither in his vocabulary nor his possession. However, if he had spent time here, then my little task for him wouldn't be too difficult to explain, either. Despite his mangling of the spoken language, he obviously understood everything I said (like sister, like brother). I told him what I had in mind. I had worked out the sequence a few days ago. What I wanted was for him to go to six different courier services, let's call them 1, 2, 3, 4, 5 and 6, so they don't get in any trouble from anyone later on for having helped me out. After all, they had no idea what role they were playing in this. He was to tell service 3 that if they received a package from courier service 1, that they were to forward it on to service 5. He was then to tell service 5 to forward the package on to me at Blake and Brock, this time with the proper address filled out on a label. He was then to tell service 4 that if they were to get a certain package from service 2, that they were to forward it on to service 6, and tell service 6 that the same package was to be forwarded on to me at B&B. Once all that was set up, Miguel was then to take packages to services 1 and 2, and from there, have them sent on to services 3 and 4, who now had instructions as to what to do with the packages when they arrived. Miguel would provide services 3, 4, 5 and 6 with the tracking numbers given the packages by courier services 1 and 2, so they knew which packages to forward where.

I then had our shipping department make up four boxes – two with two bottles of ginger ale and two with three bottles. I slipped my little pre-printed notes to Stef into each package just as the boxes were ready to be closed. I told our driver to hand these particular boxes, addressed to me but with no street number, to Miguel at the drop-off point where he was shipping the rest of the company mail. Miguel was to meet our driver at the drop-off point, then take one box each to courier services 1 and 2 and start the sequence. They were to travel normal, next-day service—no express service or anything conspicuous, just a "Fragile—Glass" label on each box. Our office shipping department had used plenty of straw while packing to ensure that the bottles wouldn't break in transit. And finally, Juanita had explained to Miguel that this was a little test I was conducting for security, and he thought the idea sounded like great fun.

After lunchtime, before the van that took our packages to our usual drop-off departed, I pulled our driver aside and explained that when he got there, the first two boxes with my name on them were to be given to Miguel and not sent anywhere. He was used to occasional instructions that didn't conform to our usual procedure, and even though this was a major departure from the norm, I was the one who was responsible for organizing this kind of thing for the firm, so he just shrugged and said OK. The second pair of boxes was to be sent the same route and in the same manner two days later. Both Monday and Wednesday, I sent one box with two bottles and one box with three bottles. Each route got one box of each size.

If Stefano and friends were watching me at the firm, even if they saw Miguel and saw him talking to me (which I tried to avoid anywhere that might be seen from the outside), they wouldn't have known who he was and wouldn't have seen him leave with any packages. I told Juanita and Miguel never to arrive or depart the firm together.

The likelihood of Stefano making a connection with the wine at the beginning was rather remote and was a risk I thought worth taking. Sure enough, Monday's delivery to courier services 1 and 2 by Miguel went off without incident. Earlier that day, Miguel had already gone to services 3 and 4, to arrange receipt from services 1 and 2, and to arrange for onward delivery to services 5 and 6. Tuesday, when no deliveries of my ginger ale, from or to the office, were to be made at all, he was to go to services 5 and 6 to arrange receipt from courier services 3 and 4, and arrange for onward forwarding from services 5 and 6 back to me at B&B on Wednesday. I told Miguel to pay each courier service on the day the delivery was to be made. Therefore, he paid services 1 and 2 on Monday, would pay for services 3 and 4 on Tuesday, and services 5 and 6 on Wednesday. He would also pay services 1 and 2 again on Wednesday for the second round of boxes. The whole cycle, with the second round of boxes, was then to be repeated on Thursday, September 2, and Friday, September 3. If Stef and his goons were still around, they could catch wind of some action and have an easier time of making the connection if they saw Miguel actually make a payment for a courier service to deliver something to me. They might not have associated him with packages that looked like they might contain bottles in the beginning, but if they were as thorough as they should have been, they would have figured out a connection by the end of the week. This was all a little complicated to remember and set up. Dan Brown would have been proud of me.

I told Miguel one last thing: if anyone showed up to try to take the packages from him by force, he was NOT to put up any kind of fierce resistance, but to give them the packages if it looked like they would use force to take them from him. Miguel looked a little disappointed. "No resist at all, señor Roberto?" I said he could put up a little argument, but he was not to defend these packages with his life. He actually looked a little disappointed, but agreed.

After all, if he were to demolish any of Stef's hired help, even assuming his "maa shalats" were up to the task, then Stef would never get my little note, would he?

During lunch, I went down to shipping and got the first two boxes, one with two bottles, one with three bottles, packed nice and tight, with the notes for Stefano tucked inside each one. I didn't expect either of the two to be seen by him, but maybe his surveillance was more extensive than I thought. He might not have been monitoring my activities so closely as to intercept either of the first two packages, but I didn't want to bet the farm on it. Fifteen minutes before the driver was to leave with the firm's packages, I sent Miguel off to the drop-off point so he could intercept the first two packages and take one each on to courier services 1 and 2, with instructions to forward them on to courier services 3 and 4 the next day.

I then called Josh at California Coin and asked him about progress with his friends in Dallas. He said that all 51,000 coins had been ordered. The wire went out from Dallas to Zürich today and would be received tomorrow, the thirty-first. Josh explained that the Europeans all knew this firm in Dallas and dealt with them regularly, so the coins should be on their way for export clearance from Switzerland on Tuesday. The Swiss are used to big transactions of gold, it seems, and they only needed a day to process the paperwork. There were direct Swiss Air Lines flights from Zürich to Los Angeles, and to avoid unnecessary logistics expenses and time loss, Josh's friends in Dallas would have the gold shipped directly to L.A. instead of to Dallas and then on to L.A. That way, a plane with the gold would land at LAX on Thursday. Delivery would be made in Josh's name, and Brinks would take care of the customs clearance paperwork and store the coins over the long (Labor Day) weekend, whether or not they cleared U.S. customs before then. I would tell Josh on Tuesday where and when I wanted delivery made.

He assumed I would want such a fortune delivered to some huge bank safety deposit box. He assumed incorrectly, but I didn't need to tell him that right then. He thought I had some odd quirks as it was, so I didn't need him thinking I was completely out of my mind—not just yet, anyway. It was already enough of a chore convincing myself that I wasn't.

I called up Aldo and told him I would have some more great bottles this week. He said, fine, just bring them along. I figured I'd bring the first five on Wednesday, after Miguel's first installment of ginger ale arrived back at B&B—*if* it arrived.

37.

At this point, it would have been too late to place any more big orders for additional quantities of French gold from Josh and have them arrive from Switzerland in time for me to take delivery before my grand finale. But I didn't want to leave the bank account empty and, above all, I didn't want to give anyone the impression that there would be any break whatsoever from the routine of the last couple of months. I had told Tom Nakano of the two checks to California Coin, but had also told him that more money would be flowing into the account. He knew about estimated tax payments as well as anyone else and knew that I would have been expected to make one on September 15. Drawing the account down to zero and leaving it there would have set off a few alarm bells to Tom, and that's the last thing I wanted to do. Having a couple more five- and six-figure checks from Aldo continue to replenish the account would be reassuring. I even had an idea of what to do with the balance when I was ready to hit the road for the last time. Some people would be happy. Some would not.

Steve Clark stopped by to say that Stan Chase had requested a preliminary meeting when it was convenient. I thought for a minute, and then asked, "Is it urgent, or could we do this after Labor Day?"

Steve said that he didn't detect any sense of urgency in the request, so I said, "How about Wednesday, September eighth?" Steve said he thought that would be agreeable and would call Stan Chase to set a time and place unless Chase and/or Caro had any objection to the date. He stopped by again later that afternoon to say that the meeting was scheduled for 10:00 a.m. on the eighth at B&B in one of our conference rooms. I said that was fine, mustering as much indifference as I possibly could, hoping that if the meeting actually ended up taking place, it would be to discuss how something horrible had happened to poor old me. Come to think of it, I don't think there would have been this many people concerned for my welfare concentrated in one room since I was in the delivery room putting in my initial appearance.

That evening, I almost was tempted to bring Anne some fun food from my time. Chinese take-out, Greek Gyros, Burger King, whatever. I didn't, of course. I didn't dare bring anything that could possibly be in a wrapper that might escape destruction or biodegradation. Even one panel of a Kung Pao chicken holder with an L.A. address or date on it or a paper fast food wrapper getting somehow preserved for posterity would have serious repercussions. Plus, with all the additives that we put in our food these days, I might have ended up inadvertently making Anne violently ill, and that was right up there on my list of things to avoid doing. I did stop off at a Korean place for some take-out bulgogi, but didn't bring any when I went to see Anne after dinner. Each time I saw her, it was like this reality vertigo coming back to hit me. "You've been a good boy today, so you may go live your fantasy again tonight (thank you, Santa!)" I told her, in between embraces and kisses and all sorts of displays of affection that were very pleasant to me (and you don't need to hear about) that I was ready for my wardrobe to be fitted. The shoes would be the hard part, and I was almost tempted to bring some of my own. Also, I had never had button-down pants before, and Anne was completely broken up with laughter to the point of tears, fascinated by my boxer shorts, and watching me desperately trying not to imitate some clumsy Chevy Chase routine in my pitiful attempt to put them on. I loved the sound of her laugh, even when it was at me, and I was finally laughing, too. I made it a point to look up on the Internet when the zipper was invented so as to get pants with a zipper if they had been invented any time during my projected lifetime. I feared not; the zipper was just one more convenience I would be sacrificing to be with Anne. But it only took about 0.015 seconds of watching her face or hearing her laugh to be reminded that this was worth it all.

I told her something else: the date I would be coming to stay with her forever. It would be in eight days. As we were not on the same calendar, we had to calculate out what date this meant for her. For me, it was September 7. For her, eight days hence would have meant the fourteenth of August. "Yesterday, August 14, 1860, a day that shall live in obscurity…(don't cry for me, California)."

Yeah, well, excuse me for getting a little giddy here. The day was approaching when I was planning to live in primitive bliss with my ultimate ideal of feminine pulchritude, and there were only about 200 things that could possibly go wrong to prevent it, max. Maybe as few as 100. The portals could fizzle out before I was ready. The plane with my French gold from Zürich might crash. Brinks might deliver it to the wrong address. Aldo might decide I knew too much about his plans and have me eliminated from the face of the earth. The Incredible Hulk might accidentally flatten my car with me in it. Who knew what might happen? Actually, that last one was just in case Stan Lee ever reads this. Hey, you never know. Excelsior!

I knew, and presumed that Anne knew as well, that this stage of our relationship (man, do I hate that word!) was all wonder and glorious infatuation, and there would be quite a few reality checks along the way. I didn't care. I don't care. I mean, sure, I'll care if something awful happens to either one of us, but what the hell has my personal life been up to now? I lost my virginity with Marnie and found some temporary companionship with Caro, but contentment? Happiness? Hell, they might have been expressions in Coptic for which I didn't know the English translation. My only rollicking success up to now had been professional, and by Caro's standards, even that had been inadequate. I am appreciated by the people I work with, and I do like that and treasure it. But for all the office camaraderie I might enjoy with Jim Hernández, Juanita or the other people at B&B, it's not enough. I thought it would do while I was still with Caro, as stupid as that now seems. But the storm changed everything. Maybe I'll grow tired of life in 1860 and go crazy. But maybe not. I think all anyone would have to do is promise I will get to hear Anne's laugh and touch her face for the next month (let alone next forty years) and I think I'd still make the trade. It's like being told I can drink some cheap supermarket wine for the rest of my life, or drink Jefferson's bottle of thirty-one-year-old 1787 Margaux that he gave me and risk never drinking wine ever again. Before meeting Anne, I was looking at drinking the supermarket wine for the rest of my life and accepting that as my fate. Now I had the chance to sip the Margaux and take my chances. This was a major fork in the road, and not one I ever saw myself taking. Hell, I never saw myself being offered the choice. But this crazy, impossible situation had been shoved under my nose by fate, and whether or not I manage to pull this off, by Jove, I was going for it.

Anne might not have understood my musings, at least not in terms I could explain coherently, so I kept these to myself for the moment and just relaxed in our (so far) chaste intimacy. But she saw that my mind was wandering a bit when she looked into my eyes and asked what was on my mind. I told her I was thinking of what we would do with our lives. She asked if I would not be content to work at the château's vineyards. I thought about that for a moment. What wine enthusiast in the year 2010 would not jump at the chance to hang around Château Lafite in the year 1860, after all? But it was surely backbreaking work, and I had just risked plenty to make sure I would bring a king's ransom with me next week. I told her I wouldn't mind doing that part-time for the experience, but I also wanted to travel, see places such as Barcelona in Spain, the major cities of Italy, Vienna and the like. I wanted to meet people I knew who would be of interest to me, and I wanted to help her raise our children. *"Nos enfants,"* not just *"mes enfants."* She liked that (so did I). I wanted her to be not just my companion, but my partner. I wanted to know the simplicities of her life as well as tell her of the complexities of mine; I wanted us to be a very special couple who would have the advantage of knowing all about both.

Anne listened to all this and gave me a very penetrating look. She may not ever have been within eyesight of a university, but she was as perceptive as a Ph.D. in psychology. She and Juanita would have gotten along famously. *"Tu vas apporter beaucoup d'argent quand tu viendras, n'est-ce pas?"* (You're bringing a lot of money when you come, aren't you?) I just stared at her, speechless. I mumbled, *"Un peu, oui."* (Some, yes.)

She was still looking at me. *"Non, beaucoup."* (No, a lot.) What was I going to say? Women know when men they care about lie to them outright. I don't know how, but they do. So I didn't. I nodded, *"Oui, beaucoup."*

She continued, *"Et comment l'as tu obtenu?"* (And how did you get it?) *BIG* sigh of relief from me, and she relaxed a little, not yet knowing my answer, but observing that her question obviously didn't bother me. Her concern was that she hadn't fallen in love with the most successful thief of three centuries! I said, *"D'accord, pas de secrets entre nous,"* (OK, no secrets between us,) but she could NOT tell anyone ever—not her father, not our children, not her best friend, no one. She was perceptive enough to know I meant it and intuitive enough to know that whatever she was about to hear wouldn't disturb her. She was definitely *not* prepared for the story I was about to tell her.

I spent over half an hour explaining the whole culture of rare wine in the late twentieth and early twenty-first centuries and how perfectly preserved bottles of wine from her era were wildly expensive rarities in my era. I told her about Thomas Jefferson, his own wine interests and the other portal. She nodded and said she vaguely remembered hearing some stories about a famous American who had traveled extensively in her area around the 1780s, even visited Château Lafite. I told her about Aldous D. George and his thugs. I told her in detail about the weird characters at the wine tastings, along with some of the descriptions given vintage wine in auction catalogs. She howled with laughter at some of them—*"Du café dans le vin, vous êtes fous!"* (Coffee in the wine, you are crazy!) It's not easy explaining our version of pomposity to someone living in France less than a century removed from Marie Antoinette. I told her about Josh, the friendly neighborhood coin expert, and how he had helped me. I told her that I had used my profits to buy *"une somme modeste"* of French money of her era that had survived until my era, and that I would be bringing it with me when I came. The eight days was the time I needed to get it delivered to where I could bring it through the portal. The only detail I left out was just how much I'd be bringing with me.

Anne listened with what could only be described as rapt attention. She finally said that what I had just told her was the most ridiculous fantasy story she had ever heard, and she only believed me because she had never seen a zipper before. I didn't know if she was being serious or not. But then she broke out into her captivating laughter and kissed me, saying that no one was capable of inventing such a wild tale of fantasy, so I must have been telling her the truth. I said I wouldn't blame her if she didn't believe me, but I wasn't going to lie to her and it was up to her to believe me or not. She said her only regret was that I was not going to bring a zipper (*"zee-PAIR"*) with me when I came for good. I asked why not? She said that if I did, she could study it, replicate it, invent it and make a fortune! We both laughed at that one and just held onto each other for a long time. If anyone or anything was going to mess this up for me, I would NOT be a happy camper.

Our conversation had lasted a while this evening and both of us sensed that neither the mood nor the timing was quite right for Anne to show me that place *"une petite demi-heure"* from there where more intimate matters might be addressed. "One Of These Nights," as the Eagles sang—just not *this* night. But now that I had given Anne (and myself) a set date on which I intended to cross over to her world forever, there was somehow less urgency. We had our usual (and increasingly difficult) parting scene and then there I was, back in my basement. I didn't really know squat about life in rural France in 1860, and made it a point to start looking up information on the Internet. Even if someone saw me searching at work, all I had to say was that I was doing some research on wine-related subjects. As everyone at B&B knew my passion for wine, it would hardly raise an eyebrow if they saw me searching the Web for information on the Bordeaux region of France. Well, Juanita might figure something was up, but she could keep her mouth shut. I would make sure I left her a nice parting gift.

38.
Tuesday, August 31

When I got to the office, in between handling B&B's logistics and accounts, I started to burn up the search engines in an effort to find out what I could about life in southwestern France around 1860. Needless to say, there weren't too many guides for twenty-first century people wishing to move there (and then).

I figured I could handle the food OK. I hoped the beds were dry and that the sheets (wow, did they even have sheets?) were changed more often than monthly. Maybe I should bring a lifetime supply of toilet paper with me? I found that a woman in France had written, for fun, a history of toilets called *"Le Grand Livre du Petit Coin."* (The Big Book of That Little Place.) I doubted Barnes & Noble had it, so I would have to find out the details of that aspect of nineteenth century French life during on-the-job training, or maybe on-the-john training, as the case may be. At least I didn't have to wonder if I'd like the wine.

My research helped me with a few minor details, but apparently many historians weren't overly concerned with the details of daily life in rural Bordeaux in 1860. I didn't need Theodore H. White to know that I wouldn't be sleeping on a Sealy Posturepedic.

There was also the question of how far my million francs would go. It wouldn't buy me Versailles, but I didn't want Versailles. That was Caro's department, and she wasn't going to be joining me. From what I could find out, the annual budget of France in those days was something like a billion francs, so, a million francs was something like one tenth of 1% of that—a rather healthy sum for one individual. I'm sure there were plenty of rich nobility with far more than that, but all I wanted was to be comfortable. I had no aspirations to emulate Louis XIV, or even become the *Duc de Chèrmanne Auxe*. I figured I was going to be just fine—if I could hang on for another week, that is. The portal to Château Lafite had to stay intact for seven more days, Caro's friend, Wendy, had to keep her nose out of my bank account, Tom Nakano had to keep the lid on, the IRS had to stick to waiting until September 16, and Stefano had to keep his distance, which I doubted he was doing. Oh, yeah, and my online course in chemistry had to give me a passing grade on my final (and only) exam.

Miguel arrived at B&B just after lunchtime and told me he had gone to courier services 5 and 6 to arrange the onward forwarding of the first two packages of ginger ale back to me when they arrived from courier services 3 and 4. He was sure he had not been followed so far. I was almost disappointed, but then, nothing had yet been assigned to be delivered to an address with my name on it. Come tomorrow, this would now change. If Stef and friends were watching what was delivered to B&B and saw a package that looked like a box that might contain wine bottles, they might pay a little more attention to who was doing the delivering, as well as to whom it was addressed and, if they could, who the sender was. If they felt there was no risk to themselves, they might even try to intercept and open a box. I was, in fact, counting on this (hence my prepared note to Stef in each package). Or maybe I was being a little too paranoid, and the most dramatic outcome of my little circus would be boosting the business of a few L.A. courier companies and sending some ginger ale on a "tour de suburban L.A." I'd find out soon enough.

Nothing else of great import happened at the office that day. Most people were making plans to go away for the upcoming Labor Day long weekend, and were looking not to have too much of a workload during the week prior to it. After all, no one else was planning to move to another century any time soon. I called Josh from my cell phone, so as not to have any trace of a call from B&B to him, and asked about progress on my little "order." He said that my checks had cleared and the wires had gone out. If all was well, the coins would be in the air on Thursday, in L.A. on Thursday night, and cleared by U.S. customs by Friday. Brinks would store them in their vault at LAX until delivery Tuesday, and had said I would be expected to provide them with the address as early as possible on Tuesday, with a preferred delivery time as well, please. I asked Josh to get me a fax number for Brinks so that I could fax them an address and a time Monday evening. This way, they would see my fax first thing Tuesday, and Josh wouldn't have to come to the shop three hours early in order to pass it on. Josh got me the Brinks fax number and the name of the man to whose attention it was supposed to go. I buried the information in my cell phone. I then asked Josh to have Brinks bill him for the storage fees. He asked why, and I said that I would be going on vacation immediately afterward and would not see the Brinks bill in time to pay it in a timely manner. I asked him to get a reasonable estimate as to the cost for the storage fees (he had agreed to pick up the cost of delivery, remember) plus an hour's extra time subsequent to delivery, for security purposes. This prompted a question from Josh: "What security purposes?" I couldn't very well tell him, "well, you see I need time to change into my nineteenth century costume, load the coins into sturdy bags with no markings, and then transport them over to nineteenth century France in my basement." So, I just said that I wanted them guarding the house to leave me time to make sure the coins were safely stored in the special place I had built for that purpose, and I wanted no one observing me while I did it. This seemed to satisfy him, and he said as much. I said I'd leave a check with him to cover the high end of their estimate. He said that worked for him, and said he'd get back to me.

That evening, I got some Vietnamese take-out: a soup with angel hair rice noodles and some chicken with sautéed onions in a strong ginger sauce with white rice. I figured where I was going, there wouldn't be any of this kind of food to choose from, so I was going to get my last licks in. It did occur to me that aside from a bottle of wine (not the worst thing), I hadn't sampled any food or drink of Anne's world. There would undoubtedly be some stuff I would have to get used to, but she and her family looked healthy enough, so whatever it was they ate, it obviously was good for somebody. I had been able to leave a half hour early due to the generally light workload. Some of the lawyers, and even the partners, had gone for the whole week so as to profit from ten days of vacation while only using up five of their allotted vacation days from work. I hadn't made a set time to meet Anne, but I got down to my basement earlier than I had yesterday by a full hour (the Vietnamese were quicker with their chicken in ginger than the Koreans had been with their bulgogi). Anne was there.

39.

I asked her how she knew I would be there so early today. She replied that she had no idea at all that I would be there early. She just thought she might get lucky. *She* might get lucky? I was in seventh heaven every second I could be with her, and she thought *she* might get lucky seeing me an hour early. She tossed me my clothes through the portal and told me to put them on before coming over. This was a departure from the norm, so I asked her how come. She just smiled a little sly smile, and said, *"Tu verras bien."* (You'll see.) I hoped she wasn't planning to have me kidnapped so I could never return. Not that I was wavering in my determination to join her permanently, but I hadn't prepared my move yet, had none of my emergency medicine on me, and was penniless (well, centimeless) so far. But I did trust her. Not that the past was free of scheming women, as Lucretia Borgia had proved, but this was just not her. I realized I had not been the top expert in judging women's character in the past, but even if I hadn't learned from all my mistakes, I also knew that what I had with Anne was like nothing I had ever felt with any woman of *any* century. And she now made three different centuries for me. How many guys can boast a romantic career that spans three centuries?

I got out of my clothes and put on my nineteenth century outfit. I almost felt like I was getting ready to trick or treat for Halloween again, except that with this stuff on, I wouldn't stand out in her world. That was exactly what she had in mind. As soon as I crossed, she sniffed at the air and then close to me. *"Qu'est-ce que tu as mangé ce soir?"* (What did you eat this evening?)

"Poulet au gingembre," (Chicken in ginger,) I told her. She closed her eyes and breathed in again, very close to me. *"C'est merveilleux,"* (It's marvelous,) she smiled. She asked me what else one ate in

Chèrmanne Auxe. I explained to her that in my time, there were all kinds of restaurants all over America, and being on the west coast, there was an especially large number of Asian cuisines, from Indian curry to Japanese sushi. She looked startled when I mentioned sushi. I had pronounced it in French, of course, with the stress on the last syllable. She asked why in the world the Japanese would eat something that sounded so disgusting? I didn't get it at first. I then thought about what the two syllables would mean in French to someone who didn't know any Japanese food. I started to laugh, and she said, OK what's the big joke? In French, broken up into two words that are pronounced the same way but with the stress on the final syllable, sushi becomes *"sous chie,"* which translates as "under-shit" and is not the sort of thing one associates with fine cuisine in most cultures. I explained sushi to her, and while the thought of raw fish didn't exactly appeal to her either, she was relieved that I enjoyed a fish dish and not munching on the leftovers of the local outhouse. Still, she said that she hoped that travelling to Japan wasn't on my "to do" list any time soon. I promised. She said, *"Et maintenant, on va visiter un endroit beaucoup plus proche."* (And now, we are going to visit a place much closer.)

I had been to Château Lafite briefly as a teenager, as well as to many other famous wine producers, but that was in the late twentieth century. Not only had it been twenty years ago in my own memory, but the layout of the area was completely different in the year 1860 anyway, so even my own vague memory of the place was useless for any kind of orientation. I just held Anne's hand and let her lead me to wherever it was she wanted to take me.

I asked her, *"C'est loin d'ici, là où tu veux m'emmener?"* (Is it far from here, where you're taking me?) She gave me a big smile and blushed a little, answering, *"Une petite demi-heure."* (Close to half an hour.) I had heard that expression from her recently enough, as in two days ago. She was telling me about a place where we wouldn't be disturbed. This was on her initiative, so I just squeezed her hand and said, *"Allons-y!"* (Let's go!) All she had brought was a little cloth sack, which she carried in her other hand. We walked through some paths out in the open, and then through some woods, with the last four or five minutes under a thick canopy of trees. Suddenly, she turned to the right at a barely discernable path, and led me to a mostly hidden little structure, best described as a well-kept shack. She opened the door to reveal a dirt floor near the door, and a large, wide covering of fresh straw at the back. There was a bolt lock on the inside, which I thought under the circumstances most helpful. There was also a small window up near the back, and that was the only light that came in from the outside.

Anne led me inside the shack and bolted the door. She then unwrapped her cloth sack. Inside was the rest of the bottle of the Lafite 1855 that we hadn't finished the other day, plus a much larger cloth, sort of like a soft tablecloth, that was folded up. It unfolded to a comfortable size and she spread the cloth over the soft straw, then turned to me and said, *"Et maintenant, mon cher Robert, tu n'as pas besoin de ton zee-PAIR."* (And now, my dear Robert, you don't need your zipper.) She started to undress, not taking her eyes off me, and I started to do likewise. I definitely didn't take my eyes off of her.

Maybe I'm a prude, and maybe I'm just too proprietary about what was undoubtedly the most wonderful hour I had ever spent up until that point, but I'm not going to share all the details. Suffice it to say that I had seen the most beautiful sight I had ever seen in my life. I heard John and Paul singing, "What do you see when you turn out the light?" and Ringo answering, "I can't tell you, but I know it's mine."

She was warm, and she moved and she called my name in French. If her purpose had been to remove any doubts either of us might have had about what we were planning, it worked. If her only motive was pure, ecstatic intimacy with me, it had the same effect. I didn't know how I was going to be able to keep a straight face for the next week, and Juanita would read my face as if it were an X-rated movie, because I'd be grinning like a Cheshire cat the next morning at the office.

Afterward, we shared half of what was left of the bottle of 1855 Lafite, and while it was still fabulous, don't let the wine experts fool you—no, it is NOT better than sex, not when the intimacy has a lot of feeling behind it.

We redressed (I was getting used to this button routine, but I still missed my *zee-PAIR*) and Anne led me back to where the portal was. Thank goodness! I would never have found it on my own. I don't even remember what we talked about on the way. We talked little anyway. I was like a high school math student who had just proved the Pythagorean Theorem for the first time on his own. I could only guess what was running through Anne's mind, but her body language was loud and clear.

By the way, I had heard that French women don't shave their underarms. I don't know if that's so for all of them, but Anne, indeed, did not. I don't know why this was supposed to be some kind of exotic phenomenon to American guys, but it seemed perfectly natural to me and was as sexy as could be. I could definitely get used to that hair for the next fifty years or so.

When we got back to the portal, she gave me that deep gaze of hers and said, *"Cette semaine sera la semaine la plus longue de ma vie."* (This will be the longest week of my life.)

"Cette semaine sera l'année la plus longue de ma vie," (This week will be the longest *year* of my life,) I replied. She smiled and nodded. *This* is what I had been looking for all my life, and I was not, no way, no how, going to let it go. The temptation to just chuck it all and stay was very powerful, but I wanted to go for the brass ring this time. Just one more week. Juanita would know that I had done something that was as momentous to me as "inventing the wheel," as Pat Conroy had put it in that novel of his about the military school, but she would be the only one, and she could keep a lid on it.

Anne asked if I was absolutely sure I wanted to go back that night, but I told her I had to and reminded her that I didn't want to arrive into her life without a cent(ime). She said she didn't care, although her curiosity had obviously been piqued by my reluctance to tell her what kind of sum of money I intended to bring with me.

Anne was reluctant to let me go, which didn't make it any easier for me, either. Crossing back to my house that night was one of the more difficult tasks I had ever undertaken, period. If the portal had disappeared during the course of the following week, I think my only options after that would have been either to fly up to San Francisco and jump off the Golden Gate Bridge, or drive down to Tijuana and loudly insult the mother and sister of a local drug lord. I'm pretty sure both methods would have been equally quick.

When back in my house, getting ready for bed provided a small but insufficient distraction from thinking about Anne. I was only able to get to sleep because of the amount of physical activity I had undertaken that evening, not that I regretted a second of it. I think I fell asleep with what Juanita would recognize as that big Cheshire Cat grin on my face.

40.
Wednesday, September 1

When I got to the office, my cell phone beeped with a message from Josh to call him back at my convenience. He must have left it for me before his usual office hours, so I waited until 10:00 to call him in the shop. He confirmed that my "chocolate" would be on Thursday's flight and that when I had the airway bill number (Dallas would call him with it), I should call Brinks and set up a time and place for delivery. He gave me a phone number and the name of a guy at Brinks to contact when the shipment had touched down. I took down his information and thanked him for his help.

Shortly after that, a guy on a sturdy bike arrived from a courier service with the box with three bottles, one of the two boxes Miguel had arranged to go on a little odyssey two days earlier. He asked for me, and I said I was the one he was looking for. I signed for it, and he made no remarks about anything unusual at all. An hour later, the other box, the one with two bottles, arrived with another guy on another bike. Same routine, "I have a delivery for Robert Packard," and after saying I was the intended recipient, please sign here, etc., etc. But before leaving, this guy remarked that he thought he had been shadowed by a big, black limousine for the last part of his trip and hoped he wasn't transporting anything illegal. Knowing where I had placed the notes to Stef, I said it was all part of a little game and I would be glad to show him what was going on. Before he could say, "Don't bother," I ripped open the box from the side where one would not see the note unless you took all the wrapping out. I pulled out the bottles of ginger ale and offered him one.

"I don't think the CIA would be overly excited to get involved with this particular brand of ginger ale, do you?" The delivery guy looked at them, shook his head, and agreed, "No, I guess not." I purposely said CIA, and not "the Mafia" so that the next time he saw the same limousine, he wouldn't panic and have an accident. This little exercise was most definitely not intended to cause any harm to some poor guy who was probably earning minimum wage and poisoning his lungs slowly in the street traffic of southern California in the process.

Still, this told me what I wanted to know. Stefano was, indeed, keeping an eye on me, and since I never got deliveries to my house, and the house was, as he had noticed, far too small to contain a vast wine cellar, deliveries at work were the most logical explanation of where I was receiving my rare wine bottles. As I was putting the wine from my basement into my car behind the closed door of my small garage, Stef and his pals never saw this happen.

Miguel stopped by that afternoon to say that he had put the second round of boxes of ginger ale on their merry way, for which I thanked him. He, in turn, gave me no more demonstrations of his expertise in "maa shalats," for which I was at least as grateful.

I took a break and went outside to call Tom Nakano to ask a favor. My bank balance was now around $500,000 and about to head northward again with some more sales to Aldo. I asked Tom to prepare $50,000 in cash for me on Friday and to keep it as quiet as possible. Tom explained that these days, in the era of debit cards and gold credit cards, that almost no one ever deposited or withdrew cash in that kind of amount. It would require two days to prepare, and even then, I'd have to fill out some kind of form, blah, blah. I said I would be happy to fill out whatever kind of form he wanted, and that the cash was a one-off special occasion. Tom remarked that it must be some kind of occasion. I assured him it was. I said that there was a special Labor Day charity thing I wanted to contribute to and make a big splash this way. He said that it should certainly do the trick. I wasn't completely lying. I knew someone who was making barely over the minimum wage who deserved a *lot* better.

Tom said he couldn't keep the request for an amount like $50,000 in cash a secret around the bank, but he didn't have to disclose who it was for until the account was actually debited. I said that, in that case, I would not make the actual withdrawal until the morning of Tuesday, September 7. I would make my charity pledge over the weekend, but not deliver the actual cash until Tuesday. Tom said that they usually didn't like to keep that kind of cash in the vault over a long holiday weekend, so he would arrange for the armored truck to make delivery first thing Tuesday morning. I thought about how I wanted to do this, and then asked our mailing department to prepare two sturdy, cardboard mailing boxes for me. One should be just big enough to pack about five or six paperback books in securely, but flat enough to fit inside my briefcase, and the other should be big enough to contain two boxes the size of the first box. I would pick them both up Friday afternoon. They said no problem, they would be ready. In the course of the years, I had often had to ship out books and documents in various sizes of boxes. Almost all of it had been either legal documents or books, and there was never a regular schedule for this kind of thing, so the shipping guys didn't give my request a second thought.

Juanita took time from her whirlwind activity of making my life easier to ask me when I would be leaving for my exotic vacation destination so she could plan to work the longer hours necessary to compensate for my absence. I had to be careful how I answered this. I couldn't very well tell her I was leaving next Tuesday evening without telling everyone else. Juanita is nothing if not efficient, and all I needed was for her to offer to arrange transportation for me to the airport of my choosing. That would have been slightly awkward, trying to explain to her that I didn't need a chauffeur-driven limousine to get me from my living room to my basement. Smart as she was, I doubt she would have been able to figure that one out, even if I had been willing to explain it to her, which I was not.

I told her it would be soon, but it was dependent on some transportation that was not regularly scheduled and had to be planned on relatively short notice, depending on availability. She looked at me like the kid in ET saying, "Gimme a break!" but just muttered, *"seguro,"* plus a few things that sounded like Cantonese expressions I was probably better off not understanding, and went on her merry way. She didn't like being lied to, and she was smart enough to know I was feeding her a line, which I had never done up to that point. It was obvious that it pissed her off, and I hated doing it. But telling her the truth, besides inviting disaster, would not have exactly earned me any more credibility, would it? I think the $300 I had given to pay Miguel for running my errands had bought me at least a week's postponement of a cross-examination along the lines of "OK, Señor Roberto, djoo gonna tell me wa's goin' on or not?" Submitted in writing, coming from Juanita, it would have read more like, "Very well, Mr. Packard, sir, would this be an appropriate moment for you to dispense with all pretense?" The gap between her erudite written English and the ethnic stereotype of her spoken English remained as wide as ever. With any luck, she would not threaten me with any in-depth demonstrations of her brother's command of "maa shalats" to get me to satisfy her curiosity.

41.

I avoided needing too much time alone with Juanita for the rest of the day and headed down to Beverly Hills and Aldo's shop on Rodeo. I sold him a big package—all fifteen bottles Philippe had sold me on Sunday, plus the last bottles from Thomas Jefferson that I had left (minus the 1787 Margaux, of course). It was an unusually large sale, just over half a million dollars. Aldo didn't haggle or even blink at the quantity. I asked him to divide the amount into two checks. He didn't even ask why, just did as I asked. When I had pocketed the two checks, I ceremoniously "informed" him that, as I had mentioned last Saturday, due to circumstances beyond my control, my stint as sole representative of the "secret" wine cellar would be over very soon, and that others would be delivering the rare bottles to him. I said I understood I was to receive a residual small commission, percentage to be determined, on each delivery. He just nodded, said, "Mmm-hmm," and acted about as surprised at the news as he might have been if I had told him that scientists had just discovered salt water in the Pacific Ocean. He might just as well have said, "Well, DUH, it's about time. Stefano doesn't do this strong-arm stuff for free, ya know." But he just said nothing, and I left it at that. He gave me one more small pat on the shoulder, like last Saturday, and a half-hearted wave goodbye, and I almost thought he had written me off then and there. He hadn't, of course, but he obviously thought all was going according to plan—*his* plan, *bien entendu.* One major regret of mine was that I would never find out his reaction to how well his plan had worked out for him. I had no sympathy for the expense of his having hired either Gordon Mercer or Stefano and his goons. Aldo had made millions off the bottles I had sold him, and had obviously whipped his moneyed clientele into a feeding frenzy for bottles from this incredible, unique cellar, for which he was (as far as his clients were concerned) the sole representative. They must have been frothing at the mouth for more. Froth away. Lassie was not coming home this time.

It was too late to deposit the checks with Tom Nakano at the bank, and I was not comfortable leaving this kind of amount in the night deposit drawer. This was definitely *not* the time to carelessly risk deposits of this magnitude being seen by Caro's friend, Wendy. I just took them home with me so I could bring them to Tom myself. I'd bring him one tomorrow, Thursday, and one more on Friday. I didn't want any one deposit to give the impression of a grand finale, especially now that this was exactly what was approaching. I had had checks for more than $300,000 before, even twice inside the space of a week, so two separate ones totaling $540,000 and change would not raise an eyebrow. I did want them to both have cleared by Tuesday, however, so the last one would go in on my way to work Friday.

I picked up some Thai chicken in red curry before heading home, and when there, changed into my 1860s clothes. I felt as if I knew how Clark Kent felt changing into Superman in a phone booth, now. But Anne was there waiting, so I would have dressed up as Big Bird if I had to. She smelled the Thai curry on me and asked what it was this time. When I told her, she said it smelled just as enchanting as the Vietnamese ginger I had had the night before. I coyly asked her if it would lead to a similar result, and she gave me a reasonable imitation of Mae West (not bad for someone who would never hear of Mae West), inviting me to come find out. I did, and it did.

Before getting dressed, we polished off the rest of the 1855 Lafite and I told her that next week I would bring a special bottle to celebrate my change of residence. I told her about Jefferson's last gift to me (to us, as I had told him about her) of the bottle of 1787 Margaux. She sniffed, and commented that Margaux was, after all, not Chateau Lafite. This bit of snobbery was *so* out of character for her that I looked at her for a second to see if she was being serious. She

218

kept her straight face for about three seconds before dissolving into peals of laughter, saying that the look on my face was worth her little act. She then assured me that it would be an honor to open a seventy-three-year-old/thirty-one-year-old bottle of Margaux to celebrate my permanent move, but on one condition. This was also not like her, but I wasn't going to fall for it twice in a row. I smiled and asked her what her condition was. She said I was not allowed to start in about whether or not I tasted raspberries or coffee while tasting it. I promised I would only comment about whether or not I tasted roses or azaleas. *"Je te tire les oreilles!"* (I'll pull off your ears!) she answered, giggling, and tugged at my ears to emphasize that she might not be joking, *"Ou bien quelque chose d'autre,"* (Or maybe something else,) she threatened, demonstrating, though mercifully gently. It was, after all, still a twenty-five-minute walk back to the portal, and that was *without* limping.

She then got more serious, and reminded me that when I came to stay with her, I would not be able to just run out and get Thai or Vietnamese food whenever I wanted. I reminded her that if I stayed in California in 2010, I wouldn't be able to reach out and touch her and hear her voice whenever I wanted either. That comment resulted in a wide smile on her part, and a half hour longer in the cabin than we had intended to stay. I didn't limp on the way back, but a half hour more in the cabin with Anne and I might not have been able to make that statement. I never met the guy who left her to go live in Spain, but I kept going back and forth between whether to erect a monument to his memory or to recommend that he be committed to the nearest loony bin.

The walk back to the portal was mostly in blissful silence, both of us just enjoying the touch of each other, the light buzz of the 1855 Lafite remnants slowly wearing off. When we got back to the portal, she pushed up against me and we whispered at the same time, *"Que six jours."* (Just six days.) She giggled and I smiled. I didn't even know if there was a French expression for "great minds think alike," but I'd teach her what it meant, and if there was no local expression, we'd make one up.

Back in the house, I came down from my high and settled back into my twenty-first-century reality mindset as best I could. Thursday had little on my work schedule, but I was running like a jet at full throttle, waiting on the runway for the pilot to release the brakes so it could take off. How I managed to get to sleep that night, I'll never know. For all I can remember, I didn't.

42.

Thursday, September 2

After a minimal stab at making myself breakfast, I showered, got dressed, and brought the first of Aldo's two checks to Tom Nakano at the bank. I called ahead to his private line, so he was expecting me. I didn't see Wendy, but she could have just been in the ladies' washroom for all I knew. Handing Tom the envelope, letting him peek inside, see the check and the deposit slip, and having him nod wordlessly, was not what you'd call a long, drawn-out process. I was out of there within two minutes.

Tom would make sure the deposit was duly recorded. If Naomi Roganov was somehow keeping an eye on my transactions, she would have noted my making the big checks out to Josh for the French gold coins, but also that deposits were flowing into the account with the same regularity as before, and if the pattern were to remain steady, I would be able to make my big estimated tax payment with no difficulty. As long as Wendy caught no whiff of what was going on with my account, she wouldn't be making any reports to Caro.

As Aldo was paying Stefano's bills, good old Stef wouldn't have even been informed about the checks. However, as I had, for all practical purposes, given Aldo my "notice," Stefano had to be aware that his "big introduction" was impending. I didn't know (yet) if this meant he would relax any close surveillance of me or intensify it. I figured it would be better to play it safe and assume the latter, which turned out to be correct. Maybe he thought there was a danger I'd try to pull a "fast one" and mess up his plans. If he did, *he* was correct, but there was no way he could have guessed to what extent. He may have been prepared for some intrigue, but he would have been thinking along the lines of Orson Welles, not H.G. Wells.

I made it into the office at around 9:00 and Juanita clearly hadn't forgiven me for not coming clean with her about my travel plans. She was somewhat less miffed about it, but while she was ten times smarter than I was, she didn't hide her emotions—either that or she wasn't even trying to. Even a "wise Latina" is still a Latina. Miguel was off making sure the two boxes sent off from courier services 1 and 2 got to services 3 and 4 and were forwarded on tomorrow to services 5 and 6. Tomorrow, he would go to service 5 to receive the box from service 3, and then to service 6 to receive the box from service 4, and then pay 5 and 6 to forward them on back to me—if they made it that far. The one cyclist had told me the day before about possibly being observed by a black limousine, and I was pretty sure Stef would not be driving around in a Subaru.

At 9:30, the personal secretary to Emmett Blake, Richard Brock's co-founder of the firm, told me that Mr. Blake needed to get to Frankfurt am Main, Germany, in a hurry, and I was to make sure he was on the next nonstop flight. Emmett Blake certainly looks the part of the senior partner. He is in his early sixties, about six-foot-three, trim, and has a shock of thick white hair, always impeccably combed. Except for the fact that his eyes were nondescript grey instead of the "piercing ice blue" these guys were always required to have in novels, he could have been the "representing counsel" in any one of a dozen law drama movies. He had met Richard Brock while they were students at the University of Pennsylvania Law School in Philadelphia in the 1970s. Richard Brock was a native of southern California. Emmett Blake was from North Carolina. After deciding to open a practice together, it didn't take long for them to settle on Brock's home turf and not Blake's. Blake never lost his Carolina drawl, but was able to temper it into something that sounded vaguely "aristocratic" and not hillbilly, which is what he reverted to on the rare occasion he was publicly seen to be upset or excited about something. This had happened fewer than ten times during the time I had worked there, and I didn't want this to be the eleventh.

I, of course, was saddled with the job of hounding Lufthansa about reserving a first-class seat for him on today's flight out of LAX. They were being difficult, as some other passenger was on the line with them at the same time for the same seat. As the other passenger was looking to buy his seat with frequent flyer miles, and I was trying to buy Mr. Blake's seat with cash, I won. Emmett Blake wanted to be able to enjoy his Labor Day with his family as much as anyone else, which meant that he *had* to be in Frankfurt in time to complete the firm's business there tomorrow, September 3, and get on the Saturday flight home, which had all first-class seats open. Lufthansa's flight 457 out of LAX left at 2:50 p.m. and got him into Frankfurt at 10:35 the next morning—plenty of time for him to make his noon appointment. I found the $14,000 plus airfare appalling, but if this was a big enough deal for Emmett Blake to be handling it personally, then the firm was being paid a fee that would be more than enough to cover the ticket out of the proceeds. A private, intercontinental jet would have cost at least five times that but, like I said, America's addiction to litigation had made us recession-proof. Had it been necessary to order a private plane, I would have done so. Maybe business wasn't going that well for the legal profession as a whole, but our firm still seemed to be very much in demand. Who said that nice guys always finish last? I had a fleeting thought, wondering about how good the sand business might be out in Elko, Nevada, and realized that I couldn't care less. I hoped that was a good sign. Emmett Blake's limo service picked him up at 10:45, in plenty of time for him to make his flight from LAX, even taking freeway traffic into account. He had brought a small suitcase, apparently having anticipated the trip.

The rushed departure of Emmett Blake, Esq., to the land of Riesling and Liebfraumilch was the only remarkable event of the day at work, other than my noticing a black limousine driving by the office at a slower speed than traffic would have normally dictated. I doubted that it was Tom Cruise scouting out locations for his next Mission Impossible film, as Sherman Oaks was somewhat less photogenic than the Na Pali Coast, or wherever it was he liked to shoot those movies. But besides Anne, there was no one I could go to in order to discuss my options, and so I did nothing. I wished I could have confided in Juanita, but that would have meant either convincing her that I had completely lost my mind or showing her the portals. Neither the rock nor the hard place was an option. If I had told her without showing her the portals, she would have had me committed to a mental institution out of pure loyalty to me, thinking this would be the only way to recover my sanity. If I had shown her the portals, I would have been putting her in danger just giving her the knowledge that they existed. If I had told her about Stef, she might well have had some friends who could have "intervened" in a forceful manner. However, if Stefano's people responded in kind or worse (not everyone is content to rely on "maa shalats"), some of Juanita's friends could get hurt, or maybe even killed, and that was one burden I refused to carry around with me for the rest of my life.

One thing I didn't quite understand was why Stefano hadn't yet called me or paid me a visit. Aldo had to have told him on Wednesday evening that I had made my final direct sale to him, and that could only mean (to him) that I was getting ready to acquiesce to Stefano's (i.e., Aldo's) demands to turn "the account" over to him. So how come Stef hadn't yet dropped by for a "friendly" chat? Or at least called? I could only think of one logical explanation. At our first "meeting," I had told him that the people supplying me with the rare wine had quite a security apparatus of their own and that they would cut us both off if he got too aggressive. He might well have been waiting to see if he could find out their identity all by himself, check out their security measures on his own, and thus know how much danger, if any, he would be in if he got too aggressive. Tempted as I was to run out and flag the limo down (I was positive he was inside behind those tinted windows), I decided to wait until tomorrow (I'm the decider, don'tcha know) and see if he would contact me on his own.

Emmett Blake called in just before his plane was to take off and said he had made the flight and that it was leaving on time. That constituted most of the excitement of that afternoon. When I slipped a personal letter of my own in the outgoing mail that day, no one even noticed, and it was sent along with the rest of the firm's mail. Considering all that was going on with me, I'm lucky no one noticed that I was a little on edge. Well—that is, with the exception of Juanita, who knew *something* was going on with me. She just didn't know *what*.

Josh called me on my cell phone to say that he had heard from Dallas that my French gold coins would be on the Swiss Air Lines flight from Zürich to LAX in the afternoon. The flight landed at 4:40 p.m., so the coins, while pre-cleared with U.S. Customs, would not be released until tomorrow. I said that was fine, that we would stick to a Tuesday delivery, and that Brinks should hold them at their secure facility until then. Josh assured me that he had already told them this, and that they would assess a $400 a day storage fee starting with Saturday (tomorrow, being the first day, was a freebie), but that they would deliver Tuesday with no additional charges, as these had been shared by him and his friends in Dallas. I said fine, and I brought him a check for $2500 on the way home that afternoon. This was more than the $1200 for three days of storage at $400 (Saturday, Sunday, Monday) I needed, but I included $500 more for the extra hour of security guarding I would want their delivery truck to provide on Tuesday, plus $800 for two extra days of storage in case any of my plans changed. Josh thought I was including more than would have been necessary, but I told him to keep the change if so. He said he wasn't *that* hard up for a tip, and that we'd find an equitable solution. Ah, so nice to do business with an honest man! He also reminded me that "keep the change" was a particularly appropriate expression to use on a coin dealer. I guess he had a point.

"What's the extra hour of security for?" Josh asked. "You can't need more than five or ten minutes to load those coins into a vault."

"Oh, nothing out of the ordinary. It's just so I can feel secure while I change clothes to my nineteenth century French attire, remove all 51,000 coins from their original packing and into something nondescript, post a blog of the last three months of my life on the internet, activate an apparatus to blow up my house and disappear forever into the year 1860 before the explosion" I thought.

"I just want to make sure I will have some armed protection so that no one decides to hold a gun to my head the second after a Brinks truck makes a big delivery to me," I told him.

Josh thought I was being overly cautious, but understood my apprehension at having so much value transferred to me, regardless of the location.

From California Coin, I headed home. I had some travel arrangements to make.

43.

For my dinner, I just made a sandwich from some leftover smoked salmon, some lemon juice, and some spicy creamed horseradish that was so strong, I'm sure it could have doubled as rocket fuel. I don't even remember what kind of bread I used, not that I would have tasted it through the horseradish anyway. It was time to start paying some serious attention to a few necessary details. I went down to the portal and Anne was there. I jumped over to her, and after a rather enthusiastic reception, I reminded her that next Tuesday I would need her to come with the sturdy horse-drawn cart I had mentioned earlier, and it should be capable of transporting four grown men. Although she hadn't indicated it would be a problem the last time I had mentioned it, I asked if she had access to such a vehicle and if she could drive one. She saw I was serious and repressed a laugh. She said that of course she had access to such a cart, and that every child over the age of ten knew how to drive one. But she was confused about one thing.

"Tu m'as dit que tu venais tout seul. Qui sont les autres trois personnes qui vont t'accompagner?" (You told me you were coming by yourself. Who are the other three persons coming with you?)

I smiled and assured her I was definitely coming alone, but would be bringing a little bit of baggage. She said that the way I had put it, it sounded like my baggage consisted of two uncles and a nephew. I said no, it was only a few essential belongings.

"Plus de trois cents kilogrammes de bricoles essentielles?" (More than 300 kilograms of essential stuff?) she asked with more than a little skepticism. I was rather reluctant to tell her before I absolutely had to about the gold. From what little I had been able to find out about the economy of her era, it represented a nearly unimaginable amount of wealth for one person to have unless he were old nobility

and his family controlled vast stretches of land. It also probably represented a danger from thieves, both amateur and professional, and I knew neither the personalities nor the rules here. I hadn't checked, but renting a large safety deposit box in the local branch of Crédit Lyonnais didn't seem like a possibility. The local constabulary, for all I knew, might represent a greater threat than the bad guys. Since the gold could probably not be stored very safely, it would have to be stored very quietly. If Anne couldn't keep her mouth shut, we would both be in danger.

I tried to be as unspecific as I could. I told her I would be coming with *"toute ma fortune."* (all my wealth.) This was not entirely true, as I would leave behind a plot of land worth a few hundred thousand (maybe even a bit of house left on it—that's for posterity to know), plus close to a $100,000 in my bank account for the IRS and Caro to fight over. I didn't care. Put Naomi Roganov and Caro in a room and let the fur fly. There was about $1.15 million in the account now. I had already told Tom Nakano to have $50,000 in cash for me Tuesday morning, so that would leave $1.1 million, give or take some small change in accrued interest. As I had no time to order more French gold from Josh, and didn't want to start making waves with other dealers at this late date, I just made plans that I deemed fitting. "Fitting" to me meant sending a check for $1 million as a contribution to the American Cancer Society. That was the letter I had sent out from the office that afternoon. I hadn't told Tom Nakano about this one, but my signature was genuine, the September 2 postmark, too, and the bank would have no legal reason to refuse to pay it. I had sent it to their address on Wilshire Boulevard in Los Angeles, so with any luck, it would get deposited tomorrow, Friday, and clear by next Tuesday or next Wednesday at the latest.

Anne had no clue about the American Cancer Society, of course. She was still concerned with how in the world *"toute ma fortune"* could possibly weigh as much as 300 kilograms. Even if I had been talking about 300 kilos in silver 5 franc coins *("écus"),* it would already be 50,000 francs, a sum more than sufficient to make a simple vineyard worker wealthy in the eyes of his peers. A million francs would be beyond the scope of the imagination of most of the Boudreau family's peers, and I had to be very careful to break this to the right people at the right time. I wasn't worried about Anne, but she had a big family, and I only really had gotten to know her father, Philippe, to any extent. It would have been sufficient for just one of her relatives to have a bad apple in his circle of friends to cause my whole plan to fall apart as soon as I was there with no way to return. I impressed upon Anne that she was to keep this a secret—as tightly as the story of who I was and how I came to be there. She appeared to understand the need for keeping her lips sealed. She said she would tell her family that she would be needing the horse and cart just to help me bring a few things that were too bulky to carry, and she was sure that would suffice to get her the use of the cart without having anyone else insist on helping us out with the move. She told me she had asked her father for a little money to get me a second set of contemporary clothes, and that he had been immediately forthcoming with the necessary few francs. It seemed to both of us that Philippe was trying to remit back to me some of the money he felt he had been overcharging for the wine bottles since we met. If he only knew!! I told Anne to let him continue to think this way until I was there for good and could inform him to what extent his help had been to, well, us.

It was getting late, and Anne told me that the cabin was *"reservée"* by someone else this evening, so we wouldn't have had its use even if we had wanted to. She asked if I was *"très déçu,"* (very disappointed,) and I told her not at all, that I hoped we'd have the rest of our lives to make up for the lost time. She looked up at me, put her hand on my cheek, and said, *"Tu es plus sage qu'on penserait, tu sais?"*

(You are smarter than one might think, you know?) I thought I had made enough mistakes in my life to able to answer that with a firm negative, but it wasn't the answer she was looking for. In fact, I don't think she was looking for an answer at all. I just kissed her hand and kept smiling at her very, *very* beautiful face. I could forego flat screen plasma TVs forever as long as I had her to look at for the rest of my life, no sweat.

We went over the details for Tuesday evening again: the horse-drawn cart, the additional set of clothes, and Anne said that we would have a room for ourselves—*"un peu modeste,"* she apologized, but I would be able to buy us some fancier digs soon enough if all went well. I think she had figured that out by now, especially when I wasn't all bothered by that particular revelation. All Brinks had to do would be to deliver my shipment and guard the house safely long enough for me to get the gold down to the basement, through the portal, and loaded onto the horse-drawn cart, and then I could take the final steps to ensure my—no, *our*—safety from Aldo/Stef, Naomi Roganov/the IRS, and Stan Chase/Caro. Then Anne and I could ride peacefully off into the sunset. Ha! Depending on the hour and the weather, maybe even literally. But that won't be part of my story. If I make it that far, I won't be in a position to post about whether it goes down that way or not. Use your imagination, how about that? Come to think of it, if you've read this far, you've been doing more than a little of that already.

We parted in our usual fashion—i.e., with great difficulty and a lot of affectionate touching that I don't need to describe in any more detail than I have for the past two nights. I slept a lot more peacefully Thursday night than I had in a while. "Sweet dreams are made of this, who am I to disagree?" Sing on, Annie…

44.
Friday, September 3

After another minimalist breakfast, on the way to the firm I deposited the last of Aldo's checks with Tom Nakano. He noted me stealing furtive looks around the office, and asked if I was expecting an attack from Taliban suicide bombers that morning or something? I shook my head and said that I was merely hoping not to run into Wendy Etxeverría. Tom laughed and said I could drop my counter-espionage moves, as Wendy had taken yesterday and today off for an extended long weekend at her parents' home in Nevada, and that she had driven up there with another girlfriend from the Elko area early Thursday morning, as they anticipated an eleven-hour drive. That had to have meant Caro, which meant she wasn't having long strategy sessions with Stan Chase prior to our planned meeting next Wednesday. She could always spend Tuesday with him, but that would be fine with me. They wouldn't be planning anything drastic until the meeting, and that would, all going as planned, be none of my concern. I felt a little foolish, acting like I was paranoid about running into my wife's friend, but any report from Wendy that might have spooked Caro into getting Stan Chase to ask for my account to be frozen would have been uncomfortable, although no longer fatal, to my plans. Any subpoenas or injunctions would be forthcoming on Wednesday at the earliest. The withdrawals that were most vital to my plans had already taken place, although the $50,000 cash "charity" donation and the $1 million to the American Cancer Society were nonetheless transactions I very much wanted to go through.

Relieved at the news that I didn't have to hide from Wendy that day, I stayed to chat with Tom for a few minutes. He said that he had ordered the cash yesterday and that it would be ready for me first thing Tuesday morning. That is when I would have to look out for Wendy, as she would be back then, but even if she saw me there, anything she told Caro would just be relayed to Stan Chase that day and be filed for shoving in my face during the Wednesday meeting. Even if Caro were to hear of the $50,000 cash withdrawal, she would figure me for such a nerd that she would have a field day the next day watching me squirm in my chair trying to explain it. I had spent so much of my life being an open book and a nerd that she would never figure me for having some great master plan in mind. Indeed, my not having any kind of a plan at all was one of the things she most faulted me for. *"Si seulement tu savais, ma chérie."* (If only you knew, my dear.) But she didn't know. She didn't even know enough French to have understood what I just wrote.

Tom told me he would try to make the cash withdrawal as discreet as possible, getting the necessary forms ready that afternoon, so all I had to do was spend a minimal amount of time in the bank Tuesday morning. He said he also would have the cash brought to his office for counting, so that I would not have to take delivery at the teller, where everybody and his brother (and Wendy) could watch me. I should be out of the bank by 9:00 a.m. at the latest, and that suited me just fine. I wanted to be done with the office a little early on Tuesday, and the office would surely have plenty of tasks for me, being the first full day of work after a long holiday weekend.

I thanked Tom again for all his help and he wished me a good Labor Day weekend. I wished him the same and left for the office.

I got to the office at about 9:15, and Miguel was already there waiting for me. I told him it was too early to set off to courier services 5 and 6, but he said he had some errands to run for Juanita as well, so he would attend to them first. I didn't have the faintest idea what Juanita would be sending her brother off to do, but figured there were plenty of Guatemalteca things that I would never understand, me being a dumb Anglo and all. All I cared about was his little errands for me, and work was filled with so many little pre-holiday things that I hardly even noticed the clock stealthily creeping up on 11:00. Miguel materialized out of nowhere and told me he was setting off to arrange for courier services 5 and 6 to receive the packages of ginger ale from services 3 and 4, and pay for immediate, same-day service to me back at the firm. His appointments were nearly an hour apart, one at high noon at service 5 and the other at 12:45 at service 6.

At noon, Miguel called me on his cell phone from service 5 to tell me that he had received the package from service 3, had paid for the delivery to me at the firm, when two big, unsmiling (*"Caras muy serias, ¿sabes?"*) guys in sunglasses muscled their way into the small courier service shop just as the bicyclist was leaving with my package and looked after him in frustration. I told Miguel to make his way to courier service 6 very slowly, so as to give the guys in sunglasses a chance to show if they were following him or not. He said no problem. At 12:50, he called me again and said that the two Mafiosi (even Miguel was now calling them that) had showed up again at service 6 and told him that they would be delivering the package to me themselves and that he should just pay the courier service and get lost. He told me he remembered what I had told him about not offering too much resistance. He said that he had knocked one of them to the ground, half unconscious, but let the other one pull a gun on him and take the package, then drag his companion back to a waiting black limousine. He said the one with the gun was really slow and that he could have knocked them both unconscious and broken their arms to boot before they had known what hit them. I told him, no, thank goodness he didn't do that (or have to!). I thanked him for having done exactly as I had asked. Courier service 6 was not happy (I'm rather confident Miguel was understating their reaction) about the incident and requested that both Miguel and Stefano's two goons please use another courier service in the future. I told Miguel to leave them the delivery fee and then tell them that their request would certainly be granted.

45.

Before the bicyclist from courier service 5 had even arrived at the office, I got the expected call from Stefano, who had read my note nestled in with the bottles of ginger ale.

"Hi Bob," he started in, voice almost friendly. "Nice to see that you have retained a semblance of a sense of humor. Your Bruce Lee clone was quite a touch. So was the ginger ale."

I adopted an equally friendly tone. "Hey, I thought you guys might be thirsty. Now, look, first off, the Bruce Lee clone is not mine. I've been told he has a black belt in three disciplines, and if his employers had ordered him to do so, he would have left your two guys as corpses without a second thought—and been back home in Hong Kong in time for a Kung Pao chicken dinner tomorrow night," I answered in as good-natured a voice as I could muster. I was rather furious that one of his goons had pulled a gun on Juanita's brother, which had brought our little adversarial relationship to a new level. "Furthermore, Stef, you didn't exactly leave me a P.O. box or a cell phone number, so I really didn't have another sure way of contacting you, did I?"

"No, you didn't," he admitted, seeming a little surprised that I appeared to be the one wanting to contact him, and not the other way around. "But I wasn't expecting you to be looking for a way to get in touch with me. Frankly, I was expecting you to be doing your level best to avoid us. OK, so you have my attention. I take it you have some news for me?"

"I do and I don't," I replied in a neutral tone.

"What the hell is that supposed to mean?" he asked with undisguised irritation. "Do you have the meeting set up or not? And if not, why not? I was led to believe that you had everything lined up for the transfer."

Led to believe? He didn't hear *that* on the eleven o'clock news. He must have been talking with Aldo every hour if he knew that. Aldo is the only one to whom I had ever said anything like that, and the biggest reaction Aldo had shown was to give me a token pat on the shoulder. Stefano was practically confirming to me who was paying his bill, not that I had ever suspected anyone else.

"I *did* have it all lined up," I lied.

"So what's the impediment?" he inquired impatiently. "Impediment," eh? Wow, four-syllable words from a Mafia enforcer. Their education budget must be flush these days, and here we all thought there was a recession on.

"The impediment, as you so aptly described it, is you," I stated, some irritation carefully creeping into my tone (convincingly, I hoped).

"How have I been impeding anything?" he shot back. "Up to today, all I have been doing is observation and surveillance."

"The problem is that you haven't been doing it very discreetly," I answered.

"You haven't noticed a thing!" Stefano barked. He was guessing, and mostly correctly, but still guessing, and I wasn't about to let him regain his balance. Doubt had been inserted and I was going to drive the blade in a little deeper.

"It's like I spelled out in the note with the ginger ale," I told him. "You're right, *I* hadn't noticed anything. But my contacts noticed everything, right down to your license plate number." I read it off to him. "Nevada plates. That's you, right? Who do you think the Bruce Lee clone works for, anyway? Me? Do you know what it costs to fly guys like that in here?" Was I good or not? Miguel had told me their license plate number not fifteen minutes ago. Miguel's Asian features and expertise in "maa shalats" had been enough to convince Stef and friends that he was Chinese. As always, let your adversaries make erroneous assumptions and then let them convince themselves that their assumptions are correct. They are always less dangerous that way, and I certainly didn't want anyone gunning for Miguel on my account. I sure didn't want them gunning for me, either. At least, if they hadn't the slightest clue that Miguel was from Guatemala, they would never look for him there.

Stefano came back, "I couldn't care less what his air fare cost, and you can thank me now for not having him shot. The same goes for you, by the way. If my guys had gotten seriously hurt, I might not be in such a charitable mood. And anyway, if Chop Suey wasn't yours, then whose is he?"

"Ling is nobody's," I told him, as if I had known "Ling" for years. "However, in this case, he was temporarily working for the owners of the wine cellar, who already called me about your little confrontation. Oh, and you'd probably be interested to know that Ling told the people who hired him that your guys were so slow, he could easily have broken both their necks before they could have gotten their guns into firing position, so I think everybody's even in the charitable mood department."

Stef was revealing his true professional ethics here. I had to tread carefully. A bullet in my leg, my shoulder or my heart could seriously delay my schedule. Witty remarks were starting to look inadequate as a viable defense. I adopted a more serious tone.

"I told you when we first met that the cellar's owners were very old, discreet money and had connections and means far beyond anything you or I could imagine," I continued. "They trust me, but they apparently had been keeping an eye on me anyway. I didn't know that, but because of you, they have decided to inform me and you have just confirmed it. Keeping an eye on me necessarily meant keeping an eye on you as well, if you have been following me around. Their eye on both of us is what led to this whole episode. I told you in the beginning that if you kept too close, that you would spook them and put the sale of their wine in serious danger. Congratulations, you have now done exactly that. They were some kind of pissed that I had attracted the kind of attention that got me a shadow, and that was you. They had offered me this account with the proviso of complete discretion. Your shadowing of me means to them that discretion has somehow been compromised. They know who you are, probably to a greater degree than they have told me, which is just about nothing, and that you have been shadowing me. So you tell me now, how am I supposed to introduce you to them as strangers and be convincing?"

"You mean to tell me that they have had someone shadowing *me* all this time?" asked Stefano. "Sorry, I doubt that."

"Doubt it all you want," I told him, "but you know full well that a guy like Ling costs more for a week's work than I make in two years." (At least I *hoped* he knew that. I sure didn't.) "Besides, they weren't specifically following *you* until *you* started following me. Before that, there was some guy named Mercer, but he apparently pulled out before the family decided to do anything about it." Stef might not have known this, but Aldo would confirm it, and thereby enhance my credibility. "I suggest you have a back-up team of two or three guys, all of whom know a lot—like a *whole* lot—about wine, and train them to be the 'new' go-betweens that I'll be introducing to the family. You and your present two pals have been made. You wouldn't get a bottle of Perrier out of these people, and that's assuming you had enough firepower to make it past their front door in the first place."

"Get off it," he said, confidence nonetheless eroding from his tone. "You haven't been anywhere near a place like that since I met you."

I laughed. "Stef, I haven't been anywhere near their place for two years! They deal through me precisely because no one has seen us together in ages. Why do you think I couldn't just invite you over for tea and crumpets the first time you introduced yourself? My showing up uninvited at their residence would automatically terminate my participation in this little business arrangement, and therefore, yours as well. This isn't old money as in Lucky Luciano. This is old money as in Charles Louis de Bourbon, if the name means anything to you."

Surprisingly, it did. "Yeah? Well Old King Louie XVI got his head chopped off, as I recall." My, my. Not just four-syllable words, but history, too. Stef must have been in the top ten of his class at Thug U.

"That's true," I replied, "but he wasn't exactly the only one in the Bourbon family, and others had seen the writing on the wall way before he got amputated at the neck. As you now know, they've been very good at watching out for their own ever since."

"Uh-huh," Stef rejoined, not thoroughly convinced, but definitely not as cocky as he was at the beginning of the conversation, either.

"By the way," I continued, "when they called with your license plate, they told me to ask you something."

"Oh? And what's that?"

I couldn't resist. "They told me to ask you if you seriously thought they would be sending me $50,000 bottles of 150 year old wine through the streets of Sherman Oaks by bicycle in a cardboard box?"

Gotcha! A moment's pause, and in a voice somewhat more subdued, he said, "OK, OK, look, this is a holiday weekend. I guess nothing will be shaking from now until the middle of next week, so I can ease up. I gotta make some phone calls and I'll get back to you after the long weekend."

"That works for me," I answered. "You know where I'll be, anyway."

"Yup," said Stefano. "Make sure you don't forget that," and he hung up.

He had lied his head off, of course. He wasn't going to lighten up his surveillance of me, whether he thought he was being watched or not. He might, however, take a little extra time to occasionally look over his shoulder and see if he could detect who was watching him. Probably not much, as he'd come up empty every time. Anyway, that was Aldo's call. Aldo was paying the bills, after all. They'd have a hard time placing "Ling" in all this, but outside of that, I very much doubted that Aldo would call off Stef and his pals unless some of them started disappearing without a trace, and that was not in my repertoire. Even so, "Ling's" appearance had shown them that something was going on that they had neither observed nor expected, and over which they had no control. I was pretty sure I had unsettled them enough to relax their chokehold-like close surveillance of me for a day or two. They might spend a little extra time looking over their own shoulders, and this would give me enough breathing room to make my final preparations. Or so I thought, anyway. Of course, after the phone call with Stef, I now had to consider getting shot by him or one his pals as a constant threat. Maybe at first just in the leg, so

I would still be alive to give Stef what he wanted, but that would be enough to ruin my day, not to mention my schedule. Wonderful.

That afternoon, I got my two cardboard boxes from shipping. They were flat and collapsed, but could be snapped into shape in a matter of seconds. I put them behind my desk with my briefcase. It was important I not forget them when I left for home over the weekend. I got enough wrapping tape for the small box as well. These I put into my briefcase. Emmett Blake left a message from Frankfurt that all had gone well and that the quick trip to Germany had been time wisely invested. I was not privy to all the high-brow projects the firm was working on, but if one of the senior partners had thought it necessary to go to Germany for a day, then it was probably to help broker the sale of the state of Bavaria to the Disney Corporation or some such momentous deal. Our senior partners did not run off to Europe for a day to sample the beer at Oktoberfest.

I called Josh at California Coin to ask if he had any more specifics from Brinks for me. He said he did and asked if I had a few minutes. I said that frankly, I didn't right then, but could swing by his shop on the way home. He said that worked for him. I wanted to do as much work as I could, in order to leave as few loose ends as possible for—and, especially, after—Tuesday. I got busy with so many menial tasks that Juanita remarked that I was trying to put her out of a job. I said the situation was quite the opposite—that I didn't want her to have too much of a job when I went on vacation. She gave me a stern look.

"Señor Roberto, djoo ebber fine me sane I got too moch work?"

I had to smile at that one. "Juanita, I have never heard you say anything of the sort. If the firm had discovered you before I did, I'd be sweating in a T-shirt somewhere, asking people how they want to have it their way at a Burger King."

Now she had to smile, too. "Dats right, an' doan djoo forget it eeder!" Juanita would always remain a phenomenon in my memory. As an example, I got a written note from her earlier today: "Fire marshal desires building inspection at some point. To what end, I cannot fathom, as our inspection is current, but they are irritatingly persistent, and demand we acquiesce to an appointment during business hours. Please advise." I swear, this is from the same woman who just told me, "Doan djoo forget it eeder!" When she had gone off to attend to other duties, I smiled to myself as I printed out her home address from my computerized roster of the firm's employees. Almost no one was privy to this information, but as I had to make up reports and employee lists for the senior partners, I had access to everyone's home address and phone number.

46.

I transformed a take-out chicken, tomato and green pesto sandwich into lunch and booked Emmett Blake's limousine to pick him up from LAX when he returned from Frankfurt the next day. The major issues of my "department" being resolved, and with most of the firm leaving work early for the long holiday weekend, I finished everything I was working on, packed my briefcase, grabbed what would become my two sturdy cardboard boxes, and headed to California Coin. Traffic was, as expected, horrendous, and I was glad not to be fighting the holiday traffic down to Aldo's store in Beverly Hills on a Friday afternoon.

After a brief stop at a post office to pick up a generic mailing label, I pulled into the now-familiar parking lot and walked into California Coin. Josh was assisting a few collectors when I got there, but they knew what they wanted and were gone within fifteen minutes—two of them happy, one disappointed. The disappointed one was grumbling under his breath.

"What was his problem?" I asked, immediately realizing I probably would not understand the answer.

"Oh, him," Josh laughed. "He wanted to look through all my 1916 nickels and was a little miffed that I was not an idiot."

"OK, I don't understand, but it sounds like a fun story," I said. "Enlighten me."

Josh explained, "There's a rare variety of 1916 Indian head nickel where the date is doubled, and you can clearly see the second date under the first one. It's called a 'double die.' It is pretty rare and is worth thousands of dollars if you can find one in decent shape. Some people think that out here in the boonies, if you consider this to be the boonies, some coin dealers might not know that and would sell one of these things for the price of a normal 1916 nickel, which would be less than $15. He did not find one in my modest stock of 1916 nickels. To add insult to injury, he saw that I *did* have one of the rare variety priced at $6500. When he saw that, he made up some lame excuse and took off. I get that all the time—occupational hazard. Most people who come in here either know what they want and expect me to have a professional's knowledge to help them out, or, like you, come in as novices and have no problem telling me they are novices and letting me guide them. But every now and then you get someone whose only motive is greed and think I'm today's easy mark. Those are the ones who leave in a foul mood, finding that I'm not the idiot they expected to find, just because I don't have a storefront on Wilshire Boulevard."

"Or Rodeo Drive," I added, half to myself.

"Or Rodeo Drive," he agreed. "But location isn't always a guarantee you'll get the best deals. There was a woman in here just yesterday, must have been around eighty years old but sharp as a tack, with this amazing collection she said she inherited from some ancestor in Europe. There were six different New England shillings, several 1796 half dollars and quarters, 1793 chain and liberty cap cents, 1802 half dimes, *five* 1794 silver dollars, just amazing stuff, almost all of it in high grade, too." He stopped and looked at my blank face. "You have no idea what I'm talking about, do you?"

"Afraid not," I admitted. I remembered that some cents of 1793 were worth a lot, having seen one that looked pretty beat up priced at $10,000 in his shop a couple of months ago, but that was about it. I hadn't studied that Red Book thoroughly enough. My bad.

"Well," he went on, "she had about 150 coins, mostly U.S., but some rare Thai coins as well. They were housed in an ornate old coin cabinet that must have been over 100 years old, and the collection must have been worth somewhere between $20 and $25 million. She seemed to know it, too. What's weird is that she hadn't gone to any of the big guys with her collection, but came right to me, left it with me for a detailed evaluation. She said that if her collection was to be auctioned off, it was to go to 'those guys in Dallas who sold the $4 million nickel.' She insisted upon that, as if they had done her some big favor in the past, but that I was to act as her broker, and she was cool with my earning an honest fee for doing it. I had never seen her before in my life and have no clue as to how she came across my name or my address. Yet here she was, tossing maybe a half million-dollar commission my way. Maybe she liked my ad in the yellow pages or something.

"Anyway, here's what I wanted to talk to you about. Brinks now has possession of your shipment from Switzerland. They'll be charging you the $400 a day for storage starting tomorrow, and the fact that Monday's a holiday is your tough luck. Therefore, it'll run you $400 times three for tomorrow, Sunday and Monday, since today's a freebie, remember. As delivery is being made on Tuesday, they won't be charging you for storage for Tuesday, so you're only down $1200 for storage. When you state the place and time of delivery, they allow half an hour for unloading. There are twenty sacks with 2500 coins each, plus one small sack with the last 1000 coins. Half an hour should be plenty, but you said you wanted them for an extra hour after delivery. They said they don't usually do that, but as long as it's late in the day and they have no other rounds to make after yours, they would have their guys stick around an extra hour for $500. I said that was OK, as I had to say yes or no on the spot. Is that all right with you?"

I said it was perfect, and the extra hour was costing exactly what I had figured they'd ask (hey, I'm not head of Security and Logistics for nothing). "You did absolutely the right thing—thanks."

He continued, "OK, but that still means you overpaid me by $800 for the Brinks expenses. Do you want me to write you a check for the difference?"

I thought for a second. I had already let him make $255,000 off of me for ordering the gold coins from his friends in Dallas. It might seem suspicious if I was so nonchalant that I was willing to blow off an $800 refund on a $2500 check. I had an inspiration.

"Tell you what, do you have any more French 10 franc coins?"

"There's an idea," he admitted. "Ever since you started buying those things on a regular basis, I always ordered a few more from the guys in Dallas so I wouldn't get caught short if you came in needing more than anticipated. Any chance you could use some silver five franc coins as well?"

I hadn't thought about this. "How much do they run?" I asked.

"They're about $25 apiece for Louis Philippe head. I could give you six 10 franc coins at $120, three five franc coins for $75, and I'll toss in a mixture of one franc and half franc coins of that era to more than make up the extra $5. Would that be OK?"

I thought for a moment. Louis Philippe. That meant dates between 1830 and 1848. Perfect! But wait: if four five franc coins, making twenty francs, cost only $100, why did I just buy all those 20 franc coins in gold at more than double that?

I said it would be OK, but how come four five franc silver coins cost $100 when one 20 franc gold coin cost $245? Josh explained that the silver coins, despite their low cost, were far more difficult to get in quantity than the gold. Banks didn't stock them, and so it would be a struggle to assemble five hundred pieces in a month, let alone fifty thousand of them in a week.

"Ah, got it," I said. "You've got a deal, then."

"Great." He smiled. "I'll put that together right now. It shouldn't take me more than ten minutes to find the silver coins and write them up."

While he was busy doing that, I looked through some of the auction catalogues and literature he had lying around the shop. It would probably be my last time, I suddenly realized. It looked like a really fun hobby and one that really spanned the gamut—from little albums for kids starting out all the way up to $3.74 million nickels like the one sold by Josh's friends in Dallas. Maybe I'd get into it with some of my spare funds when I was with Anne. I could study that Red Book that Josh had given me, and possibly be able to find some coins destined to be future mega-expensive rarities. Only I would know, of course, but it could be fun, and I'd certainly be able to afford it. In leafing through some of the catalogues Josh had, I noticed that an American named Virgil Brand had been collecting American and foreign coins around the turn of the twentieth century. Coins he had bought for $10 were selling ninety years later for $10,000 and more, sometimes a lot more. Maybe I could scour France, England and Europe for cheap, old American coins that were destined to be worth a fortune and leave them to *my* descendants to be sold starting in 2010, like Josh's visitor yesterday. Just a thought, anyway. A guy should have a hobby, right?

This train of thought was interrupted when Josh came back with my $800 worth of French coins.

"That should make us even," he said.

"Looks good to me, thanks!"

"Pleasure's all mine," he said. "I wish all my novices turned out like you have. Don't forget to get that fax to Brinks by Monday night."

"I won't. I'll be leaving for a vacation soon, so if I don't see you beforehand, thanks for all your help. If I know anyone in need of coin expertise, I'll be sure to send them your way."

He stuck out his hand. "I definitely appreciate it, Bob. Have a wonderful trip."

I took his hand and said, "I certainly hope to!"

47.

I started on my way home from there. I had two stops to make.
I didn't know if Stef was on top of me or not, but at this point,
his following me around, as long as he didn't enter my basement,
would make him no wiser. As my house was far too small to have
a vast wine cellar, and he himself had said it at our first meeting,
I wasn't overly worried about that. I don't know if he swallowed my
story about my not having visited the mysterious vast estate owned
by nebulous French aristocracy in two years, but, as he had told
me himself, I had obviously not been to any such place since he had
been tailing me, and that's what he cared about.

My first stop was at the garden center, and my request was a
little unusual, even for them. What I wanted was a supply of small
burlap or jute bags, twenty-one of them to be exact. They didn't
stock them as a rule, but they regularly got in plants and small trees
packed in earth kept in place by burlap bags, and instead of tossing
them away, they sometimes kept them around in case someone had
a use for them. The woman that I had asked said that if I could wait
ten minutes, she would run to the storage area and see if there were
any such bags that were slated for discarding. Sure enough, about ten
minutes later, she came back with twenty-five small burlap bags and
an equal number of small ropes with which to tie them shut—more
than enough for me. I asked her how much I owed her. She
remembered me from when I had bought the ammonium nitrate and
said there was no charge, as I had saved them the trouble of disposing
of them. I crammed them into a large nondescript shopping bag she
gave me, thanked her profusely, and gave myself a proverbial pat
on the back for the idea of the burlap bags. The gold coins might
arrive from Switzerland in canvas bags, like they use at banks today
to transport coins, with the name of some Swiss bank stenciled
on them. I didn't even know if all Swiss banks had been founded

by 1860, and I didn't intend to have such anomalies accompany me on Tuesday night.

On the way out of the garden center, while stopped at a traffic light, my car got an almost imperceptible bump from the car behind me. I turned around to see who the careless driver was. Oops. Not so careless. It was a black limousine with tinted windows. When the light changed, the limo speeded up and passed me with a hand waving to me from an opened tinted window as it turned a corner. I wondered if I should look for shops that sold bullet-proof vests.

Trying, with limited success, to forget my little traffic mishap, I stopped at the Vietnamese place again for another round of ginger chicken, brought it home, and ate it at an atypically unhurried pace. I changed into my "costume," as I was beginning to call Anne's set of contemporary clothes for me, put my extra $800 worth of French coins from Josh into a small paper bag, and crossed over to Anne, who was waiting. She smelled the ginger again.

"C'est connu en France, mais on ne l'utilise pas dans la cuisine d'habitude," (It's known in France, but we don't usually use it to cook with,) she explained.

"Vous l'utilisez pour quoi, alors?" (Well, then what *do* you use it for?) I asked.

She blushed, and said softly, *"Toi et moi, nous n'avons pas besoin du gingembre pour ce but en tout cas."* (You and I don't need any ginger for that purpose, in any case.)

An aphrodisiac! This great tasting stuff, and they think its best use is as an aphrodisiac? That got a laugh out of me. I told her that maybe they could learn a thing or two from the Vietnamese. She sniffed again, up close. *"Peut-être bien,"* (Maybe so,) she commented. Of course, if she was to swoon like this every time she smelled ginger on my breath, maybe its reputation as an aphrodisiac wasn't so overblown after all. I'd have plenty of time to find out. I was still looking forward to getting a chance to sample about fifty years' worth of Châteaux Lafite, Margaux, Latour, and all their little neighbors. If I got to munch on some ginger chicken, 1860 Bordeaux style, in the meantime, well, so much the better. Man does not live by vintage reds alone (although I wouldn't bet on my trying to live without them either). Come to think of it, I had never asked what she had for dinner, so I did. She said just a little bread with some marmalade and some cheese. That sounded rather modest, and I was about to say so until I remembered—this is France, hello? They eat their big meal at midday, not in the evening.

I got out the little bag of coins I had gotten from Josh for my last $800. She looked at the three five franc coins of 1847 and 1848. *"Ces pièces trainent encore en quantité dans l'année 2010?"* (These coins are still around in quantity in the year 2010?) she marveled.

"À ce qu'il semble," (It appears so,) I replied. *"En tout cas, elles n'ont pas coûté cher."* (At any rate, they weren't very expensive.)

"Cinq francs, c'est déjà cher," (Five francs is already expensive,) she commented. Wow, if five francs was real money to her, wait 'til she found out I was coming with a million francs. When she saw what the 325 kilograms of my baggage consisted of, her head would spin. But not to the tune of the song "Money Makes the World Go Around" from "Cabaret." There are light years between Anne and Caro, and not just in terms of the fourth dimension. Caro comes from a world where your worth as a person is measured in numerical terms. Anne comes from a world where your character is your wealth, as material wealth was always something "others" had. Her social strata never got rich and, therefore, she never expected to, never aspired to it, never was jealous of anyone else. Her (our) net worth was about to experience a modest upward adjustment.

I had no idea yet how I was going to explain it to her, and I'd have to be somewhat discreet or I'd attract enough attention for the history books. Plus, having people hate us out of jealousy is something I would try very hard to avoid.

"On m'a filé quelques pièces pour me rembourser une dette," (Someone gave me these coins to repay a debt,) I told her, and poured out the rest of the contents of the little paper bag. There were six gold 10 franc coins of Napoleon III, plus two worn silver one franc coins and three silver half franc coins of Louis Philippe. I had just handed her the three five franc coins, so this meant seventy-eight francs and fifty centimes. Her eyes went wide. This wasn't in payment for anything, after all—just some pocket change.

"Soixante-dix-huit francs et cinquante centimes! C'est un mois de salaire, même plus!" (Seventy-eight francs and 50 centimes! That's a month's salary, more even!)

OK, not *just* some pocket change. That gave me a basis to do some quick mental calculation. If sixty francs was a month's salary, then a year's salary, even with a small bonus at the end, would be less than 800 francs. Fifty years of a vineyard worker's salary would, thus, be less than 40,000 francs, and I would be bringing twenty-five times that much with me. I might not be nineteenth century France's John D. Rockefeller, but we would not be facing budgetary shortfalls by any means. Moreover, while I had every intention of following Thomas Jefferson's advice to not make a name for myself, by the same token I did not intend to sit on my derrière for fifty years and drink Bordeaux wines until gout set in or my liver gave its two weeks' notice.

If purchasing power was a measure, and one figured that a poorly paid worker in my day made $2000 a month, then I had just poured out the equivalent (to Anne) of $2500 in 2010 cash into her hand out of a small paper bag. But she was the one who was going to impress me.

She looked at the money, and opened my hand and gave it back. *"J'espère que tu sais quoi faire avec une petite fortune comme ça."* (I hope you know what to do with a small fortune like that.)

I grinned and put it back in her hand. *"Je ne sais pas ce que l'on peut faire chez toi avec une somme pareille. J'espérais que tu allais m'expliquer."* (I have no idea what one does in your world with a sum like that. I was hoping you'd lay it out for me.)

She started to protest, but I insisted and told her that French money couldn't be spent in California in 2010. Besides, the franc no longer existed. That one stopped her. I reminded her again that she could never tell anyone anything I told her about my world, or the future in general. I knew of several bad situations that would arise in the coming years and would do what I could to shield us and our children from them, but I couldn't very well lay out all I knew about the coming Franco-Prussian War or the horrors of the two World Wars of the "next" century. I would have to find a way to make sure my family would be safe, but not give away *how* I knew what I knew so far in advance. Well, I'd figure it out somehow. I may not have been a lawyer, but I had worked in a law firm long enough to know that you sometimes have to keep things you know to yourself for them to be of any use.

Anne asked me what would take the place of the franc and when. I told her that starting in the year 2002, there would be a pan-European currency used almost everywhere—in France, in Spain, in Italy, in Germany. She stopped me right there, gaping in disbelief. *"La France et l'Allemagne vont s'unir en utilisant la même monnaie?"* (France and Germany will unite using the same currency?) I said yes. There would be horrible conflicts between the two beforehand.

"Comme d'habitude," (As usual,) she commented bitterly. I said yes, but that in fewer than 100 years, the leaders of France and Germany would be friends and work out a system where the two countries would be the core of a European Union. Indeed, they would be so politically and economically dependent upon each other that open borders would result and a further war between the two would become a virtual impossibility.

"Ça semble tout à fait impossible," (That seems totally impossible,) she commented.

"Pour toi, j'ai peur que celà ne reste impossible. Mais nos petits-enfants vont le voir, parce-que je l'ai vu," (For you, I fear it will remain impossible. But our grandchildren will see it, because I have seen it,) I told her.

"Tant pis pour moi, alors, mais si tu restes avec moi pour me rassurer, je peux l'accepter." (Too bad for me, then, but if you stay with me to reassure me, I can accept that.) I assured her that I had no intention of going anywhere unless she was with me.

She took my hand. *"La cabine est libre demain et dimanche."* (The cabin is free tomorrow and Sunday.) There seemed to be some kind of underground, unspoken reservation system here for this kind of thing. Apparently, the unobtrusive roadside motel hadn't been invented yet. But I didn't want the 1860 Bordeaux version of the unobtrusive roadside motel to be our only chance to "be alone." So I asked her flat out, what would be the necessary protocol for us to live together openly? She seemed surprised at my ignorance. *"Il faudrait se marier, que penses tu?"* (We'd have to get married, what do you think?"

"Sounds like a plan," I commented to myself. *"Comment?"* she asked. Oops. Anglicisms were not part of the French vocabulary in 1860. *"J'ai dit, je n'ai rien contre ça."* (I said, I have nothing against that.)

„Mais tu es déjà marié!" (But you're already married!)

"Officiellement, oui, mais pas ici," (Officially, yes, but not *here,*) I said, pointing to my head. *"Et, n'oublies pas, une fois que je suis avec toi ici, je ne suis même pas encore né."* (And, don't forget, once I'm here with you, I haven't even been born yet.)

„Tu es né en quelle année, en fait?" (What year *were* you born in, anyway?)

I chuckled and asked her if it bothered her, marrying a man more than 140 years younger than she was? She gave me a poke in the side, and said, *"Pas de faux fuyants! Parles!"* (Don't avoid the subject! Out with it!)

"D'accord," (OK,) I relented. *"Je suis né le 23 juin 1974."* (I was born on the twenty-third of June in the year 1974.)

"Invraisemblable. C'est dingue, tout ça," (Incredible. Completely crazy, all this,) she said, more to herself than to me.

I told her I agreed with her completely, but here we were. I reminded her of the "housewarming" gift from Thomas Jefferson, and that I would bring it tomorrow night, but that we were not to open it until I had crossed over for the last time on Tuesday. I also told her my view about our situation—that I could go on drinking low-grade wine for the rest of my life or drink the prestige vintage and have it be the last bottle I ever touch. I explained to her that, by that, I did *not* mean that Caro was low-grade wine or that Anne was the prestige vintage, but that *my life* (and its prospects from 2010 on) was the low-grade vintage and that my meeting her and coming to stay with her was the prestige vintage that I wished to go for, even if it would be a short-lived pleasure.

She kissed me and whispered, *"Tu as bien l'air de savoir exactement ce que je veux m'entendre dire."* (You seem to know exactly what I want to hear from you.)

I caressed her smooth cheek and said, *"Ce n'est pas dificile quand tout ce que tu veux entendre est la vérité."* (It's not difficult when all you want to hear is the truth.)

48.

She asked me to tell her about Thomas Jefferson. She said that I had already explained that in my time, there were transportation vehicles that could fly 300 people from Paris to California in a single day and that we could eat food from all over the world in any big city and so on, but I had never talked of my encounter with this wine-collecting ex-president that had so impressed me.

How was I to explain Thomas Jefferson to a bright, but relatively unworldly, woman from France in 1860? Sure, he was far less removed from her world than from mine, but America might as well have been another planet as far as she was concerned. She knew that we didn't have kings, but the concept of a president who was head of state but had far less power than a king was difficult to explain to her, even if the recent kings of France were not as powerful as the absolute monarchs of the eighteenth century. I tried to impart upon her what a visionary Jefferson was. The separation of church and state, so there was no official religion, appealed to her—more so than I would have imagined to someone from a country so predominantly Catholic. She said that some of their priests were extraordinarily good men and that they had served their parishes well, but that others wielded close to absolute power in their parishes and abused their position in society to either enrich themselves or engage in behavior that was in flagrant violation of their vows. No one dared speak out against them, and they thus felt they could carry out their evil activities with no fear of punishment. I told her that this was a heavy issue even in my time, when no one religion held sway in my country or, at least, wasn't supposed to. She nodded. *"Les traditions des siècles sont comme les tortues,"* (The traditions of the centuries are like turtles,) she commented.

I told her about Jefferson's writing of the Declaration of Independence when he was just thirty-three, alone in a room in Philadelphia. I told her about his stays in France, as sort of an ambassador of the brand new (1784—not long after the victory at Yorktown) United States, until the French Revolution of 1789 (this, of course, she knew about). I reminded her that he had traveled in her own native Bordeaux region, as she had heard tell, checking out the wines, including her own Château Lafite, and how he had been so impressed by them that he had cases and cases of them shipped to him in America. He had had the vision to send an expedition to the west coast of North America at a time when we had no claim to it. He had engineered the purchase of the Louisiana Territory from Napoleon at a time when our country could scarcely afford it, but Napoleon was so distracted with his obsession of conquering Europe that he was willing to complete the transaction, forever changing the history of North America. I also told her that he had founded a university, the University of Virginia ("*l'Université de la Virginie*" to you) in Charlottesville, and that his collection of books formed the nucleus of the Library of Congress. I translated Library of Congress as "*Bibliothèque Nationale,*" or "National Library," as there really was such a thing in France. I also told her about how he had sold me some wine out of his collection, and reminded her that he had given me (well, us, since I had told him about Anne) a special bottle for us to share when we were together for good. She marveled about that information. "*Quelle voyage pour cette bouteille!*" (What a trip for that bottle!) She was right—from Bordeaux in 1787 to Virginia until 1818, then to California in 2010, and back to Bordeaux in 1860.

Finally, I spilled my guts and told her that I had also discussed my situation with her with Jefferson. I told her that he had had a relationship that was not socially acceptable in his time and was distraught about the need to keep it secret. I also told her that

Jefferson had advised me to follow my heart, and that if I did that, it meant being right where I was now—with her.

"Il est très avisé, votre Président Jefferson," (He is very wise, your President Jefferson,) she commented, pronouncing it "Jeh-fair-SUN," and then corrected herself. *"C'est à dire, **était**, même pour moi."* (*Was,* that is to say, even for me.) I nodded. She continued, *"Dommage—je crois que j'aurais bien aimé ce monsieur."* (Too bad—I think I would have liked this gentleman very much.)

"Au secours, un concurrent!" (Help, a competitor!) I said in mock despair. She poked me in the side sharply. When I winced, she said defiantly that if I could chase after a woman born 140 years before I was, then she had every right to want to hear about an interesting man born ninety years before she was. Oh, no, chérie, I don't fall for *that* one anymore. I knew her too well by now. I made a pouting face and she burst into that laughter of hers I loved so very much. I laughed, too, and remarked on how *good* it felt.

It struck me. *That's* what Caro needed. She never laughed. I don't know if it was my fault or if she was just incapable of it anymore, but she never laughed, or hadn't laughed that I could recall in the last five or more years. If I couldn't make her laugh, then she needed someone who could. She needed that more than all the mansions and Rolls Royces in Los Angeles (or all the sand in Nevada). I couldn't give it to her, and she probably didn't even realize that she missed it, but I'd bet the château that she did. I never knew what would do the trick. Maybe an antidepressant, maybe some classic Road Runner cartoons, something. Oh, well. That was for the next guy. I had tried, at first, at second, at ninety-ninth, not succeeded, and still tried, tried again, and still failed. I was succeeding now. I intended to succeed with Anne for a long time to come. Well, that is, long time gone. Whatever. You know what I mean.

To get my mind off Caro—not a difficult task with Anne's hand in mine, mind you—but also to get back to the subject we had been discussing an hour ago, I reminded her of the prospect of our getting married. She reminded me about the fact that I was still married. I said that when I came to stay—only four days away!—that my disappearance would result in my being declared dead, and that such a declaration would result in an automatic divorce. I didn't know how long it would take for the paperwork to be official, but since it would all be so far into the future for us, that it wouldn't matter. I also said that Caro had already set the process in motion, and that since I wouldn't have been contesting it in any case, that as far as I was concerned, it was a done deal. She nodded, seeming not totally convinced, but with one of those, *"Si vous le dites,"* (If you say so) looks. I told her that I thought it might be less confusing if she and her family just told everyone I was not married, instead of explaining that I was going to be divorced, but not for another 150 years or so. She nodded and said that when I put it that way, it did make a lot of sense. I told her that I actually did make sense on occasion, sometimes three times a month, but that I had used up my quota with her already, so she shouldn't expect me to make sense again for another two weeks or so. I got another poke in the ribs for my trouble.

"N'aie pas peur, cher Robert, je serai ta femme. Il y a plein de raisons, mais surtout parce que tu n'as rien d'artificiel." (Fear not, dear ro-BAIR, I will be your wife. There are plenty of reasons, but above all because there is nothing artificial about you.)

How about that? I thought she was going to tell me that our time out in the cabin had already made me a father-to-be. Maybe it had and we didn't know it yet, but that wasn't the reason she had just promised herself to me in so many words. Here she told me that what she liked most about me was what women in my world always

259

disliked about me—that I wasn't cool, that I was an open book and didn't put on enough of an impressive façade. Different strokes for different folks. Anne was definitely my kind of folks.

By now it was getting dark, and she said she had to get home. We had our usual "I-don't-want-to-let-go-of-you" parting scene, and then did just that. I was a little beat, anyway, to be honest, and I had a few chores on my calendar for tomorrow. Mad scientist at work.

49.

Saturday, September 4

I slept late. Yesterday had gone by without my realizing what a toll the day's events had taken on me. Not that I had run a marathon or anything, but I had gotten a lot done at the office, plus there were the stops at the bank and the post office, dealing with Miguel, sparring with Stefano on the phone, running by Josh's shop, then the garden center, then the Vietnamese take-out, and then the evening with Anne. I was really happy that most of the preparations were either done or close to it.

I went outside to get the morning paper to see what new disasters had befallen humanity overnight. Inside was a single printed sheet of paper. I assumed it contained 50 reasons why I should patronize some newly opened vegan steak house in Topanga Canyon, but I looked anyway. Umm, no, not from a vegan steak house, and I doubt anyone else in the neighborhood got one of these sheets stuck in their morning paper. It was a computer-printed "news" article. The headline read, "Sherman Oaks Resident Escapes Violent Attack With His Life." Uh-oh. I read on. "Robert Packard of 1136 Grove Street barely survived a brutal assault in the garage of his residence that left him missing three fingers on his left hand and a broken right leg. Paramedics who treated him said he would survive, but would need a period of several months of rehabilitation treatment. Upon regaining consciousness in Sherman Oaks Hospital on Van Nuys Boulevard, Mr. Packard said he couldn't describe his attacker(s), and didn't know of why anyone would want to harm him in such a manner. Police were investigating, but admitted they held little hope of finding the attackers with neither a description nor a motive."

Below the "article," there was some more text, just in case I hadn't gotten the message: "Bob, this is just to make sure you and your friends know that we are serious about our job, and your karate kid will not be enough to protect you forever if you should decide against cooperating with us. Let's keep this little piece of paper in the fiction section, shall we?" No signature or return address, of course.

Nothing like a little threat of grievous bodily harm to liven up my morning, right? But this was obviously a direct consequence of the previous day's events and phone call. The sequence of events I had set in motion was on course, and as far as Stef was concerned, the holiday weekend suddenly worked in my favor. He knew I couldn't receive any more "deliveries" at the office until Tuesday, since we wouldn't be open until then. Watching me like a hawk during a holiday weekend would most likely be a waste of his time. Stef was evil, but he was not stupid. As long as I hadn't announced any trips to Aldo's shop to sell him more rare bottles, then there was little reason to watch me to find out where and when I was receiving them. If I were to take any long drives out to some secluded estate somewhere, I'm sure he would be on my tail, probably following some GPS device he had hidden in my car somewhere. I may not have been evil, but I wasn't stupid either.

After a utilitarian breakfast of orange juice, tea, and some English muffins with peanut butter, I disconnected my computer from the Internet and opened the encrypted file I had saved previously. I read through all the ingredients and steps needed to transform my ammonium nitrate into a potent explosive. There were several steps that had to be followed, and a few things I had to run out and get, but it was more than a little unnerving to me to find out how little skill was required to build one of these things. This may not have been as simple as mixing oil and vinegar to make a salad dressing, but it wasn't exactly the Manhattan Project either. I would have a very potent explosive by this evening, if I wanted. I didn't want. I wanted it for Tuesday evening, but I would get all the stuff necessary by this afternoon and give the assembly a dry run, without really mixing the brew until early Tuesday morning. I didn't know to what extent anyone could snoop on my computer while I was reviewing my foray into demolition technology, but I figured disconnecting myself from the information superhighway might not be such a bad idea while going over this stuff. It would be just my luck if some upstanding geek decided to make an unannounced (and undetected) pit stop on my computer while I was busy and then turn me in, in case I was entertaining thoughts of blowing up Disneyland on Labor Day or something.

So, most of my Saturday was spent doing leisurely shopping for what would be the rest of my explosive soup, that being mostly oil, as I already had the ammonium nitrate. Then there was a stop at a stationery store for a small roll of sturdy, brown wrapping paper. I didn't see Stef or any of his goons in their black limousines, but except for once or twice in the last month, I hadn't detected them at all then, either. But they had been there, so I just went on the assumption that they were following me now. Whenever I stopped for some of the necessary ingredients, I made sure I bought a couple of completely unrelated items, in case Stef or his "companions" were versed in ammonium nitrate bombs. Bullets and broken bones seemed more their speed, but you never know what the backgrounds of these guys might have been. It was probably a safe bet that none of them had trained as florists. When I got back home in the late afternoon, I made it a point to tend to Caro's garden for a good half hour or more. Caro was in Nevada with Wendy until Monday night, so she wasn't going to be cruising by in Wendy's car to check on me, but it wasn't impossible that someone in the neighborhood might still be in touch with her, and anyway, I wanted to give Stef and friends the impression that I had so little to do with the time on my hands that gardening was now a serious pastime for me. I didn't see any more black limousines, but I was pretty sure that Stef and friends had other, somewhat less-conspicuous vehicles at their disposal as well.

I decided on some Pad Thai for dinner that night. I had only three more dinners planned in the era of readily accessible ethnic food, so I figured I'd get in my last licks while I could. Anne was having a great time smelling the vestiges of them on me when I crossed over to see her in the evenings, but much as I wanted to share them with her, so much the greater was my fear of making her ill from whatever additives they used to make the stuff so tasty. All I needed was to arrange all this and then find out that Anne had a deathly allergy to MSG. Hell, it hadn't even been invented until 1908 (no, of course I hadn't known that from the beginning; I looked it up when Anne seemed so intrigued by my oriental take-out meals).

At the onset of dusk in California (and before that in France, being at a higher latitude), I crossed over. I was wearing my 1860 clothes and I had brought Thomas Jefferson's gift, the bottle of Margaux, 1787. I told Anne that we were not to open it before Tuesday night, when I came over for good. Anne had on one of her simple outfits and her smile was of that "I-got-something-for-you" genre. Women are open books only on those rare occasions when they want men to know what is on their minds. This was definitely one such occasion.

Anne admired Thomas Jefferson's bottle of wine. She knew enough about wine to remark how amazingly well-preserved it looked. I reminded her that the bottle itself was only thirty-one years old, even if we were looking to enjoy it seventy-three years after it was produced. *"C'est fou tout ça. Fou, fou, fou."* (All this is crazy. Crazy, crazy, crazy.) She shook her head. She looked up at me. She remarked that such a bottle must be quite an expensive collector's item in my day. I said it was beyond any value she could possibly imagine in 2010. She asked why in the world I would forego the money just for a bottle of wine (asks the woman who grew up at Château Lafite).

I reminded her that I had made a promise to Thomas Jefferson that I would not sell this bottle of wine, but enjoy it with the person most important to me in my life. Anne just looked up at me, lasered in on my eyes with her big baby browns, and nodded.

I'm fairly sure that if I told her that this bottle would probably fetch around $100,000 (or, rather, 8,000 francs in gold or about nine years' wages in her terms) in my world, she would have conked me over the head, told me to take it back and sell it, the 8000 gold francs being more money than she or her family had ever seen at one time. But I was bringing a million francs in gold with me, so I figured shutting up about the bottle's worth would be the better course of action. Besides, *I wanted to taste that frigging bottle!* My only regret was that, if all went according to plan (shut up, Murphy), Anne and I would be the *only* people on earth after 1818 to ever taste a thirty-one-year-old Margaux 1787. I'll have to leave it up to your imagination, as I don't plan to be around to be able to give an account of what kind of bouquet this wine has. Probably some fruits and flowers no one remembers. I know one thing, if it tastes like stale Dr. Pepper with a dash of canned frozen grape juice, the company will more than make up for it. Still, I'm betting it will taste like every cent's worth of the $100,000 that Aldo would have grudgingly given me for it. I challenge anyone reading this to tell me *one* instance when President Thomas Jefferson *ever* sold them a bottle of wine that didn't taste great. There, you see?

On the way to the little cabin out in the woods, I asked Anne if she could find me a sturdy piece of rope for Tuesday, one about ten or so meters long. This caught her by surprise, but I explained that I needed it for a last-minute preparation, and that she was more likely to have such a thing than any store I would be visiting in my normal activities. She shrugged, and said, *"Bien sûr,"* (Sure,) but wondered how come? I just said it was something I needed. I confessed that some people that might wish us ("us," not "me," you will note) harm might be watching me, and try to use the portal for "bad (*méchant*)" purposes, maybe even follow me, and that this was to be prevented at all costs. She looked mildly worried and asked if she needed to be concerned about this. I said probably not, but it would just be one more precaution if I were not seen buying the rope, so as not to provoke questions. She understood, nodded, said she could get something like that with no difficulty at all. Where did I think she was, after all? Ah, rural life!

If it hadn't been for all the complications back home, this could almost be a science fiction version of "Green Acres." But Eddie Albert and Eva Gabor never had to contend with Naomi Roganov, Caro's divorce lawyer, or Aldo and his hired thugs. Sitcoms didn't imitate life, and life never imitated sitcoms. Well, usually, anyway. Back when I was in college, there definitely were some guys who could have come straight out of the TV series "The Big Bang Theory," but even in physics lab there were some perfectly normal types, too, like Jim "Zorro" Hernández. Funny, the obsessed nerds all had normal, banal names like Bill and Phil, and the guy called Zorro was the normal one.

50.

We arrived at the cabin and all thoughts of Eddie Albert and Eva Gabor and prudish American sitcoms of the 1960s where married couples slept in pajamas and separate beds evaporated into the Bordeaux evening. Anne and I vanished into the cabin, and if it weren't such a groaner, considering the circumstances, I'd say, "The rest is history." She was beautiful, she was wonderful, she was fabulous. I mean, if you are looking for some steamy play-by-play, you're barking up the wrong *arbre.* She reminded me once again why I was risking all this and, at this point, I hardly needed reminding. If you can't figure it out from that, you must have taken a vow of celibacy before reaching puberty and I can't help you.

Later, with Anne resting next to me, an arm over my chest, I wondered silently to myself: assuming I could make my problems go away and if Anne would learn English, would I even *want* to bring Anne to my world? Would she even look upon things we consider "progress" to be just that? Yes, we had all our great technology. We could fly to France and back in two days if we wanted to, pick up communications devices and talk to anyone in the world any time, watch any one of 1,000 movies upon demand, go out for any kind of exotic meal at any time of night or day. What's not to like, right? Well, potentially, to someone like Anne, plenty might not be to like. She had grown up her whole life without a movie or an airplane flight or a telephone. She still was a strong, well-adjusted, level-headed woman, even if (or maybe because) she had never even had a Game Boy or a cell phone while growing up. How could I even ask her to try to adapt to such a world, especially when there was zero documentation of her even existing, and where she would be considered a primitive, knowing nothing about how anything worked, even if she did learn English? I thought I had a far

267

better shot at adjusting to a world where I spoke the language and knew many of its limitations.

I shifted slightly, and her arm on my chest had to move a little to compensate. *"Non, non, ne bouge pas,"* (No, no, don't move,) she murmured. It was as if she had been following my train of thought. No way, but her words sort of capped off my internal musings perfectly. *Non, ma chère Anne.* Although I do have to go home tonight, I will be here for good soon, and I will not move.

Eventually, I did move, of course. At some point, Anne was always expected back at the family whatever-it-was. Family compound? That probably wasn't the right term. Family compound is what the Kennedys had in Hyannis on Cape Cod. I've seen photos. Huge spread, sailboats and stuff. Anne's family probably lived in some one- or two-room structure. Electricity and running water were out of the question, let alone a family catamaran.

As we dressed just before we left the cabin, Anne looked me in the eye in the creeping dusk and said, *"Je pourrais très facilement m'habituer à ça, tu sais?"* (I could very easily get used to this, you know?) I held her against me and stroked her gorgeous, dark brown hair and said, *"On va s'habituer ensemble, et très bientôt."* (We're going to get used to this together, and very soon.) Who needs electricity, running water or a catamaran? Anne wouldn't know she lacked any of those creature comforts in the first place. I'd get used to the idea of lacking them, especially the catamaran. Unlikely as it may seem, you'd be *amazed* how quickly you can get used to the idea of not owning a catamaran. I once read a great novel where one of the characters (come to think of it, a Basque, of all people) started philosophizing that there were two ways to realize contentment—either you increase your material possessions until they meet your wants or you reduce your wants until they meet your material possessions. He obviously touted the latter as the better and the more practical of the two options.

Anne didn't know the scope of the material wealth I would be bringing with me, but even so, all the money in the world wouldn't buy central air conditioning if it hadn't been invented yet. I'd have to do a lot of what that fictional, philosophizing Basque had recommended. But I knew by now that I had something that all the central air conditioning in the world couldn't offer *me*. For Anne, I was willing to sweat a little. More than a little, even. But I had two and a half days yet, during which I would sweat in a different manner altogether. The number of things that could go wrong was diminishing as the time drew near, but all it would take would be one.

I pushed thoughts of disaster out of my head—not a difficult task in Anne's presence. If going to bed with her every night and waking up next to her every morning required some serious adjustments to my material needs, I figured they would be adjustments I would gladly make. Hell, if it didn't work out, I could always wait for the Civil War to be over, move to Kitty Hawk, North Carolina, wait for the Wright brothers to grow up, and plant an idea or two about aerodynamics in their heads.

Back at the portal, it was the usual "I-don't-want-to-let-go-of-you" parting scene, but one of only three more. I think the closer we got, the more Anne and I both realized what we'd lose if, for some reason, there should be some kind of mechanical failure and we would be permanently separated from each other. I think she feared it more than I did, as I saw no reason the technology should be in danger of failing, whereas she had practically no idea what technology was. I had more to fear from my fellow twenty-first-century humans than anything else. Even so, I figured I had little to fear tonight, and I was right. I slept again in my own bed—soundly, if alone.

51.

Sunday, September 5

I woke up at around 9:30. After all, today was the Sunday before a long holiday weekend with tomorrow also being a holiday. I did a quick perusal of the news. The oil spill in the Gulf of Mexico was either capped or on its way to being finally plugged for good. Great, I thought. This thing had been gushing millions of gallons of crude oil for months, and because most of it was probably on the ocean floor and not visible to a fishing boat or a casual beach stroller, the government would just say, "Problem solved, crisis over." Yeah, you wish. I had read about some Mississippi fishermen who said they would rather go broke than sell poisoned fish to their customers. I would have nominated them for the Nobel Peace prize, but guys like that are usually just noble, and never Nobel material. They'll probably nobly go broke and be ignored by the history books. My intention was to deliberately be ignored by the history books, but definitely not to go broke.

Let's see, what else was going on today? The tone in U.S. politics was getting crazier by the minute, with people who I thought sounded like they belonged in padded cells and straitjackets winning primary elections and some poised to enter Congress. Hurricanes brewing in the Caribbean, typhoons in the Pacific likewise, mm-hmm, more good news. Pakistan had floods that made twenty million people homeless. That was something like 140% of the population of Holland. The price of gold had risen on general fears about the world economy. Ah, so I was right to fix the price of my French gold coins when I did. This was not really positive news, but at least it wasn't bad news unless you were foolish enough to have taken out a short position last year and held it. What else?

Oh, yes, and southern California was to have an unusually long spell of rain, starting later tomorrow and lasting well into the week. Now, *that* one I liked. It meant that Caro and her lawyer would have to meet with Steve Clark after a drive through the rain, and then find out that their little quest for riches was going to meet with a lot less success than Wendy led Caro and her lawyer to believe. The weather wouldn't exactly help to cheer either of them up any, especially if Stan Chase had taken Caro's case on a contingency basis. If Caro had told him that she had rock solid information (i.e., Wendy's snooping at the bank) that I could be taken for millions, he might have done just that. I almost regret that I won't be around to hear that little attorney-client conversation, but somehow I'm betting they would have invited me out of the room before that one began. There's no way I would have gotten to be a fly on that wall in either case.

I got a sudden tinge of fright. Rainstorms? As in thunder and lightning? Lightning, as in what caused the portals to come into being in the first place? What if, "What lightning giveth, lightning taketh away, whether thou likest it or not?" I looked a lot more carefully at that weather forecast—rain, not thunderstorms, at least nothing of any significance. If that changed, I'd have to run over to Anne penniless just for fear of never being able to get to her after some electrical anomaly zapped the portals back out of existence (or put me face to face with her great-grandmother at age fourteen, instead). I know I would have done it; I would have gone to stay with Anne with nothing but the clothes on my back, not even a *zee-PAIR*. But I had put a lot of time and taken a lot of risk to arrange my parting gift for Juanita and my huge wedding gift, if you want to call it that, for Anne. I didn't want to disappear without both tasks being completed, although I'm not totally dense—finding a woman like Anne is something you can't buy with all the riches in the world, and a billion dollars without Anne would have been worth less to me than a bottle of Stef's ginger ale. I knew I told her I was bringing some considerable wealth, too, and I didn't know how she would take it if I suddenly showed up for good with empty pockets. But she was one hell of an actress if the feelings I thought she had shown for me were a put-on. I was convinced she was for real and would have accepted me as a pauper. I also hoped I wouldn't have to find out. I had read that working in a French vineyard for two francs a day until you drop dead was considered less than "ideal working conditions."

I got a shudder and ran downstairs, but today, Sunday, the weather was still its usual southern California sunny self and the portals were there as always, oblivious to my sudden panic attack. It was Sunday in Bordeaux, too, and although people seemed to be out and about in the distance, most of the activity did not seem to be work-related. It stood to reason that most of the population would be going to a local Catholic church. Basque separatists weren't blowing things up in France in 1860, and the next war with the Germans was ten years in the future, so the scene seemed quite relaxed. I went back upstairs. *Calme-toi, ro-BAIR.* This is no time to lose your nerve.

I knew Anne would have calmed me down in no time flat. She would have brought along some $25,000 (to me) bottle of "Château N'importequoi." We would have opened it and watched the clouds send us their own private smoke signals. I contemplated that and actually did calm down—a lot. One of my problems this Sunday was that I had pretty much completed my arrangements and all that required the help of others couldn't be done before Tuesday. Brinks didn't deliver on holidays, and even if they did, Josh had arranged for a Tuesday delivery. My parting gift for Juanita couldn't be withdrawn from the bank before then anyway. So, what was I going to do with myself this fine Sunday? Ha! By George, I think I got it. The Borders bookstore chain was in financial trouble, but they had a store near me that was still open.

I drove out there and bought a movie with Juliet Binoche in it. "Chocolat," of course. Her resemblance to Anne was not 100%, but close, and her (or her character's) general comportment was more than just vaguely similar. Anne was younger, of course, and had no children, whereas Juliet Binoche's character in "Chocolat" did, but just seeing the film with its rural setting in (not quite the early nineteenth century) France put me in a great mood. I was almost tempted to bring a fully charged laptop with the DVD over to Anne just to show her. Almost.

But Thomas Jefferson was the good angel whispering in my ear: don't even think about it. What if the unspeakable happens, and you suddenly die, and a twenty-first-century device suddenly shows up in the history books as having appeared in Bordeaux in 1860? Who knew what ripples that could cause in the fabric of time? Maybe Hitler would win the Second World War as a result? Maybe the invention of the atomic bomb would be perfected by Stalin's Soviet Union? Maybe Sarah Palin would have become President? *Je suis désolé, ma chère Anne* (sort of "dreadful sorry, Clementine,") you will have to hear the fantasy tales of the twenty-first century from my lips without a demonstration for every seemingly impossible thing I tell you.

Juliet Binoche's character in "Chocolat" has, for most of the film, something Anne never had: a slight melancholy. The Juliet Binoche woman in the film was used to being forced to move out of almost every community she lived in. Anne, on the other hand, fit right into her world and was an integral part of it. I hoped I could come to be accepted as her partner. I didn't mind being thought of as "somewhat different," but I didn't want to stand out to the point where I might be thought of as a trouble-maker or a threat to anyone. Despite the wealth I would be bringing, I would try to be "her husband," rather than have her be "my wife." Discretion is the better part of valor, *Ro-BAIR*. Forget that at your peril. If and when you meet Pierre Curie, remember, history says *he's* the one who got the Nobel Prize, not you. Make sure you keep it that way. Aye, aye, Captain. As long as first mate (interpret that one as you will) Anne is aboard, old *Ro-BAIR* ain't gonna rock this boat.

I had been pausing my "Chocolat" video periodically for runs to the fridge or the john, but there were otherwise no interruptions. A few minutes after 4:30 in the afternoon, however, after I had finally watched the film to the end, the phone rang. I thought, *"Please,* let it be anyone other than Stef or Caro, *pretty please?"* It had been such a nice day up to this point. Stef had no reason to call, and Caro should have been with Wendy in Nevada, although I'd seen with my own eyes that they have telephone service in Nevada (imagine that!), so she could still be there and call me in California.

Yay, it wasn't Caro or Stef, but Jim Hernández, wanting to know if I felt like coming over to visit with him and Janice tomorrow afternoon. You know, as my last full day in this life, which he obviously couldn't know, I could think of nothing better I'd like to do the next day. Labor Day Monday was just another day in France, so Anne would be working anyway until evening. Jim and Janice knew all about Caro's leaving and must have noticed that I was less than devastated by it. But they also knew (or thought they knew) that I hadn't been seeing anyone else since the separation. Maybe they thought I was lonely, and maybe they were going to invite me over anyway, but I was glad Jim called and said I'd love to come over. We set it for one in the afternoon and hung up.

This definitely brightened up what was already a very mellow day. Don't forget, I'm from southern California, so I'm allowed to use expressions like that. Except for the last-minute activities that I already had planned for Tuesday, all I had to do was hang out and hope no one named Stef, Caro, Wendy, Naomi or Stan decided to throw a live hand grenade into my plans (or vinegar into my wine, or however you want to put it).

For one of my last two planned dinners alone, I opted for Thai again. This time, I opted for chicken and bamboo in red curry with basil and cilantro and plenty of coconut milk, mildly spicy, over basmati rice and with a glass noodle and papaya salad on the side. I figured I'd get enough *aubergine à la bordelaise* to satisfy my cravings for continental cuisine in very short order.

When I had cleared up the containers of Thai food and cleaned up the kitchen somewhat (hey, I was technically a bachelor), I changed into my Bordeaux outfit. I still was using my own shoes, but the pants practically covered them, so even Anne never noticed them until I took the pants off and, so far, she had been the only one in her world to see me do that.

52.

Anne was again waiting for me at the portal. At this point, I was getting so adept at hopping over, I was tempted to do some double axels while doing it, but resisted, for fear of over-estimating my ability to compete for the next summer Olympics—especially since the first Olympic Games in modern times wouldn't be held until 1896. If you started with my biological age, thirty-six, in the year 1860, then I'd be seventy-two when the first modern-era Olympics were held. I didn't know what state of health I'd be in then, but the likelihood of my qualifying for any kind of Olympic sport, even at age thirty-six (much less seventy-two), was probably minimal at best. Besides, I still didn't know what would happen if I disturbed the portal during transit. I still hadn't left any of my limbs dangling where I didn't want to, but risking it just to show off seemed plain stupid. When I showed up with a million francs in gold two days hence (I hoped, anyway!) I imagined *that* would be enough showing off for one lifetime.

When I crossed and she came up to me, she smelled the Thai food immediately. *"Qu'est-ce que tu as mangé cette fois?"* (What did you eat this time?) she demanded. I coyly told her she was better off not asking. She insisted.

"Ne me dis pas que c'était du 'sous-chie,'" (Don't tell me it was that 'sushi,') she said.

I explained that I had eaten a Thai dish, not a Japanese dish. She demanded that I tell her what it was. *"Si tu insistes,"* (If you insist,) I told her. *"C'était du* (It was) *kaeng phet gai sai naw mai."*

She got ready to give me one of those pokes in the side, but I saw it coming and warded her off. *"Non, vraiment! Ce n'est pas une blague!"* (No, really, that's not a joke!)

She just put her hand on her hips in a gesture of expectation, waiting for me to tell her what kind of spiders and caterpillars were used in this unpronounceable dish. I laughed and told her it was chicken in a Thai red curry with *"lait de coco."* (coconut milk) There was also some bamboo in it, too.

She then threw me a curve. *"Tu veux m'apporter un peu de ça demain? J'aimerais en goûter."* (Do you want to bring me some tomorrow? I'd like to taste that.) I said I'd love to, but she needed to know that in my day, they put in all kinds of additives and stuff, that some people were allergic to them, and I didn't know how to help her if she should have some kind of deathly allergic reaction to the MSG or whatever else they tossed in there in my day. She asked why such additives were even allowed? Ummm, yes. She might have asked me as well why they allow toxic waste dumps, why they allow fertilizer runoffs into the waterways, why they allow oil companies to dump a couple million gallons of toxic oil dispersant into waters from which we get our fish. I don't know. They just do.

But she continued, if these additives in the food were so bad, then why was I eating it, and why wasn't I sick from it? I told her I was used to it by now. She said if it tasted as good as it smelled, then she would be happy to get used to it, too. I told her that if she liked Thai food that much, then I'd take her on a trip to Thailand if she wanted. *"Je ne sais même pas où c'est."* (I don't even know where that is,) she confessed. I remembered—1860; she probably only knew it by its old name. *"On l'appelle aussi Siam."* She had heard of Siam, but didn't exactly know where it was, and certainly never harbored any illusions of ever seeing it. I told her it was in Asia and that it was reputed to be very beautiful.

"Peut-être bien," (Maybe so)," she commented wistfully, *"mais qui peut se payer un voyage comme ça?"* (but who can afford for such a trip?)

"On se débrouillera," (We'll manage,) I told her with a sly grin.

"Tu as intérêt!" (It's in your best interest!) she warned me playfully. I explained to her about MSG, the fact that it was invented in 1908, that almost all oriental food used it in my day, and that some people had a violent reaction to it but never knew until they tried it. I told her I didn't want to risk it with her, as there was no way I could help her if it made her ill. This, at least, she understood.

"Bon, alors, tu dois m'emmener au Siam pour que je puisse goûter ce kaeng phet gai et cetera." (OK, then, you'll have to take me to Thailand so I can taste this kaeng phet gai, etc.) I told her it would be my pleasure.

She just looked at me, seeing that my expression hadn't changed. *"Tu sais, je te crois."* (You know, I believe you.)

For a vineyard worker in Bordeaux in 1860, the prospect of a trip to Thailand was about as realistic as the idea of spending a weekend on the moon. Anne's statement that she believed me when I said I'd take her to Thailand was a huge leap of faith for someone in her position in her day. I didn't intend to let her down. For her, Thailand might as well have been the moon. I would take her there.

"Pour le moment, si ce n'est pas trop près pour toi, je voulais t'emmener à un endroit un peu moins loin que le Siam," (For the moment, if it's not too close for you, I'd like to take you to a place a little closer than Thailand,) she offered.

Distracted by thoughts of the temples of Bangkok, I asked where that might be. She squeezed my hand and said, *"Disons, une petite demi-heure d'ici."* (Let's say, not quite a half hour from here.)

The temples of Bangkok went *poof* in my mind's eye and she had my undivided attention in less time than it takes a pocket calculator to add one plus one. I didn't even have to say, *"Allons-y"* (Let's go) this time.

Afterward, in the cabin, lightly stroking her bare back, I remembered that song by Foreigner from the '80s that you hear on the oldies stations, "It Feels Like The First Time." With Anne, it did—every time. There was one thing I was wondering about, but she was way ahead of me. *"La semaine prochaine, il faudra faire attention."* (Next week, we'll have to be careful)

I asked pourquoi.

She got up on her elbows and smiled. *"Parce que si nous ne faisons pas attention, il y aura un petit Robert dans neuf mois environ."* (Because if we aren't careful, there will be a little *Ro-BAIR* in about nine months.)

I contemplated that one. *"Est-ce que ça serait une mauvaise chose?"* (Would that be a bad thing?) I asked.

"Pas si nous le voulons," (Not if we want it)," she replied, *"mais il faudrait se marier."* (But we'd have to get married.)

Fine. This was as good a moment as any. She had already said that she was willing to marry me, but it was time for a formal proposal. *"D'accord,"* (OK,) I said. "Anne Boudreau, *je t'aime et je te demande ici et maintenant si tu veux être ma femme?"* (Anne Boudreau, I love you, and I'm asking you here and now if you will be my wife?)

She just looked at me, caressed my face, and said, *"Jamais de la vie."* (Never in your life.) Not quite believing what I had just heard, I stared at her in disbelief. She managed to keep a straight face for maybe half a second and then burst into her ringing laughter. She got me again. I was 0 for 10 or something. Great, I'm a classic nineteenth century nerd. *"Mon cher Robert, je suis déjà ta femme. Il ne manque que les formalités, et de ça, nous nous en occupons dans trois jours, d'accord?"* (My dear *RoBAIR*, I am already your wife. Only the formalities are left, and we'll get started on those in three days, OK?)

Life with Anne was *not* going to be boring. And I *would* have my revenge. I would take her to the Orient, and every time she would swoon over how wonderful some exotic dish tasted, I would tell her that it was made of spiders, scorpion tails and bat wings—seasoned with the obligatory eye of newt. Hmm, I'd better look up the French word for "newt." Two more days. If I could have sped up the clock by blowing on it, I would have.

She turned and reached into a cloth bag she had brought along. She often had something like that with her, and as often as not, with nothing in it, so I hadn't paid it any attention. *"C'est des voisins,"* (It's from the neighbors) she explained. It was a bottle of Mouton-Rothschild, 1854. She started to explain that until 1853, it had been Brane-Mouton, but I told her I already knew all about that, being somewhat knowledgeable about wine. Bought by the Rothschild family, and since 1853, Brane-Mouton had been renamed Mouton-Rothschild. *"Bien au courant, monsieur Robert,"* (Quite up on things, monsieur *Ro-BAIR,*) she commented. She opened the bottle, let it breathe for a few minutes, and poured it into two glasses she had brought. It was the same situation as the last time when she opened the bottle of Lafite 1855. I just let it play and dance in my mouth, do Swan Lake on my tongue and dissipate to its aftertaste, and then repeated the ritual a couple of times. Anne seemed fascinated by my reaction to the contemporary wines of the region, which had to have been about as exotic to her as Coke Classic was to me. It must have almost been a comic scene, with me off in Never-Never Land sipping some red wine and this absolutely exquisite woman sitting naked in front of me waving, *Yoo-hoo, remember me?*

But I came down from my wine-induced high, and with Anne sitting in front of me with nothing on, I promise you, she once again became the object of my distraction in very short order.

When we could indulge no more, we got dressed and headed back to the portal. "Deux jours," (Two days,) she said. *"Deux jours,"* I repeated. She pressed up against me with her arms around me. At the same time, we both said, *"Deux jours de trop."* (Two days too many.) I couldn't see her smile, but I know it was there.

Tomorrow would be Labor Day, the day on which I would probably do the least work of any day in recent memory. I didn't fall asleep right away when I finally got back to my own bed, but when I did, I was out like a light.

53.
Monday, September 6

I woke up at around 9:00 in the morning. I think I must have felt like Eisenhower did on June 5, 1944.

I wasn't due at Jim's house until 1:00 in the afternoon, and he lived only maybe a 15-minute drive from my house, although in a more upscale neighborhood. Sherman Oaks is not like central or west Los Angeles, where a fifteen-minute drive can be walked in forty-five seconds, or even less if you're not on crutches.

I had a twelve pack of English muffins left in my fridge, so I opened it, split two of them, toasted them, and spread them with peanut butter. I like peanut butter, and don't recall seeing it offered even on my twentieth and twenty-first century trips to France. Make hay while the sun shines, right? I didn't know what my latest cholesterol readings were, but they certainly wouldn't be hurt by eliminating peanut butter from my diet soon. I knew they didn't have refined sugar in 1860 France, and had read that Russians, at least, still used marmalade to sweeten their tea. Just on a lark, I made some hot tea and instead of using sugar or honey to sweeten it, I used a couple of spoonfuls of some apricot marmalade I had. You know something? The Russians are on to something here. It tasted great. I'd have to remember that one for future (or past, as the case may be) reference.

The Boudreau family would be working today as any other day, so there was no point in looking for them (i.e., Anne) at this hour. I didn't rush in taking a shower or getting dressed. I booted up my laptop and checked in on what was going on in the world. It certainly didn't look like a mass epidemic of common sense had broken out overnight, and although there would be some major madness to follow in the 150 years after 1860, it didn't look like it was ebbing any by September 2010. For all our technological advances, the basic plagues of greed, fear and envy seemed to be just as prevalent in the world now as they were in 1860. Thomas Jefferson would have not have been pleased.

Still, now, as then, there were some truly good people in the world, and I had been invited over to share the afternoon with two of them. After perusing the news from American, French, British and Australian Web sites, I got dressed and made my way over to the house of Jim and Janice Hernández.

Caro had always whined about how much bigger and better-appointed the Hernández house was than ours, and although I had gotten tired of the whining, there was no denying that they had a *great* house. Lots of windows designed to let in a lot of light, well-proportioned rooms, and a really delightful garden and patio on which meals could be prepared and eaten. Jim and Janice had gotten some chicken filets, some shrimp from the Pacific, and some Hawaiian ono filets. I asked them which army they were expecting to feed? They laughed and said that since they both worked long hours during the week, they often did this on weekends and lived off of leftovers during the first part of the week. Some kind of leftovers! They had marinated the shrimp in a Japanese teriyaki sauce, the chicken in a kind of Texas barbecue sauce and the ono filets in a ginger-garlic mash with some lemon juice over it. Jim fired up the grill, and it was a hell of a feast. I had to watch it or I would end up gorging myself to the point where I would be useless to Anne this evening, except as a consultant.

Jim and Janice had a passable red wine (under the circumstances, that is—little did they know!), and after eating we relaxed in some very comfortable garden chairs. Jim reflected on how well work was going and about how, with so much evil stuff going on in the world, it was dangerously easy to get complacent. Janice was mostly nodding in agreement. Two years younger than Jim, she was my age and looked pretty good—sort of a cross between Pamela Anderson and Kathleen Turner. She asked me what I thought about having children and said it was OK if I didn't want to talk about that. My separation from Caro was public knowledge by now.

I told her I had no problem with the subject, although I did neglect to mention that I was about to confront exactly the same question. I thought for a moment. Anne had already said she wanted children and I always had. I told Janice that I thought that, barring living in Mogadishu or Darfur, it had to be a decision made independently of current circumstances. I thought the deciding factors had to be whether the prospective parents had the means and the desire to raise children. I thought that if both were present, then the other objects could be overcome. Reflecting on my own childhood, I said that I thought the most important thing a child needed was to be wanted. All else could be managed.

Jim and Janice thought that sounded very wise and profound, especially coming from someone who had no children of his own. I reminded them that while I had none of my own, that I had been one once, and playfully asked them if they had not? They laughed at that and said that they had been wanting to "get started" for a while, but just hadn't found the timing to be right. I said that I thought the timing was secondary to the cast of characters. With Caro, I told them, it became clear to me early on that the timing would never be right with her. They asked if this was the cause for our separation. I said that no, it was worse than that. I laid out for them more about Caro's background than I had done up to then and told them her comments to me about their house and income as opposed to ours. Jim asked me flat out if I felt in any way underpaid by the firm or mistreated?

284

I said no, not in the slightest. I explained that whatever ambitions I may have harbored, they were in the field of physics, not in the size of my house or my bank account. I also explained about the time we got invited to that gathering in South Carolina at New Year's, and how Caro's reaction had quashed any thoughts of going. Jim and Janice had never heard of the gathering in Charleston. To them, South Carolina might as well have been the dark side of the moon, but they seemed to understand where I was coming from. I told them that Caro was much more interested in growing our status than in growing our family, and that I just couldn't see asking a child to grow up in that environment. This didn't start to take into account the fact that Caro never wanted children in the first place.

"You both want children, don't you?" I asked. They both nodded. "Well, I doubt the world is going to get any better, but you have the means to provide for them and, apparently, the desire to have them and raise them. I think that you really can't ask for more than that and don't need to. The world will need someone to carry on after us, won't it?"

They looked at each other and smiled that knowing smile between a man and a woman who are devoted to each other and have been for a long time. I may be dense, but I finally caught on. I turned to Janice.

"You're pregnant, aren't you? That's what this was all about!" They nodded again and broke out into big grins.

"And you wanted me to be the first to know?"

"Well, except for our parents, yes," Janice said.

"Wow, in honor of the occasion, I'll even refrain from comments about the blade of Zorro," I said, and this got a big laugh out of both of them.

"How long have you known?" I asked.

"Since last Friday," Jim said. "I wanted to corner you at the office and discuss it, but you seemed like you were so busy, it was as if you weren't going to be around for the next month. That's why we waited to call you until yesterday."

The next month? How about the next rest of my life?

"I'm glad you did," I commented, as much to myself as to them. "I think I wouldn't have been able to process the thought with all that was going on last Friday."

"You were definitely a whirling dervish," said Jim. "I guess with the long weekend coming up, they had you working on seventy different projects at once."

"Conservatively speaking," I commented. "I can only imagine what's going to be on my plate tomorrow, too. The long weekend will certainly create a rush of work to be done the second we get into the office. You were right to choose today to discuss all this. Plus, there's no take-out place anywhere near the office with grilled ginger-garlic ono filets this good."

"I should hope not!" Janice chimed in. Jim and I laughed at that.

I said, "If there is such a place, you can bet Juanita will find it."

Jim answered, "She was really a godsend, wasn't she? How did you know to pick her when she applied for the position? When you hear her talk, you would think she was an ethnic stereotype out of some situation comedy, but when you see her writing or watch what she can do, and with what efficiency, I think we could patent her DNA and make a fortune. How did you see beyond the surface?"

I just went on instinct, really. I told Jim as much. Their "hmmmms" told me that they thought it was too bad that my accurate instinct with Juanita hadn't done me as much good with Caro. I decided to put them out of their misery.

"It's too bad my instinct didn't function as well before marrying Caro." Relieved, their faces both said, "You said it, we didn't." They didn't comment verbally, but they didn't have to.

"Hey, Jim," I changed the subject, "did you know that Juanita speaks Cantonese?"

"Along with Turkish, Swahili and Bulgarian?" He thought I was starting on one of my "Wonder Woman Juanita" routines of exaggerated praise. It wouldn't have been the first time.

"Nope. This is for real. She learned Cantonese from her ex, even spoke it with him towards the end of their marriage. When I was interviewing her for the job and saw her name and 'divorced' marital status, I had asked her as a joke if she had learned Mandarin Chinese while married. She admitted, with great shame, that since her ex was from Hong Kong, she *'only'* knew Cantonese, and was worried if that was a deficiency so major as to disqualify her from consideration for the job. I nearly fell off my chair when I realized she was serious. I guess I never mentioned that, did I?"

"Holy crap, I hadn't the slightest idea," said Jim with no small amount of awe. "Are you serious? With her pronunciation of English, her spoken Cantonese is probably just as much of a catastrophe, but if she understands it, we could use her to stand around in a meeting room like a menial coffee server while we're negotiating with businessmen from Hong Kong or Guangdong. She could translate for us what they were saying while we are out of the room. Those guys are so macho; they'd never suspect a female Hispanic coffee server of understanding every word they say. Wow!! I never knew. We've had this amazing asset in the company for like five years and completely ignored it. I'll have a talk with the partners in a day or two, and make them aware of this. We do *lots* of business with people from southern China these days."

"You might offer her a decent raise in salary just to insure she stays around, once she knows how valuable you think she is," I recommended.

"I think we'll quadruple it," Jim said. "We'll earn it back on the very first negotiation we have. Oops!"

He remembered whom he had just said that to. "I guess she'd be making more than you if we did that. I guess we'd give you a raise just for having brought it up."

I reassured him, "Hey, look, she's the one who speaks Cantonese, not me. You could quadruple my salary and I'd still never be able to learn Cantonese, so give her whatever she deserves based on her own merits and don't worry about me."

"That little bit of knowledge will probably end up being worth enough to the firm to cover a few raises, and could well end up being my ticket to senior partner. I'll take care of the worrying, OK?"

"Deal," I said with a grin, and we sealed it with the rest of the bottle of California red he had opened earlier. I almost felt bad about not telling him that I didn't plan to be around to enjoy any further raises, but I was thrilled at the prospect that Juanita might get a massive one, as well as some recognition for the brainy woman she was, rather than being judged just for the image she projected in our ignorant Anglo eyes.

We talked about babies for the rest of the time, as Janice wasn't interested in office shop talk. When the food had started to digest and the wine was starting to wear off, I thanked them both profusely for having me over, especially, as I had been otherwise looking at the prospect of spending the whole day alone. I neglected to tell them that I did not have to contemplate spending the evening alone. That would have required a few explanations that I was not prepared to give. They said it was their pleasure, and that they had both enjoyed my words on babies and families. They said they hoped that I would "find someone" again soon, so that we could make it a foursome in the future. I said that I actually had someone I was "possibly getting serious with," but she lived rather far away. Jim and Janice said they hoped it worked out and that if it did, that they would get to meet her. I didn't want to get embarrassingly evasive, so I just said, "We'll see," and left it at that. After a firm handshake from Jim and a warm embrace from Janice, I headed back home. I reflected on leaving behind such good friends, but you had to follow your heart. Thomas Jefferson was right. I hated to leave Jim and Janice guessing, and I'm still not sure how much Juanita had already guessed, but Anne was my future (my future, my past, whatever), and that's where I wanted to be. Jim and Janice and their new baby would be fine without me, and I would be miserable without Anne. Not a hard choice to make. Lafite 1860 still beats even the finest of California Cabernets.

54.

I got back to the house around 5:30 and changed into my 1860s clothes right away. At the portal, I only saw Minou foraging around, probably looking for some wayward smoked salmon that had lost its way in the vineyards. Anne popped up from just out of view of the portal and said, *"Coucou!"* She had heard me coming and wanted to surprise me (she did).

I jumped over and held her. She kissed me and asked me if I didn't want to make my permanent move a day early. I told her there was a very good reason why I, and thus we, had to wait until tomorrow.

"Plus c'est court, plus ça semble long." (The shorter it is, the longer it seems.) I nodded.

She told me that "papa (i.e., Philippe)" was aware that I would be coming tomorrow and had arranged a *"modeste"* place for me to store *"mes affaires,"* which in this case, meant "my stuff." As "my stuff," in this case (apologies to George Carlin's ghost), meant a king's ransom in negotiable, legal tender gold coins, I hoped that the modest place was so modest as to not stand out like a sore *pousse.*

I told her that I would not be bringing much more than a few *"médicaments,"* (medicines,) the clothes on my back (the ones she had made for me), and *"un peu d'argent."* (some money.)

She asked me that if this was all I was bringing, how come I needed a sturdy horse-drawn cart for transportation? That was a logical enough question, and one I didn't mind answering, but didn't want her to walk around in a daze all that night and the next day when I told her just how much my *"un peu d'argent"* was. So, I told her, *"C'est parce-que j'ai besoin de beaucoup de médicaments."* (It's because I need a lot of medicine.) She gave me a slight poke in the side.

"Tu n'as pas l'air si malade que ça," (You don't look *that* sick,) she commented.

"Je pourrais toujours le devenir," (I could always become it) I answered.

"Arrêtes," (Stop it,) she told me. *"Si tu ne veux pas me le dire maintenant, je verrai bien demain soir."* (If you don't want to tell me now, I'll see tomorrow night.)

I could see that this bothered her. I told her it wasn't that I wanted to conceal anything from her. That was the last thing I would ever want to do. I just wanted to make sure that for the last day, that her *"comportement"* (behavior) would not indicate anything more than a slight anticipation. She looked at me and said, *"C'est quelque chose qui me plaira?"* (Is it something I'll like?)

I smiled at that one. *"Beaucoup, même."* (A lot, even.)

She sighed and resigned herself. *"D'accord, un jour. Très mystérieux, tout de même ."* (OK, one day. Very mysterious, all the same.)

I emphasized again that it was only mysterious for a day, and for a very good reason.

"Bon, et maintenant, j'ai quelque chose qui te plaira à toi, j'éspère." (All right, and now I have something that *you'll* like, I hope.)

"Et ça, c'est ?" (And that is...?) My voice trailed off waiting for her to complete my sentence.

She smiled slyly and said softly, *"Anne, crue."* (Anne, raw.) I said I could think of nothing better on the menu, and off we headed to the cabin in the woods.

Lying in each other's arms in a slight sweat, she remarked that all she could detect this evening was a slight aroma of ginger and she asked if I had taken a break from my Thai and Vietnamese chefs. I told her about my visit with Jim and Janice Hernández. I told her most of the conversation, especially the part about wanting children. She asked me if Caro had suddenly come back wanting children, if I would want to go back to her. I explained that I would never want to have children with Caro, as I could never fulfill her main desire, which could only be fulfilled by material objects. I told Anne that what I loved about her was that she was devoid of such material needs and that she let me fulfill her needs with, so to speak, empty hands. She told me that I fulfilled her needs with *"ton esprit."* (your spirit.) *"Et, de temps en temps, ce qui se trouve derrière ton zee-PAIR."* (And, from time to time, what can be found behind your zee-PAIR.)

This time, I was the one laughing my fool head off, and she joined me.

"J'aime le son de ta voix quand tu ris," (I like the sound of your laugh,) she said. I told her that her laugh was music to my ears, too, and it was what I had so missed with Caro.

"La pauvre, elle doit être une fille très triste," (Poor thing, she must be one very sad girl,) Anne observed.

"Ne parlons plus des personnes tristes," (Let's not talk about sad people anymore,) I suggested. She smiled and nodded.

"Moi, en tout cas, je suis bien contente," (I, at any rate, am quite happy,) she said. I said that I was, too. She wrapped her arm around me and closed her eyes. *"Bon, alors, ne parlons pas pendant un petit moment."* (Well, then, let's not talk at all for a bit.)

And so we lay there, letting the evening drag along at its own pace without us, until she stirred and reminded me that she still had to be home that night. I got the impression that at this point, everyone in the family had to have known what was going on, but there were certain unwritten rules concerning what was said to whom and what was not. Fine, I'd get clued in by Anne and the men in her family in due time.

When the light of day started to wane to a point where the light in the cabin sent its silent signal, we got dressed and walked back to the portal. She looked at it for a second.

"Quelle phénomène t'a propulsé ici chez moi," (What a phenomenon that brought you here to me,) she mused, almost to herself.

"Quelle chance incroyable que tu aies été là quand cette porte s'est ouverte," (What incredible luck that you were here when that portal opened,) I reminded her.

She turned to me and reminded me, *"Il ne faut pas se moquer de la fortune quand elle t'offre un cadeau.* (You shouldn't make fun of fortune when it offers you a gift.) *Tu ne sais jamais si ça sera la dernière fois."* (You never know if it'll be the last time.)

"Une fois m'a suffit," (Once was enough)," I reminded her.

"Une panne suffit pour tout détruire, aussi," (One thing going wrong is enough to destroy everything, too,) she cautioned me. *"Ne manques pas de venir demain, et le reste de ma vie,"* (Don't you fail to come tomorrow, and for the rest of my life,) she whispered to me.

"Je ne te ferais pas faux bond, et tu ne serais plus jamais sans moi," (I won't fail, and you won't be without me ever again,) I promised her. In French, it somehow flows better; sorry.

I held her tightly to me, and felt her press up against me. One more day, *Ro-BAIR*. Don't mess it up.

55.
Tuesday, September 7

I got up early. The alarm I had set the previous night woke me up at 5:30 a.m.. I showered, got dressed, and made myself three English muffins, one with raspberry jam and the other two with peanut butter. It occurred to me that these might be my last English muffins and last peanut butter ever. Very weird, but not enough to distract me.

I thought that today, I must be feeling like Eisenhower felt on the morning of June 6, 1944.

I went downstairs to put together the ammonium nitrate explosive as per the instructions I had printed out on Saturday, and it was frighteningly easy. I was done by 8:00 a.m. I carefully made sure the last details were ready, but not such that it might detonate prematurely. I remembered that cartoon where an instructor for suicide bombers had a belt of explosives around his waist, and he was telling his rapt students, "Now pay careful attention. I am only going to demonstrate this once!" I wanted my little ka-boom to go off only once, too, but not before I wanted it to, and definitely not blowing me up with it. I didn't anticipate any of the Brinks guys disobeying my instructions to stay upstairs when they arrived, but in case one of them got a little overeager and followed me downstairs, even only partially, I did not want him to get a whiff of the fact that there were enough explosives in the room to turn the house into matchsticks. So, I hid the bomb parts carefully among and, mostly, behind the boxes housing the electrical circuitry for my portals. Since it looked like a bunch of electrical mumbo jumbo even to one who had knowledge of the field, it wouldn't stand out in the slightest to someone who had none. Maybe I was going a little overboard, but this was going to be my only shot. No second chances, so it was better to be overcautious then to bang my head against the wall later on for a lifetime of "if onlys."

Satisfied that I had made the presence of Hiroshima Jr. undetectable to even a curious intruder into my basement, I went back upstairs and grabbed my briefcase and the two cardboard boxes I had gotten from shipping last Friday. I assembled the big one, so it now was a real box, and put the folded up little one inside it. It was still practically empty and weighed nothing.

I called the number for Brinks that Josh had given me to make sure my fax from Monday night had been received. I got transferred to a guy I guess must have been the dispatcher for Sherman Oaks. The guy said, yes, he had gotten the fax, and he had set up the delivery for 5:30 p.m. as requested, allotted half an hour for handover, and an extra hour of guard duty for the four armed men who would be accompanying the shipment. The only thing he was nervous about was that he couldn't figure out what kind of business it was to whom he would be making delivery. I said that it was not a place of business, but my home. Understandably skeptical, he inquired if I had sufficient security measures in place to house such valuables. I assured him that I did, and that his company and his men were absolved of all responsibility the minute they left my property. He said I'd have to sign a release form his men would have on them when they arrived at my house. I said I would be glad to do so. It sounded like he was still very uncomfortable with the whole scheme—to his credit, I'd say. It would have made me very nervous if he had found nothing unusual about my request.

I went into the garage and put my briefcase and the cardboard box into my car, then I headed to the bank. It was starting to get overcast, but wasn't raining yet, so the drive was not difficult. When I got to the bank's parking lot, I took the big cardboard box and my briefcase out of the car. I made a point of clumsily dropping the big cardboard box on the ground, picking it up again and dropping it again. The plan was to give whoever was watching the idea that the box weighed so little that there could be no wine bottles in there, or anything else of consequence, for that matter.

Tom Nakano was waiting for me in the lobby. Wendy was either not there yet or with a client. He ushered me into his office, had me sign a few forms, and had me make out a check for $50,000 to "Cash." I signed the back of it, and he handed me five bundles of one hundred $100 bills.

"What's in the box?" he asked. "Roses for my wife?"

"Next time," I smiled. I opened the big box and took out the still-flat little box. From my briefcase, I took out that morning's *USA Today*. "I need to do this away from prying eyes. It will only take me a minute. Is that OK?"

"I guess," he said, curious as to what in the world I had in mind.

"Thanks!" I said, sounding relieved and not really faking it. He got a call and asked if he could leave me alone there for five or ten minutes. I said sure. Perfect! This saved me a trip to a public men's room with a borrowed pair of scissors. He left, and I took the small box and folded it into shape. I then lined it with crumpled up pages from the newspaper, placed the bundles of $100 bills in it one by one wrapped up in more crumpled up newspaper, and packed them so tightly that rattling the box around produced not the slightest amount of movement inside. The box was small and compact, although it now had a little weight to it, but it was no more than it would have weighed if I had packed three medium-length paperback novels in it. As a matter of fact, that was my whole idea. I took some wide tape out of my briefcase, taped the box firmly together, and then wrapped it tightly in the wrapping paper I had bought Saturday.

I used some scissors on Tom's desk to cut the paper to size. After taping up the wrapping paper on the outside, I peeled off the mailing label I had gotten from the post office near Josh's shop and pasted it onto the package. It fit snugly into my briefcase. I sat down and let my mind wander for the next two minutes. When he returned, I left a bewildered Tom Nakano to dispose of the debris that had once been the larger box and the leftover snips of wrapping paper. I thanked him for all his help and discretion, and asked him to see if Wendy was still absent.

Tom looked outside his office, and said, "Bad luck. Either she just got here or the client she was with left. One way or the other, she's at her desk outside. She'll see you when you leave."

Oh well. I said, "We'll at least confuse her a little." His face showed he had no clue what I meant, but he played along. We walked out of his office, and although I didn't look directly at Wendy, she noticed that Tom and I were together. As we approached her desk, I turned to Tom, and said, "Look, you may think I've been wasting my time here this morning, but I swear to you that a good vintage Lafite blows the cork off the best Mouton Rothschild any day. I want you to promise me you'll come with me to the next wine tasting I can find time for and let me convince you, all right?"

Tom knew less about wine vintages than he knew about the mating habits of tree frogs, but he went along and said, "It sounds like an exercise in futility, but if it'll get you off my back once and for all, call me, and it's a date."

I gave him the thumbs up sign, we shook hands, and I left the bank. Wendy may not have bought that we had met to discuss nothing more than wine vintages, but from our animated expressions, she might have gathered that the subject of wine was of far greater importance than whatever else I might have stopped by for. Whatever she might have thought, if she was on the phone to Caro about it, and I'm sure she would be, whatever she had to say would not raise enough suspicion in Caro's mind to feel the necessity to undertake anything prior to our scheduled meeting at B&B tomorrow morning. If Wendy were to mention the wine argument, Caro would probably interpret that as "business as usual" for me and probably dismiss my entire visit offhandedly.

56.

I left the bank, and drove to the post office near Josh's shop. The package I had prepared with the $50,000 in cash in it was all properly addressed with a neat USPS label, but I didn't know what it would cost, so I stood in line to mail it. There were only three people in front of me, although one of them seemed to speak only Ukrainian or some such language, so it took five minutes longer than should have been necessary to get a stamp for a post card. When it was finally my turn, I just put my package, addressed to Juanita's home, on the scale and paid the required postage for a registered package. The clerk filled out the form for a registered package (no special rate for "printed matter," boo hoo!), pasted the postage on it, and handed me my receipt. I'd never find out if it got to her if all went right, but I hoped so. I had slipped in a little hand-written note saying, *"Gracias para todo. Tenías razón con mi amiga, pero te ruego, no digas nada a nadie, nunca, igual lo que suceda."* (Thank you for everything. You were right about my girlfriend, but I beg you, don't say anything to anyone, ever, no matter what happens.) OK, I used an Internet translator for half of that, but it sounded right to my non-Hispanic ears. I also wrote this: "If you declare it, use income averaging! If not, *es igual* (it doesn't matter)." This was more than she made in a year, and after taking out for taxes, close to what she made in two years. In the time she had worked with/for me, Juanita had always stood up for me, been there when I couldn't or didn't want to, and been cross with me exactly once, and that was when I lied to her last Wednesday, which she had detected instantly and had every reason to call me on it.

I would have given her the million instead of the American Cancer Society, but for a few reasons. If I had sent her a check, it would have had to reach her after my disappearance/presumed demise, and might have been refused by Tom's bank when presented for payment. Besides, Naomi Roganov might have shown up on her doorstep to demand the money be turned over to Uncle Sam (or Auntie Naomi). Caro might have chimed in as well with her lawyer. Both Naomi and Caro would have had a worse time in the court of public opinion trying to take away a donation to the American Cancer Society. Besides, I left the two of them $100,000 to fight over, so it's not like they would be fighting over bread crumbs (though compared to what my account held a few weeks earlier, that's exactly what was left).

Withdrawing $100,000 in cash was probably too big for Tom not to have had big suspicions, no matter what I told him it was for, and it would have made for a far more conspicuous package, as well. I figured $50,000 was just small enough to not make too many waves, and I wanted Juanita to be able to enjoy her money with no repercussions whatsoever. If she thought it was too much, she could always give some to Miguel, so he could open a formal school for maa shalats in Guatemala. Besides, she hadn't the faintest idea that my conversation yesterday with Jim Hernández might soon lead to her getting a raise in salary so huge (I hoped) as to make my little parting gift seem paltry by comparison.

Notice to any eager IRS agent who might read this and think they have found an easy mark in Juanita: She is smarter than either of us, especially you. If she doesn't declare it as income, she'll have hidden it where you'll never find it, and although there will be a record of my having withdrawn the cash from the bank, the only evidence you have that she received any of that money from me at all is this internet posting by a guy who claims to have spent afternoons lost in pleasant conversation with Thomas Jefferson. Ponder *that* one for a minute before running to your immediate superior yelling that you have snared a live one, OK?

With Juanita's parting gift safely in the mail, I headed for the office. I had no idea how to conduct myself. If all went well, I would disappear from the face of the earth that evening and no one would have the slightest idea how or why. I don't know why I was worried—after all, except for that minor detail, today would be a day like any other, right?

When I got to the office, Juanita was waiting for me. I had to get a grip. Yes, she was smart and intuitive to the point of being clairvoyant, but there was no way in the world she could have guessed what was going on in my head that morning. As it turned out, the reason she was waiting for me was as much a mystery to her as it was to me. She handed me a sealed envelope. It was opaque, but felt like it contained another envelope inside it. I asked if it was for me.

Juanita said, "Djess, eets for djoo, bat djoo cannot open it unteel da lass t'ing djoo doo today (Yes, it's for you, but you can't open it until the last thing you do today)." And here I thought I was the one being mysterious.

"This is not from you?" I asked, now genuinely curious.

She shook her head, "No, señor." She told me that a well-dressed elderly lady, *muy elegante*, maybe eighty years old, *"viejita,"* had left it for me early that morning, didn't seem at all bothered that she didn't find me at the office, and left specific instructions to give the envelope to me, but that opening it was to be the last thing I did today in my house. This seemed incredibly weird, and the timing was most inauspicious, as I did have just a few other things planned for this evening. But OK, if it were a request for my presence at some social function, it would be ignored, and if it were a request for a charitable contribution, I wouldn't have time to honor that, either. If the American Cancer Society had already gotten my million-dollar check, even if they were to send someone to the office to thank me, I doubt they would have used an eighty-year-old woman, and they certainly would not have delivered a note of thanks with no writing on the outside. Come to think of it, I had only left my home address on the letter and on the envelope. There was no mention of where I worked at all. I have to admit, I was genuinely baffled, but if that's the way she wanted it, then fine with me. I was almost glad she had insisted on that. This way, whatever request might be made of me on a page of this elegant set of stationery, I would not be able to honor it and wouldn't have the time to worry about it. The little old lady from Pasadena (or wherever she turned out to be from) would have to come back tomorrow to hear of my absence like the rest. Whatever it is she wanted from me, she could get in line with everybody else.

I stuck the mysterious envelope in my inside jacket pocket, where it barely fit. What in the world could it be about, anyway? The thing that kept gnawing at me was the part about not opening it until it was the last thing I did today. I mean, today, of all days! That just had a rather peculiar ring to it. I couldn't fault her timing for dramatic effect, although there wasn't any way she could have known that, whoever she was. Oh, well. I had other bottles to cork today.

Emmett Blake stopped by to thank me for getting his logistics arranged on such short notice last week, which was an unexpected honor. Except for calling me in advance of the dark and stormy night, and confronting me about being followed by Gordon Mercer and Company, the senior partners rarely acknowledged my existence, and this was a nice reminder that not all lawyers were bad guys. I heard later on in the day that while he had not negotiated the sale of Volkswagen to Bill Gates or Warren Buffett, his trip to Germany had been wildly successful and his timely arrival in Frankfurt on Friday morning had been crucial to his mission being "possible." He must have landed some immense fee for the firm, and if I had helped him do it in some small way, then it was nice of him to acknowledge it. If our roles had been reversed, I expect he would have had more luck with Lufthansa than I would have had navigating the German legal system. I didn't "haff vays to make zem talk," much less negotiate the sale of mad King Ludwig's Neuschwanstein castle, or whatever it was Blake was doing over there.

57.

There were a dozen other menial tasks to take care of, since today was the first day of a short week after a holiday. Everyone was back and whatever they needed, they needed it yesterday. I went about trying to accommodate them all like there was no tomorrow, as, with any luck, there wouldn't be—not as they understood it, anyway. I delegated chores to Juanita and still had my hands full. Even so, as I watched her, I caught her stealing glances back at me, too. She *knew* something was up. Don't ask me how, but she did. At the same time, she handled everything flawlessly, and it occurred to me, not for the first time, that she could assume my position in a seamless transition. I only hoped that the partners would honor her abilities with a commensurate increase in salary. If they could listen beyond her cartoon character speech and read any of her memos, they'd realize that if she were to polish up her spoken English and go to law school, she'd be able to make partner herself, within two years, she was that smart. If Ecuador ever got into such dire financial straits that they had to sell the Galápagos Islands, I'll bet Juanita could find the top buyer for them and get a binding clause that the new buyer would agree to stiffer environmental restrictions than were already in force.

I had no time for lunch at all, but Juanita arranged that, too. She ordered chicken sunset enchiladas for me, sort of a Tex-Mex variety with two different kinds of melted cheese over them, which gave them their "sunset" appearance. A little gooey, but just spicy enough to give them a little "kick," and they really were great. I never even knew there had been a place that made Mexican food that good in the neighborhood. No wonder. There hadn't been. This place, Juanita explained, had just opened ten days ago, practically around the corner. She made it her business to always have information like this. B&B would do just fine without me.

I couldn't pack up all my personal effects without arousing more than a few questions of a nature I preferred not to confront just now, so I asked Juanita if she could take over for me if I were to leave at 4:00 instead of at 6:00 p.m. as usual. She asked me if what I had to do was really so very important. I said, yes, today, it was. She asked if it had to do with my "gir-FREHN," and I smiled and said, *"Por supuesto."* (Of course.) She grinned her knowing grin, said she *knew* something was up with me from the second I walked in the door this morning. One of the rare occasions when Juanita's legendary sixth sense got the vibes right, but the scenario wrong, if not completely. She thought I was going to propose tonight. Not quite, querida Juanita. That was a done deal. Tonight, I intended to elope, and not to Reno. But I couldn't quite tell her that, could I? So I let her think she got it right, and at 4:00, she practically shoved me out the door and said, *"¡Vete, vete ya!"* which is pretty much the Spanish equivalent of, "Go on, get outta here!"

I wanted to say goodbye to everyone, especially Jim Hernández, but also Steve Clark, Richie Genovese and a few others, but I couldn't without risking blowing the whole thing. So, I just quietly (except for Juanita) left Blake and Brock with zero fanfare whatsoever. I hoped the rest of the evening would go off with as little fanfare, but I couldn't get rid of the feeling that I would not get a waiver of Murphy's Law so easily. I'd find out soon enough.

I got home a few minutes before 4:30, everyone else having a full work day, and traffic was light. I am putting down the events of the day here in between preparations. I have the burlap bags and my medicine in place downstairs, and my set of contemporary (as in 1860 France) clothes ready to put on once the gold is finally loaded onto Anne's cart. There is one thing I have decided to take with me and risk it being found. I took the spiral out of the Red Book of American coins that Josh gave me. I tossed away the covers.

All I want is to have something I can copy onto contemporary (1860) paper, and then burn the original when I have all the information transferred. Maybe I'll be able to find some of these old, super-expensive (in 2010) coins for nothing and accumulate a cool collection for peanuts. After all, France, along with England, was one of the few nations to trade with the United States since its inception, and there could well be some old American coins in France in 1860 that made their way back over the last seventy years as pocket change, mementos of a visit or whatever. The pages of Josh's catalog would tell me which ones to look out for. I didn't know much about them yet, but if I was going to live in Bordeaux in the year 1860, a bottle of 1859 Lafite would be more common, and worth less, than a bottle of mineral water (tasted better, though). Bottles of 1859 Château Lafite would no longer be the subject of high finance. They wouldn't require much detective work to find them, either. They'd be served at lunch on a daily basis!

I did another review of my little (OK, not so little) ammonium nitrate bomb. I'm not going to go into details. It's not rocket science to make one, but it does require a bit of skill. Remember that weirdo who wanted to blow up Times Square in New York? He got the instructions wrong, or else Times Square would have looked like Oklahoma City, but with forty times the casualties. Enough nut cases have no doubt gotten the idea without my helping any of them out. Maybe it's arrogant of me to assume my motives for wanting to build one of these explosive devices are nobler than anyone else's, but if anyone else who *has* built one did it to protect his blissful life with a woman he loves 150 years in the past, let him speak now or forever shut his trap. Nobody? I thought not.

58.

At around quarter after 5:00, Anne showed up at the portal, this time driving a heavy cart pulled by two tired-looking but very sturdy horses. She had a smile on her face that I could only describe as beatific. The cart had a long, flat, wooden surface with walls on the sides about eight inches high, perfect for what I needed. Anne had brought along some coarse cloth covers and some hay as padding, just as I had asked.

"Tu es prêt?" (You're ready?) she asked.

"Presque," (Almost,) I smiled back. *"D'un instant à l'autre."* (Any moment now.)

"Je suis prête pour toi," (I'm ready for you,) she said, holding up Thomas Jefferson's present, the thirty-one-year-old bottle of Château Margaux, 1787. I'll never get to describe its bouquet in this narrative, but I'll bet Aunt Murgatroid would have been impressed.

The doorbell rang at 5:25. Brinks? I told Anne I suspected it was *"la caisse."* (The cashier.) I went upstairs to check. I told Anne I'd be right back. Of course, it was Brinks. I hadn't called for a pizza, and the Avon lady was off today. They were four men strong, and strong in more ways than one. They all looked like runners-up in a Rambo lookalike contest.

"Robert Packard?" one of them asked.

I almost answered, "No, Daffy Duck. You must have the wrong address," but besides the fact that it probably wasn't the right occasion to get sarcastic, these guys didn't exactly exude lightheartedness. Instead, I remained as serious as they were, and said, "Yes, that's right. Would you like some ID just in case?"

"Yes, please, if you don't mind," the same one answered. "This is a high-value delivery," he started.

"I'm well aware," I cut him off. "About 325 kilograms' worth, actually. Here you go." I would have been very suspicious if he hadn't asked for any ID for this kind of value. I showed him both my passport and driver's license.

He stayed formal. After examining both passport and license, he returned them to me with a, "Thank you, sir." These guys appeared to all be ex-military, which was just fine with me. Taking a quick look past the front door into my modest abode, the modesty of which had offended Caro for so many years, he asked, a little incredulous, "Is *this* the address where you want delivery?" I said that yes, it was, and that I had installed some extremely sophisticated security protection in the basement, where the delivery was to be stored. He asked if he and his men were to bring the bags down to the basement. I said no, my insurance did not permit anyone to go down there but me, but that if he and his men could deliver the bags to the door at the top of the stairway, I would take them down to the secure area, one by one. He told his companions, and I could practically see them rolling their eyes, but I was certainly not the first rich nut case they had delivered to, and would doubtlessly not be the last. He made sure to have me sign the release forms his dispatcher had told me about that morning.

"How do you want us to do this?" the same guy asked. Very good question, and not at all obvious. These guys were pros. Thank goodness.

"Let's do it this way," I said. I had parked my car off to the side at the curb and the garage, while not completely free of accumulated debris, was free enough so that the Brinks truck could back up and fill the entrance to the garage. From the outside, no one could get a good look at what was happening inside, and certainly not at what was being offloaded out of the back of the truck and into the house.

"I've put my car out at the street. Why don't you back the truck up to the garage so that no one can see what is being offloaded, nor by how many men? There is a door to the interior of the house at the back of the garage, and your men can work from the back of the truck, unseen from the outside."

He walked over to the garage, took a quick visual assessment of the dimensions, and decided that it would work. He nodded his approval and went back to the truck, got in, and had a few words with the driver. They gave me a thumbs-up, and I hit the switch that opened the garage door. As soon as it was open, the big Brinks truck backed neatly into it with only the front half sticking out. I saw two black limousines pull up directly across from the front door of my house. I locked the front door. The Brinks guys noticed the limos as well. It looked like Stef and his goons wanted not only a ringside seat (which they would not get), but were like sharks smelling blood (which they figured they would get), waiting to circle for the kill.

"Friends of yours?" one of the Brinks guards asked, with a tone that implied he suspected exactly the opposite and was ready for trouble.

"Doubtful," I answered. "Those stupid jerks from the British Consulate again, I'd guess."

That stopped them. "The British Consulate?"

I said, "Yeah, they're scouting for houses for their diplomats in lower-priced areas than west L.A. and Beverly Hills, and they've been by more than once, asking if I'd consider selling. When they came around before, it was always on a Tuesday, just like today."

"I see," said the biggest one, clearly not entirely convinced, but thrown somewhat off by my immediate response and my apparent lack of concern. Another round of eye-rolling and mumbled "whatevers" ensued. The lack of diplomatic plates on the limos probably would not have escaped their notice. Either they had not seen the limos' license plates, or they had not taken the trouble to get a closer look when they could have. Miguel had told me, and Stef had confirmed by not denying it, that their vehicles had Nevada plates. The Brinks guys would have smelled something fishy, knowing that a British consulate in California would not be driving vehicles with Nevada plates. But as long as they didn't see the Nevada plates, and no one interfered with them while they were doing their job, it wouldn't be an issue with them. They were armed and knew how to use their weapons, too. A couple of them looked like they might have shot it out with the Taliban and survived. They probably figured they could handle some domestic bad guys if they had to. I'm sure they could have, too, but a gunfight would have delayed my plans, and possibly led to the discovery of the portals. I hoped Stef and his thugs would keep their distance as long as the Brinks guys were there. That's me, the eternal optimist.

The Brinks guards started unloading the canvas sacks. They had a big "UBS" logo on them. I didn't remember all I had read about the various Swiss banks on the Internet, but I was pretty sure the UBS had been founded later than 1860, so I had been wise to get the burlap sacks. As soon as one sack was at the door to the stairway down to the basement, I carried it down, took a sharp pen knife I had for the occasion, and cut the cord. I then poured the 2500 gold 20 franc coins into a burlap sack, tied it shut, brought it over to the portal, and handed it over to Anne on the other side. As I emptied them, I tossed the canvas UBS sacks into a deep recess of the wine cellar. The bags, when full, weighed something like thirty-five pounds each (it sounds like less if you say sixteen kilograms), but

Anne was used to hard work and didn't flinch. This went on for about twenty minutes until the last sack of the twenty-one had been loaded. Anne kept looking at me as I kept handing her the sacks. She held her tongue, but it was obvious she wanted to ask me something, and I knew what it was. Heavy sacks full of gold coins clinking against each other do make a rather distinctive sound when tossed, one after another, on a hard, wooden surface. After the last sack, the lightest one with only 1000 coins instead of 2500 coins, she couldn't hold back any longer. She sat down on the edge of the cart, the heavy sacks behind her, and crossed her arms.

"*Bon, mon cher Robert, ces sacs sont bien lourds.* (All right, my dear Robert, these sacks are good and heavy.) *Vas-tu me dire en fin qu'est-ce qu'il y a là-dedans, vraiment?* (Are you finally going to tell me what is really in them?) *Et n'essaies même pas de me dire que ces sacs sont pleins de zippers.*" (And don't even try to tell me these sacks are full of zee-*PAIRS.*) She hadn't been able to see me make the transfer from the UBS bags, as I had done that at the other end of the basement at the foot of the stairwell.

I told her, "*Tu fais bien de rester assise, chère Anne.* (It's a good thing you're sitting down, dear Anne). *Il y a des pièces de vingt francs en or dedans.*" (There are gold 20 franc coins in there.)

Her eyes grew wide, wider and wider still.

"*Tout ça?*" (All that?) she breathed in, jerking her thumb backwards, pointing to the burlap bags.

"*Tout ça,*" I confirmed.

"*Combien y-a-t-il?*" (How much is there?) she whispered, awestruck.

"*Un million et vingt mille francs,*" (One million and twenty thousand francs,) I replied.

She turned and stared at the bundle of sacks behind her on the wooden platform of the cart. *"Eh, bien,"* (Well, well,) she said, now back to a matter-of-fact voice, but still staring.

"Tu avais raison hier ,"(You were right yesterday,) she remarked, turning back to me.

"Comment, ça?" (How so?) I asked.

"Ça me plaît." (I like it) She grinned. *"Et tu avais raison hier, j'aurais eu du mal à me comporter normalement si je l'avais su!"* (And you were right yesterday, I would have had a hard time acting normally if I had known.)

I changed quickly into my 1860s clothes and crossed over, bringing one last little bag, the one with the paper bags of medicine Juanita had gotten for me and the pages from Josh's Red Book. I noticed briefly that one of Josh's California Coin business cards was stuck to one of the introductory pages—good advertising for him in 2010, but less useful to him a century before he would be born. I was in a hurry, and so didn't try to remove it right away, but I'd have to remind myself to destroy it before long, not that a card from a shop in California that wouldn't open for another 140 years would attract a lot of attention in Bordeaux, 1860. Even so, I had to remember to remove it at some point—forgetting little details like that could have consequences.

The cart had some leftover hay on it and a pitchfork for pushing the hay around, but still had plenty of room for the sacks of gold. Together, we arranged them up on the wooden cart. They really didn't take up as much space as the number "one million" implies. The cart had shifted a few feet during the process of heaving the sacks up onto the wooden plank, but the horses shifted with it, used to loading on uneven ground and probably with heavier loads.

The portal was now off to one side, no longer visible from the cart, but we kept working. We were done in a matter of minutes. I took the piece of rope she had found for me, crossed back over to my basement, and tied it around the thick power cord that had been providing the electricity for these devices since I had started tinkering with them and, more importantly, since the portals to Château Lafite and Monticello had come into being. Then I coiled the rope in a corner near the power outlet. Less than an hour to go.

We arranged the straw around the burlap sacks with the gold 20 franc coins that were now all loaded onto the cart. The cotton pillow case with my medicine and the pages from Josh's Red Book were with Anne. I had a couple of details to take care of back in my basement before my last au revoir. I crossed back over in order to write the last bit of my one-shot blog (i.e., this here) on the laptop upstairs, bring out my homemade fertilizer bomb stowed down in the basement, see the Brinks guys off, hit "Enter" to send my blog out into the world, set the timer on the bomb, and, when safely on the Bordeaux side of the portal, yank the rope tied to the power plug to my little creation. I assumed, but didn't know for sure, that the portals would disappear if I pulled the plug. I didn't even know if they would reboot, so to speak, if the power were restored, but I hoped not, just in case I had gotten a failing grade in my Internet course in homemade explosives.

59.

I went upstairs to my laptop to type out the events of the day, got that done, went back down to the basement, and figured I was finished. Fat chance. Those two black limousines with the tinted windows were not the British Consulate's real estate scouting team after all. Down the basement stairs comes a guy I recognized as one of the two strong, silent types that accompanied Stefano to our first meeting about a month ago. Maybe six-foot-two, athletic build, dark blond hair, cut on the short side, but not a buzz cut by any means, dressed casually. He carried a very unfriendly looking black pistol and had a smug, arrogant grin pasted on his face. Now I know why people instinctively put up their hands in the movies when being confronted by a gun. It is *very* intimidating. What I didn't get was how this guy was able to waltz into the house with the armed Brinks guys still in the truck in the open garage in front of my house? How did he even *dare* in the first place?

Today's thugs are nothing if not accommodating. He told me before I asked.

"When Stef saw the Brinks truck backed up to your house, we figured there might be something in it for us, so he had me sneak in the back when your pals were done loading whatever it was into your house from the front. Piece of cake. They were their own distraction. They're relaxing right now inside their truck, all four of them. Thought we'd never catch on, did ya? Bet your wine cellar must be a million or two more valuable than it was an hour and a half ago, isn't it?" I nodded slowly. "Trying to get in the mother lode before we take over, right?" I nodded again. Luckily, he had no clue, so at least Anne was in no immediate danger. She could hear this guy menacing me, but, knowing no English, couldn't understand a word of what he was saying.

"You planning to go to a costume party or something?" he sneered, taking in the clothes Anne had had made for me.

"Something like that," I answered." "This isn't standard office attire where I work, if that's what you're asking."

He looked at the portal, went up to within a foot of it, and remarked, "Hey, **very** cool hi-def TV you got here," he remarked. "I ain't **never** seen one this big with this kind of sharpness. What the hell make is this?"

"It's an experimental model. It has kind of a long name," I answered. *"Il veut me tuer. Je ne pensais pas à ça. Je ne sais pas qu'est-ce que je peux faire."*

"What the hell kind of brand is *that*?" Stef's goon demanded. He said "the hell" a lot. "Longest name I ever heard, and it sure as hell doesn't sound Japanese or Chinese."

I had just told Anne, "He wants to kill me. I didn't think of this. I don't know what I can do." Luckily, Stef's thug was not a French major. When he again turned toward me, I saw her nod from a corner of the portal. She was quite aware that whoever she could see could just as easily see her back, and she obviously knew what a pistol was. She kept out of visual range until his back was turned to her.

"It's not just a brand. Like I said, it's an experimental model. I've been working on it with some friends from France. That's how come the long French name. It's not anything you can order just yet," I explained.

"Too bad," the guy said." "I don't know if you're going to survive long enough to build me one."

315

Trying to keep him talking (as in trying to keep myself alive),
I continued, "Look, if you're interested, I really could build you one.
It would take a while to get all the parts from France, but if it'll keep
me alive, believe me, I'll find them!"

"That's Stef's decision, not mine—as long as you don't make any
sudden moves, that is. I don't want to get into a firefight with the
Brinks guys, and you don't want it to be over your dead body, so
why don't we just stay the hell right here, nice and quiet, until your
Brinks buddies leave, and Stef and the others can join us and debate
whether or not you're gonna have another birthday?"

"Hey, we're friends," I assured him. "Your wish is my command. Nice
and quiet it is."

"You are being incredibly sensible about this," he remarked.
"You don't have a private army stashed in the next room, by
any chance?"

"I wish," I said. "I'd be a lot more confident about my next birthday
if I did, that's for sure." The Brinks truck would be pulling out
in maybe another forty minutes max, maybe less. I wasn't exactly
looking at my watch, which was in the bundle of my twenty-first
century clothes in a heap in the laundry room. There weren't a lot
of places to buy batteries for it where I had been intending to go.
The Brinks guys had specific instructions—from me, no less—not
to come down into the basement. This meant that Stef's thug
could train his gun on me as long as he wanted and would be in no
danger of the Brinks guards seeing him. The best laid plans of mice
and men...

He took his eye off me for a second, briefly looked back over his
shoulder through the portal (just missing Anne), and then turned
back to me. "This is definitely one cool set-up. What the hell,

316

maybe I'll take you up on your offer. That has to be a better deal for you than bequeathing it to me in your will, right?"

"It would definitely be my pleasure, as I work much better while alive, you know?"

He snickered, "Yeah, don't we all," and lowered the gun somewhat, relaxing in the confidence that he was in complete control of the situation, which he certainly was—for the next five seconds, anyway.

Suddenly, he lurched forward, his over-confident sneer instantly giving way to a look which could only be described as 50% shock and 50% agonizing pain. I think. I've never seen anyone up close with an expression like that. Half a second later, I saw the cause of his sudden change in demeanor. A medium-sized pitchfork was sticking out of his back, the four stakes driven up to the hilt in him. I got out of the way as he surged past me and onto the cement floor, face down, twitching, but otherwise not moving. The twitching didn't last more than half a minute, either. The hell, you say. How about *to* hell?

Anne's anxious voice came to me from the other side of the portal. "**Ro-BAIR***!! Tu vas bien?*" (Are you all right?) She had understood the situation and made her first and last contribution to the history of the twenty-first century. She also probably had saved my life in the process. I wasn't about to debate the nuances of justifiable homicide with her. I just told her that she had just saved my life from a killer, etc., etc., at which point she cut me off, and said, "*Dépêche-toi, tu me raconteras quand il y a du temps!*" (Hurry up, you'll tell me when there's time!) Ah, oui. When there's time. I guarantee you that with her, there was *definitely* no pun intended.

I ran to the top of the stairs and called to the Brinks guys at the garage, "How much longer do I have the pleasure of your presence?"

One of them called back, "Thirty-two minutes, sir, to be precise, although we can hang for a few if you need us."

"OK, thanks. That should be fine until the cavalry gets here." Muffled snickers from the garage.

I let Stef's goon ferment where he fell, and then set up the fertilizer bomb. I hope I set it up, anyway! It's not like I had asked the neighbors to let me blow up *their* houses for practice. Next, I went upstairs to the laptop, where I am now writing all this extra stuff down—not exactly the peaceful ending I had planned, but like I said, I'm telling what happened, and I couldn't care less who believes it. After all, the rest of my story is hardly a candidate for publication in *True Confessions*. I'll add a few details in the middle here and there where they make sense, and then I'll put a little note at the beginning so that no one who reads this thinks the body of Stef's thug is me.

There, that took all of ten minutes. Anne is waiting at the driver's seat, looking a little shaken up (I guess she doesn't kill twenty-first century gangsters as a part of her regular Tuesday evening aerobics workout), but ready for me to join her on the cart, which is now back in front of the portal, horses ready to go.

I took the rope attached to the power cord and pulled the other end through the portal, where Anne had set it on the cart, ready for me to pull it after I crossed for the last time. The Brinks guys had another fifteen minutes or so on the clock, then they'd ride off into the sunset, which meant Stef would be in here, I figure, no later than five minutes after that—maybe less when he realized his goon wasn't answering his cell phone. So here's my schedule: I'm going to grab my jacket from work and peek at the old lady's envelope from this morning, see what she wanted. Then I'll post this whole story on a few sites I have already had scouted out, hope that Caro and Aldo see it, as I have changed no names to protect the innocent, the guilty or the plain greedy. Then I'm going to wait until the Brinks truck takes off, set the timer on my fertilizer bomb for about three minutes after that, and then cross over to Anne and use the rope attached to the power cable to pull the plug and hope that the portals disappear. If they don't, then I hope the bomb works. If it doesn't *and* the portals are still there, then I guess Stef and friends will be following in my footsteps into the nineteenth century. If that happens and the portals stay, then I guess I'll be back to face the music at some point. Stefano is not likely to look kindly on the demise of his "associate." If all goes well, then all that will remain is this one-shot blog and a story that no one will ever believe. Time to check that letter I left in the jacket I was wearing at the office. This shouldn't take a minute.

60.

Oh. My. God. That envelope from the mysterious old lady at the office this morning—I just opened it. "About 80 years old." Like the equally mysterious eighty-year-old lady who showed up out of the blue at California Coin last week with the "$20 to $25 million collection" of old American and Thai coins she had "inherited from an ancestor in Europe." No, Josh, it wasn't your ad in the yellow pages. She had known exactly where to go and when. Little details do, indeed, have consequences. The inside envelope was addressed to "M. Robert Packard, 7 Septembre 2010." The handwriting was very ornate, a style hardly anyone used any more. Inside was a single piece of paper with a brief, hand-written note in French. It said, simply, *"Cher arrière-grandpère, vos descendants vous souhaitent un agréable voyage!"*

I'll say it again. Oh. My. God. The little old lady was *not* from Pasadena, and she would not be back tomorrow looking for me. She had known before anyone that I would no longer be there. Her note translated out to "Dear great-grandfather, your descendants wish you a pleasant journey!"

I'll still enjoy the wine for the rest of my life, but I guess Josh got me into a new hobby after all, and I returned/will be returning his favor in spades.

I now have this whole story ready to post. All I have to do is hit "enter." The Brinks truck will be leaving any minute now. When it does, the timer on the fertilizer bomb gets turned on for its three-minute countdown. One minute after that, I'll be sitting on Anne's cart, the rope attached to the portal's power cord in my hand, ready for me to pull it. Ten minutes after that, courtesy of Thomas Jefferson, Anne and I will be enjoying a 31-year-old bottle of Château Margaux, vintage 1787.

So, with any luck, au revoir for now, au revoir *to* now, and *santé!*

EXPLOSION DEMOLISHES RESIDENCE
IN SHERMAN OAKS, GAS LEAK SUSPECTED

Los Angeles Times, September 9, 2010

Michiko Taniuchi

Sherman Oaks, September 8—Sherman Oaks homicide police Detective William Engstrom said in a prepared statement that a gas leak is suspected as the cause of an explosion on Tuesday evening, September 7. The explosion devastated the house of Robert H. Packard, 36, of 1136 Grove Street. A severely burned body, presumed to be Mr. Packard, has been found in the area of the basement. Engstrom said that the gas leak was a preliminary theory and that the investigation is still ongoing. The Sherman Oaks Fire Department is also finishing its forensic investigation of the house's wreckage.

Mr. Packard was last seen entering his residence about 4:30 p.m. that afternoon and was not seen leaving it. According to Detective Engstrom, the cause of death may or may not have been from the explosion. There appeared to be major puncture wounds in the victim's back, he said, although the force of such an explosion would certainly have been sufficient to have driven heavy, sharp objects into a human body with deadly force. Engstrom stated that the force of the explosion rendered a definitive assessment impossible for the moment, and that the forensic report would furnish more concrete information. Parts of what appeared to be a pitchfork were found nearby among the debris. A Beretta 9 millimeter pistol was also found, although Engstrom said it was too early to determine if it had been fired. Mr. Packard had never applied for a handgun permit, and the police were checking the serial number for its registration.

Mr. Packard's car was in front of the house, parked on Grove Street, and suffered no serious damage. A passer-by, Mr.

Stefano Contini of Las Vegas, NV, was thrown to the ground by the force of the blast and slightly burned by a piece of flaming wood that fell on his arm. He was determined not to have a concussion, and after treatment by paramedics on the spot, was released after police had determined that he had no obvious connection to Mr. Packard or the explosion. "I was just out for a stroll," Mr. Contini told the press, "when this house just went up with a big boom. Just like that!" Mr. Contini explained he had been visiting friends in the neighborhood at the time, but did not specify who they were. No one else interviewed at the scene of the blast said they knew Mr. Contini.

At the time of the explosion, two large, black limousines were seen parked in front of or near the Packard residence, according to neighbors, but they left immediately after the explosion. This was of interest to the police, said Detective Engstrom, but no license plate numbers had been recorded and, therefore, it would be difficult to determine if the vehicles in question were related to the blast or not. Several neighbors said they had seen a Brinks armored truck backed up to the garage of the Packard residence for about an hour and a half prior to the explosion, but that it had left before the explosion occurred. A Brinks spokeswoman in Los Angeles confirmed that they had made a delivery at that time to the Packard address, but would only furnish details to the police, not to the media, as was their practice in such cases. She stated that Brinks would be making no further public comment.

Packard's wife, Carolyn A. Packard, formerly of Elko, NV, was not in the house at the time of the explosion and was not available for comment. She had recently been staying with a friend, Wendy Etxeverría, also of Sherman Oaks, and was apparently involved in divorce proceedings against Mr. Packard. She referred all inquiries to her attorney, Stanley Chase, of the firm of Barry and Berke, also of Sherman Oaks. Detective Engstrom said that she was not a suspect in the blast, although the police would be talking to her as a matter of routine, in case she could furnish any information that might prove helpful.

Mr. Packard worked at the Sherman Oaks law firm of Blake and Brock as head of their Security and Logistics Department, according to his assistant, Ms. Juanita Chang. Mr. and Mrs. Packard had no children. Despite his impending divorce, Ms. Chang said that Mr. Packard had never seemed happier with his life than he had recently. She said she had no idea why anyone might want to do Mr. Packard any harm. Richard Brock, one of the firm's two senior partners, said that Mr. Packard had been a most valuable employee at his firm for many years, and that his death would mean a great loss to Blake and Brock.

Detective Engstrom said that from the degree and manner of the damage done to the Packard house, a gas leak looked to be the most likely cause, although he stressed that he was just giving a preliminary opinion and it would be several days before the police could make a definitive statement as to the cause of the blast. They would await the results of the Fire Department's forensic investigation before any official statements were made on the matter. Detective Engstrom said that the basement area, where the body was found, was a chaotic jumble of wiring and what appeared to be wrecked parts of several as yet unidentified electrical devices. He further stated that a quantity of broken, dark green glass had been found in the vicinity of the basement, but he suspected nothing more exotic than a modest wine cellar. Further statements will be forthcoming as new evidence emerges.

**** **

"The phylloxera plague of 1870 virtually wiped out the grape vines of the Médoc region of Bordeaux, although a very few apparently did survive. This was not enough to repopulate the region, but it is almost as if someone knew the plague was coming and made an effort to safeguard a few vines for posterity and/or future personal use. Bottles of pre-1870 Bordeaux wines, especially if the bottles are in such condition as to indicate little change in the content, are considered great prizes and command great attention, as well as great prices, when offered for sale. They are a highlight of any wine tasting."

Excerpt, "The Great Wines of Bordeaux" by Aldous D. George, Harper, Los Angeles, 2015.

Thanks to, in alphabetical order:

Marc Birnbaum, Dallas

Sabine Bourgey, Paris

Dawne Brooks, Illinois

John Emory, Virginia

Kit Emory, New Jersey

Dr. Stanley Flegler, Lansing, Michigan

James Halperin, Heritage Auctions, Dallas

Wade Hinderling, New York

Stan Lee, Beverly Hills

Frank Martell, Heritage Auctions, Dallas

Michel Prieur, Paris †

Andrew Sather, New Jersey

Karlyn Thayer, Cheraw, Colorado †

Ruth Westheimer, New York

Elisabeth Wichmann-Emory, Düsseldorf

Cover illustration by Kerstin Wichmann,
Hamburg, Germany

Cover art by Mary Hermann and Lisa Fox

© 2012 by Marc Emory

Afterword

As far as the characters in this story go, my friends Ruth Westheimer and Stan Lee are perfectly real. Thomas Jefferson was obviously real, too, although I was not, alas, blessed with the personal access that Robert Packard managed to obtain for himself. Jefferson really did travel to Long Island with James Madison to try to preserve the Unkechaug language for posterity, and he really did have to butt heads with Alexander Hamilton to get the United States to adopt a decimally based currency, as opposed to one based on the cumbersome English system. If my admiration of Jefferson shows through, it is all too genuine, and I make no apologies for it.

Christie's, Sotheby's and Heritage Auctions are quite real. Heritage does, indeed, have a formidable wholesale trading operation in gold coins in Dallas, and they really did sell a 1913 nickel for $3.74 million. California Coin is fictitious, although there is a coin store in the Los Angeles area with a pleasant man named Josh who can and would accept the order given him by Robert Packard.

The Renaissance Weekend gatherings in Charleston, South Carolina every New Year are very much real, and I would be remiss if I didn't express my appreciation to Phil and Linda Lader, as well as to Debbie Shaw and Alison Boyd Gelles for the good times I have had there.

The price of a troy ounce of gold at the time the story was being started in 2010 was hovering between $1200 and $1250. The prediction by the fictitious Josh Crane that the gold price would jump to over $1500 in 2011 was correct.

The law firms of "Blake and Brock" and "Barry and Berke" are also fictitious, although a certain very able attorney in New York City will get a chuckle out of one of them.

Research by Thom Hartmann in his book, "What Would Jefferson Do?" proved extremely helpful in providing timelines and insight into Thomas Jefferson's views on slavery.

The dispute over whether the bottles sold as being from Thomas Jefferson's wine cellar were, in fact, genuine, is ongoing as of this writing. Heritage also has a rare wine department that was helpful in confirming much of the information I used here, some of which was also found in "The Billionaire's Vinegar," by Benjamin Wallace. Wade Hinderling, as well as being knowledgeable about rare coins, is a highly regarded expert in the field of French wine and speaks the language fluently, albeit with a prominent New York accent.

Aldous D. George and his wine store on Rodeo Drive were made up, although that fabulous ice cream shop on Santa Monica Boulevard was not—if you're in the area, stop in! You won't regret it. Stef, Juanita and Miguel, Jim Hernández and, of course, Anne Boudreau and her family are complete figments of my imagination. Juliette Binoche, fortunately, is very much real.

The few phrases of Latin that are included really did come from Miss Hobson's ninth grade Latin class.

My thanks as well to Dawne Brooks and the late Karlyn Thayer, most patient editors, from a most neophyte writer. If Karlyn Thayer had been a gardener, she could have taken a daisy, and pruned it until it became an orchid.

My exquisite wife, Elisabeth, does not resemble Juliette Binoche in the slightest. She cannot receive enough praise for allowing me the time to spend on this story. I can only attribute her patience to the fact that she is a professionally trained social worker.

Düsseldorf, Germany/Dallas, Texas/Truro, Massachusetts, 2010-2012

© 2012 by Marc Emory

Some of the coins mentioned in "The Time Cellar"
Photos courtesy of Heritage Auctions, Dallas, Texas

France, gold ten francs
1856, A (Paris) mint

USA "Bust" half dollar

France 20 gold francs, pre-1860

USA "chain" cent of 1793

South Africa, gold Kruger Pond

USA 1794 Silver Dollar

Colonial U.S. New England Shilling, ca. 1652

USA 1796 half dollar

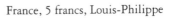

France, 5 francs, Louis-Philippe

France 10 francs gold, "BB" mint, (enlarged)

Pattern $4 gold piece, USA

"Bust" Half Dime

1802 Half Dime

Some of the vineyards mentioned in "The Time Cellar"

Château Lafite, 1870

Rausan, vintage unknown

Château Latour, 1865

Cheval Blanc, 1982

37147283R00191

Made in the USA
Lexington, KY
19 November 2014